The Apocryphal Acts
of Paul, Peter, John, Andrew and Thomas

Ancient Texts and Translations

Series Editor
K. C. Hanson

Robert William Rogers
*Cuneiform Parallels to the
Old Testament*

D. Winton Thomas, editor
*Documents from
Old Testament Times*

Henry Frederick Lutz
*Early Babylonian Letters
from Larsa*

Albert T. Clay
Babylonian Epics, Hymns, Omens, and Other Texts

Daniel David Luckenbill
The Annals of Sennacherib

A. E. Cowley
*Aramaic Papyri of the
Fifth Century B.C.*

G. R. Driver
Aramaic Documents of the Fifth Century B.C., rev. ed.

Adolf Neubauer
The Book of Tobit

August Dillman
The Ethiopic Text of 1 Enoch

R. H. Charles
*The Apocrypha and Pseudepigrapha
of the Old Testament*

R. H. Charles
The Book of Enoch

R. H. Charles
The Book of Jubilees

R. H. Charles
*The Testaments of the
Twelve Patriarchs*

R. H. Charles
The Apocalypse of Baruch

Herbert Edward Ryle
& Montaque Rhodes James
*The Psalms of the Pharisees,
commonly called
The Psalms of Solomon*

H. B. Swete
The Gospel of Peter

Richard Adelbert Lipsius
& Max Bonnet
*Apocryphal Acts
of the Apostles (3 vols.)*

The Apocryphal Acts
of Paul, Peter, John, Andrew and Thomas

Bernhard Pick

New bibliography by K. C. Hanson

Wipf & Stock Publishers
Eugene, Oregon

THE APOCRYPHAL ACTS OF PAUL, PETER, JOHN,
ANDREW AND THOMAS
Ancient Texts and Translations

Copyright © 2006 Wipf & Stock Publishers. All rights reserved. Except for brief quotations in critical publications or reviews, no part of this book may be reproduced in any manner without prior written permission from the publisher. Write: Permissions, Wipf & Stock, 199 W. 8th Ave., Eugene, OR 97401.

ISBN: 1-59752-6738

Cataloging-in-Publication data:

The Apocryphal Acts of Paul, Peter, John, Andrew and Thomas / [translated] by Bernhard Pick ; new bibliography by K. C. Hanson.

    xxii + 376 p. cm.

    1. Bible. N. T. Apocryphal books. 2. Apocryphal books (New Testament). 3. Apocryphal Acts of the Apostles. I. Pick, Bernhard (1842–1917). II. Hanson, K. C. (Kenneth C.). III. Title. IV. Series.

BS2870 .P5 2006

Manufactured in the U.S.A.

Series Foreword

The discoveries of documents from the ancient Near Eastern and Mediterranean worlds have altered our modern understanding of those worlds in both breadth and depth. Especially since the mid-nineteenth century, chance discoveries as well as archaeological excavations have brought to light thousands of clay tablets, stone inscriptions and stelae, leather scrolls, codices, papyri, seals, and ostraca.

The genres of these written documents are quite diverse: receipts, tax lists, inventories, letters, prophecies, blessings and curses, dowry documents, deeds, laws, instructions, collections of proverbs, philosophical treatises, state propaganda, myths and legends, hymns and prayers, liturgies and rituals, and many more. Some of them came to light in long-famous cities—such as Ur, Babylon, Nineveh, and Jerusalem—while others came from locations that were previously little-known or unknown—such as Ebla, Ugarit, Elephantine, Qumran, and Nag Hammadi.

But what good are these remnants from the distant past? Why should anyone bother with what are often fragmentary, obscure, or long-forgotten scraps of ancient cultures? Each person will answer those questions for herself or himself, depending upon interests and commitments. But the documents have influenced scholarly research in several areas.

It must first be said that the documents are of interest and importance in their own right, whatever their connections—or lack of them—to modern ethnic, religious, or ideological concerns. Many of them provide windows on how real people lived in the ancient world—what they grew and ate; how they related to their families, business associates, and states; how they were taxed; how and whom they worshiped; how they organized their communities; their hopes and fears; and how they understood and portrayed their own group's story.

They are of intense interest at the linguistic level. They provide us with previously unknown or undeciphered languages and dialects, broaden our range of vocabularies and meanings, assist us in mapping the relationships and developments of languages, and provide examples of loan-words and linguistic influences between languages. A monumental project such as *The Assyrian Dictionary,* produced by the Oriental Institute at the University of Chicago, would have been unthinkable without the broad range of Akkadian resources today.[1] And our study of Coptic and early gospels would be impoverished without the Nag Hammadi codices.[2]

---

[1] I. J. Gelb et al., editors, *The Assyrian Dictionary of the Oriental Institute of the University of Chicago* (Chicago: Univ. of Chicago Press, 1956–).

[2] James M. Robinson, editor, *The Nag Hammadi Library in English,* 4th ed. (Leiden: Brill, 1996).

The variety of genres also attracts our interest in terms of the history of literature. Such stories as Athra-hasis, Enumma Elish, and Gilgamesh have become important to the study of world literature. While modern readers may be most intrigued by something with obvious political or religious content, we often learn a great deal from a tax receipt or a dowry document. Hermann Gunkel influenced biblical studies not only because of his keen insights into the biblical books, but because he studied the biblical genres in the light of ancient Near Eastern texts. As he examined the genres in the Psalms, for example, he compared them to the poetic passages throughout the rest of the Bible, the Apocrypha, the Pseudepigrapha, Akkadian sources, and Egyptian sources.[3] While the Akkadian and Egyptian resources were much more limited in the 1920s and 1930s when he was working on the Psalms, his methodology and insights have had an on-going significance.

History is also a significant interest. Many of these texts mention kingdoms, ethnic and tribal groups, rulers, diplomats, generals, locations, or events that assist in establishing chronologies, give us different perspectives on previously known events, or fill in gaps in our knowledge. Historians can never have too many sources. The Amarna letters, for example, provide us with the names of local rulers in Canaan during the

---

[3] Hermann Gunkel, *Einleitung in die Psalmen: Die Gattungen der religiösen Lyrik Israels,* completed by Joachim Begrich, HAT (Göttingen: Vandenhoeck & Ruprecht, 1933). ET = *Introduction to the Psalms: The Genres of the Religious Lyric of Israel,* trans. James D. Nogalski, Mercer Library of Biblical Studies (Macon, Ga.: Mercer Univ. Press, 1998).

fourteenth century BCE, their relationship with the pharaoh, as well as the military issues of the period.[4]

Social analysis is another area of fertile research. A deed can reveal economic structures, production, land tenure, kinship relations, scribal conventions, calendars, and social hierarchies. Both the Elephantine papyri from Egypt (fifth century BCE) and the Babatha archive from the Judean desert (second century CE) include personal legal documents and letters relating to dowries, inheritance, and property transfers that provide glimpses of complex kinship relations, networking, and legal witnesses.[5] And the Elephantine documents also include letters to the high priest in Jerusalem from the priests of Elephantine regarding the rebuilding of the Elephantine temple.

Religion in the ancient world was usually embedded in either political or kinship structures. That is, it was normally a function of either the political group or kin-group to which one belonged. We are fortunate to have numerous texts of epic literature, liturgies, and rituals. These include such things as creation stories, purification rituals, and the interpretation of sheep livers for omens. The Dead Sea Scrolls, for example, provide

---

[4] William L. Moran, *The Amarna Letters* (Baltimore: Johns Hopkins Univ. Press, 1992).

[5] Bezalel Porten et al., editors, *The Elephantine Papyri in English: Three Millennia of Cross-Cultural Continuity and Change,* Documenta et Monumenta Orientis Antiqui 22 (Leiden: Brill, 1996); Yigael Yadin et al., *The Finds from the Bar Kokhba Period in the Cave of Letters,* 3 vols., Judean Desert Studies (Jerusalem: Israel Exploration Society, 1963–2002) [NB: vols. 2 and 3 are titled *Documents* instead of *Finds*].

us with biblical books, texts of biblical interpretation, community regulations, and liturgical texts from the second temple period.[6]

Another key element has been the study of law. A variety of legal principles, laws, and collections of regulations provide windows on social structures, economics, governance, property rights, and punishments. The stele of Hammurabi of Babylon (c. 1700 BCE) is certainly the most famous. But we have many more, for example: Ur-Nammu (c. 2100 BCE), Lipit-Ishtar (c. 1850 BCE), and the Middle Assyrian Laws (c. 1150 BCE).

The intention of Ancient Texts and Translations (ATT) is to make available a variety of ancient documents and document collections to a broad range of readers. The series will include reprints of long out-of-print volumes, revisions of earlier editions, and completely new volumes. The understanding of ancient societies depends upon our close reading of the documents, however fragmentary, that have survived.

—K. C. Hanson
Series Editor

---

[6] Florentino Garcia Martinez, *The Dead Sea Scrolls Translated: The Qumran Texts in English,* 2d ed., trans. Wilfred G. E. Watson (Grand Rapids: Eerdmans, 1996).

Select Bibliography

Baarda, T., editor. *Text and Testimony: Essays on New Testament and Apocryphal Literature in Honour of A. F. J. Klijn.* Kampen: Kok, 1988.

Bovon, François. *Les Actes Apocryphes des Apotres: Christianisme et Monde et Païen.* Geneva: Labor et Fides, 1981.

———. *New Testament Traditions and Apocryphal Narratives.* Translated by Jane Haapiseva-Hunter. Princeton Theological Monograph Series 36. Allison, PA: Pickwick, 1995.

———. *The Apocryphal Acts of the Apostles.* Religions of the World. Cambridge: Harvard University Press, 1999.

———. *Studies in Early Christianity.* Grand Rapids: Baker Academic, 2005.

Burrus, Virginia. *Chastity as Autonomy: Women in the Stories of the Apocryphal Acts.* Studies in Women and Religion 23. Lewiston, NY: Mellen, 1987.

Cameron, Ron, editor. *The Other Gospels: Non-Canonical Gospel Texts.* Philadelphia: Westminster, 1982.

Charlesworth, James H. et al. *The New Testament Apocrypha and Pseudepigrapha: A Guide to Publications, with Excursuses on Apocalypses.* ATLA Bibliography Series 17. Metuchen, NJ: Scarecrow, 1987.

Davies, Stevan L. *The Revolt of the Widows: The Social World of the Apocryphal Acts.* Carbondale, IL: Southern Illinois University Press, 1980.

Ehrman, Bart D. *Lost Christianities: The Battles for Scripture and the Faiths We Never Knew.* Oxford: Oxford University Press, 2003.

Elliott, John K., editor. *The Apocryphal New Testament: A Collection of Apocryphal Christian Literature in an English Translation.* Oxford: Clarendon, 1993.

Jones, F. Stanley, editor. *Which Mary? The Marys of Early Christian Tradition.* Society of Biblical Literature Symposium Series 19. Atlanta: Society of Biblical Literature, 2002.

Lapham, F. *Introduction to the New Testament Apocrypha.* Understanding the Bible and Its World. London: T. & T. Clark, 2003.

McDonald, Dennis Ronald, editor. *The Legend and the Apostle: The Battle for Paul in Story and Canon.* Philadelphia: Westminster, 1983.

———. *The Apocryphal Acts of the Aposties.* Semeia 38. Atlanta: Scholars, 1986.

———. *Christianizing Homer: The Odyssey, Plato, and the Acts of Andrew.* New York: Oxford University Press, 1994.

Robinson, James M., editor. *The Nag Hammadi Library in English.* 3d ed. San Francisco: HarperSanFrancisco, 1990.

Schneemelcher, Wilhelm, editor. *New Testament Apocrypha.* 2 vols. Rev. ed. Translated by R. McL. Wilson. Louisville: Westminster John Knox, 1991–92.

PREFACE

The publication of the epoch-making work by Lipsius on the Apocryphal Acts of the Apostles comprising about 1800 pages closely printed; Schmidt's Coptic Acta Pauli, more especially the critical edition of the Apocryphal Acts by Lipsius and Bonnet, have opened a large, but very little cultivated field of ancient Christian literature. The oldest of these Acts are those which are treated in the present volume. They give us a picture of Christianity towards the end of the second century. They are important for the history of the Christian cultus in the second and third cent., and by their description of the divine service in the houses they supplement of picture delineated in the Acts of the Apostles. They are also important for the history of Christian poetry which commences among the Gnostics; in short: though these Acts contain both "truth and fiction," they cannot be ignored by the teacher and preacher, the missionary and historian. What has hitherto been a *terra incognita* generally speaking, has now been made accessible, especially by the beautiful edition of Lipsius and Bonnet, whose text must now be considered as *textus receptus*. Tischendorf's text which was published in 1851, is now superseded by this later publication, and what is said of the text concerns also the English translation of Apocryphal Acts based on Tischendorf's work. As an illustration we only refer to the fact that chaps. 39–41, 62–158 now found in the Acts of Thomas are wanting in Tischendorf's edition. The Acts of Paul and Thecla formerly regarded as a separate book, are now proven to be a part of the Acts of Paul, to which also belongs the so-called third epistle to the Corinthians. Without calling attention to many other points, it is obvious that the Apocryphal Acts, as far as they have been translated into English, need a thorough revision, if not a new translation. For the present we offer the oldest and therefore most important Acts. That these Acts cannot be ignored because they form an important contribution to the primitive literature of the Church, the reader can readily see from the special introductions and literature. In the preparation of the present volume the work edited by Edgar Hennecke has been of great help. I have also made free use of the English translation of the Apocryphal Acts by A. Walker in the Ante-Nicene Christian Library (Edinb. 1867), as far as was possible. In other respects the present work is entirely independent, and whatever its shortcomings may be, we have the satisfaction that it is the first effort to make the researches of Lipsius, Bonnet, Schmidt, etc. accessible to the English reader.

B. P.

Newark, New Jersey, Nov. 1908.

TABLE OF CONTENTS

	PAGE
PREFACE	iii
GENERAL INTRODUCTION TO APOCRYPHAL ACTS	vii

I. THE ACTS OF PAUL 1
   A. THE ACTS OF PAUL AND THECLA 8
   B. PAUL'S CORRESPONDENCE WITH THE CORINTHIANS 35
   C. THE MARTYRDOM OF THE HOLY APOSTLE PAUL 43

II. THE ACTS OF PETER 50
   1. THE DEED OF PETER 52
   2. PETER'S AFFAIR WITH SIMON 57
      Martyrdom of the Holy Apostle Peter . . 106

III. THE ACTS OF JOHN 123
   1. ACTS OF THE HOLY APOSTLE JOHN THE THEOLOGIAN 126
   2. ARRIVAL AT EPHESUS AND WORK THERE . . 136
      Lycomedes and Cleopatra 136
      The picture of John 142
      Healing of the old women 145
      Destruction of the Artemis Temple . . 148
      The Raising of the Priest 152
      The Parricide 154
      John and the Partridge 157
   3. RETURN TO EPHESUS AND SECOND ABODE THERE 159
      From Laodicea a second time to Ephesus . 159
      End and Raising up of Drusiana . . . 161
   4. PERTAINING TO THE LIFE OF JESUS AND HIS DEATH 175
   5. THE END OF JOHN 188
      Appendix: John and the robber . . . 196

TABLE OF CONTENTS

	PAGE
IV. THE ACTS OF ANDREW	200
1. THE DOUBLE FRAGMENT OF EUODIUS	201
2. ANDREW IN PRISON	203
3. THE DEATH OF ANDREW	215
V. THE ACTS OF THOMAS	222
THE DEEDS OF THE HOLY APOSTLE THOMAS	225
First deed of the Apostle Judas Thomas. How the Lord sold him to the merchant Abban, that he should go down and convert India	225
Second deed of the Apostle Thomas. His appearance before King Gundafor	238
Third deed. About the dragon	250
Fourth deed. Concerning the colt	260
Fifth deed. About the demon that dwelt in the woman	262
Sixth deed. Concerning the young man who killed the maiden	270
Seventh deed. Concerning the commander	279
Eighth deed. About the wild asses	284
Ninth deed. About the wife of Charis	294
Tenth deed. How Mygdonia receives baptism	323
Eleventh deed. Concerning the wife of Misdai	333
Twelfth deed. Concerning Vazan, Misdai's son	338
Thirteenth deed. How Vazan and the others were baptized	348
Martyrdom of the Holy and Famous Apostle Thomas	355
I. INDEX OF PASSAGES	363
II. INDEX OF SUBJECTS	366

GENERAL INTRODUCTION TO APOCRYPHAL ACTS.

LITERATURE

Zahn, Th., *Acta Joannis*, Erlangen,
Lipsius, R.A. *Die apokryphen Apostelgeschichten und Apostellegenden*, I, Braunschweig, 1883; II, 1, 1887; II, 2, 1884; supplement, 1890; see also Lüdemann, "Die apokryphen Apostelgeschichten und Apostellegenden von R.A. Lipsius," in *Prot. Kirchenzeitung*, 1887, Nos. 42-46; H. Lietz, "Der gnostisch-christliche Character der apokr. Apostelgeschichten und Legenden im Anschluss an R.A. Lipsius" in *Zeitschrift für wissenschaftliche Theologie*, 37 (1894), 34-57.

Zahn, *Geschichte des Neutestamentlichen Kanons*, II, 2 (1892), 797-910.

"Die Wanderungen des Apostels Johannes" in *Neue Kirchliche Zeitschrift*, X, 1899, p. 191 ff.

Forschungen zur Geschichte des Neutest. Kanons VI (1900), p. 14 ff., 194 ff.

Preuschen in Harnack, *Geschichte der Altchristlichen Litteratur*, I (1893), p. 116-128, 131-134.

Batifoll. Art. "Actes apocryphes des Apôtres" in Vigouroux' *Dictionnaire de la Bible*, I (1895), p. 159-165.

Duchesne, "Les anciens recueils de legendes apostoliques," in *Compte rendu du III. congrès scientifique international des Catholiques tenu à Bruxelles*, V. section (Sciences historiques), Brux. 1895, p. 67-79.

Krüger, *Geschichte der altchristlichen Litteratur in den ersten drei Jahrhunderten*, 1895, with supplement 1898, §§ 30, 102.

James, M.R., *Apocrypha Anecdota* II (Texts and studies, V, I, 1897), p. ix ff.

Ehrhard, A., *Die altchristliche Literatur und ihre Erforschung von 1884–1900*, 1900, p. 151 f.

Liechtenhan, R., *Die Offenbarung im Gnosticismus*, 1901, p. 49 ff., 150 ff.; "Die pseudepigraphe Litteratur der Gnostiker" in *Zeitschrift für die Neutest. Wissenschaft* III, 1902, p. 287 ff.

Bardenhewer, O., *Geschichte der altchristlichen Literatur* I, 1902, p. 414 ff.

Schmidt, C., *Die alten Petrusakten im Zusammenhang der Apokryphen Apostellitteratur*, 1903.

Hennecke, *Neutestamentliche Apokryphen*, 1904.
Handbuch zu den Neutestamentlichen Apokryphen, 1904.

Clemen, *Paulus*, I (1904), 333 ff.

Leipoldt, *Geschichte des Neutestamentlichen Kanons*, I (1907), 258 ff.

Bruyne, D. de, "Nouveaux fragments des Actes de Pierre, de Paul, de Jean, d'André et de l'Apocalypse d'Elie" (*Revue Benedictine*, 25 (1908), No. 2).

Editions. Fabricius, *Codex apocryphus Novi Testamenti* II, 1703.

Tischendorf, *Acta Apostolorum apocrypha*, 1851.

Lipsius — Bonnet, *Acta Apostolorum apocrypha*, Vol. I, 1891 (containing the Acts of Peter, Paul, Paul and Peter, Paul and Thecla, and Thaddæus); Vol. II, 1, 1898 (containing the Passion of Andrew, Acts of Andrew, Martyrdom of Andrew, Passion of Andrew and Matthias, Acts of Peter and Andrew, Passion of Bartholomew, Acts of John, Martyrdom of Matthew); Vol. II, 2 (1903), containing the Acts of Philip and Thomas together with the Acts of Barnabas. The first volume was edited by Lipsius; the second by Bonnet.

The late Professor R.A. Lipsius, of Jena (d. 1892), thus opens his epoch-making work *Die apokryphen Apostelgeschichten und Apostellegenden* (1893–91):

"Under the name of Acts or Deeds (*praxeis, acta, actus*), Circuits or Journeys (*periodoi*), and Martyrdom or Consummation (*martyrion, teleiosis*) of the various apostles was comprised in the times of Christian antiquity a widely spread and manifold literature, of which very important remains exist. As early as the second century numerous legendary reports concerning the fates of the apostles were in circulation, in part, at least, of a very romantic character. The real history of the lives and deaths of most of the apostles being shrouded in obscurity, a pious imagination was very early busily employed in filling up the large lacunæ left in the historical reminiscences of the church. Not a few of such narratives owe their origin simply to an endeavor to satisfy the pious curiosity or taste for the marvelous in members of the primitive church; while others subserved the local interests of particular towns or districts which claimed to have derived their Christianity from the missionary activity of one of the apostles, or their line of bishops from one immediately ordained by him. It likewise not infrequently happened that party spirit, theological or ecclesiastical, would take advantage of a pious credulity to further its own ends by manipulating the older legends, or inventing others entirely new, after a carefully preconceived form and pattern. And so almost every fresh editor of such narratives, using that freedom which all antiquity was wont to allow itself in dealing with literary monuments, would reveal the materials which lay before him, excluding whatever might not suit his theological point of view — dogmatic statement, for example, speeches, prayers, etc., for which he would substitute other formulæ of his own composition, and further expanding or abridging after his own pleasure, or as the immediate object which he had in view might dictate. Only with the simply miraculous parts of the narrative was the case different. These passed unaltered and unquestioned from one hand to another, ecclesiastical circles the most opposed in other respects having here equal and coinciding interests, while the critical spirit, usually so acute in detecting erroneous opinions or heretical tendencies, was contented here to lay down its arms, however troubled or suspected the source from which such legendary narration might flow. Therefore, although these fables originated for the most part in heretical quarters, we find them at a later period among the cherished possessions of ordinary Catholics, acquaintance with them being perpetually renewed or their memory preserved in Catholic Christendom, partly by the festal homilies of eminent Fathers, and partly by religious poetry and works of sacred art. Like all legends or myths preserved in popular memory, however, they present great difficulties in the way of a satisfactory treatment from a literary point of view, perpetually springing up, as they do, afresh, now here, now there, now in one shape, now in another, and again withdrawing themselves in a tantalizing way, for a longer or shorter period, from the eyes of the historical inquirer. The older church martyrologies and calendars, subject as they were to continuous processes of change and augmentation, and the collectanea of later chroniclers and legend writers, who for the most part copied one from another, have furnished us with rich stores of legendary matter, which only in rare instances can be satisfactorily traced back to their original sources."

There can be no doubt that numerous apocryphal apostle-legends were current during the second century, and that certain written recensions existed, as may be seen from allusions and references by early writers. But with the fourth century the testimonies as to the existence and use of apocryphal Acts become numerous. Most explicit in this respect is the testimony of Photius, patriarch of Constantinople, A. D. 858, who in his Bibl., cod. 114, speaks of a volume purporting to be written by Leucius Charinus,[1] and containing the travels of Peter, John, Andrew, Thomas and Paul. Photius describes the book[2] as both foolish and heretical. It taught the existence of two Gods — an evil one, the God of the Jews, having Simon Magus for his minister; and a good one, whom, confounding the two Persons it identified with Christ. It denied the reality of Christ's incarnation, and gave a Docetic account of his life on earth, and in particular of his crucifixion; it condemned marriage, and regarded all generation as the work of the evil principle; and it told several silly and childish stories. We can satis-

---

[1] Schmidt (loc. cit. pp. 27–77), after examining the direct and indirect testimonies of tradition, comes to the conclusion that the authorship of Leucius can originally only be claimed for the Acts of John.

[2] The passage is given by Zahn, *Acta Joannis*, p. 215 f.

factorily trace these Acts back to the fourth century by means of references in writers of that date. At that time they were chiefly in use among the Manichæans; yet there are grounds for looking on them as more ancient than that heresy, which only began toward the end of the third century. We do not find, indeed, the name of Leucius in any writer earlier than the fourth century; yet earlier writers show acquaintance with stories which we know to have been in the Leucian Acts; whence the conclusion has been drawn that these Acts are really a second-century production, and that they found favor with the Manichæans on account of the affinity of their doctrines. From Epiphanius we know that these Acts were also largely in use among other heretical parties, and much that still remains to us seems frequently to favor older sectarian opinions, although in our present texts the most characteristic passages have been toned down or removed. Scarcely one of these Gnostic Acts of the Apostles has come down to us wholly untampered with; while, on the other hand, even in works which have already passed several times through the reforming hands of Catholic revisers, some of the old Gnostic features, despite all their efforts, are still distinctly traceable.

The original purpose with which these apocryphal writings were composed was that of diffusing a knowledge of the doctrines and customs of the various Gnostic schools,[8] and of setting up against the Catholic tradition another which appealed with no less confidence to the authority of apostles and their immediate disciples. And yet it was hardly as a sort of rival or additional canon that these writings were presented to the Christian public of those times. They aimed, rather, at supplying a popular kind of religious reading in the shape of tracts set forth by the Gnostic propaganda, which, professing to contain historical reminiscences from

---

[8] Schmidt contends that these Acts have their origin within the Catholic Church itself — "probably in the reign of Septimius Severus, about the beginning of the third century, at a time when Gnostic views, in a hazy form, were widely held, and had not yet taken a shape definite enough to provoke the hostility and condemnation of orthodox Church Councils."

apostolic times, and composed in the credulous spirit of the age, seemed to satisfy the demands of pious curiosity and soon obtained an extensive circulation. Catholic bishops and teachers did not know how better to stem this flood of Gnostic writings and their influence among the faithful, than by boldly adopting the most popular narrations from the heretical books, and, after carefully eliminating the poison of false doctrine, replacing them in this purified form in the hands of the people. That this process of purification was not always complete need not surprise us when we consider how changeable or uncertain on some points was the boundary line between Gnostic and Catholic doctrines. Thus originated the many castrated and revised editions of the Acts of Peter, Paul, John, Andrew, Thomas, Philip, Matthew, and others, which are found in Greek, Latin, Syriac, Armenian, Arabic, Coptic, Ethiopic, Anglo-Saxon, and ancient Slavonic languages.

In general, however, says Lipsius whom we follow for the most part, these Gnostic productions, apart from any more or less marked assertion of heretical dogmas or rules of life, betray their real origin by the overgrowths of a luxuriant imagination, by their highly colored pictures, and by their passionate love for mythical additions and adornments in excess even of the popular belief in signs and wonders. The favorite critical canon — "the more romantic the more recent in origin" — does not hold good as against this branch of literature, in which exorcising of demons, raisings of the dead, and other miracles of healing or of punishment are multiplied endlessly. The incessant repetition of the like wonders baffles the efforts of the most lively imagination to avoid a certain monotony, interrupted, however, by dialogues and prayers, which not seldom afford a pleasant relief, and are sometimes of a genuinely poetical character. There is withal a rich apparatus of the supernatural, consisting of visions, angelic appearances, voices from heaven, speaking animals and demons, who with shame confess their impotence against the champions of the truth; unearthly streams of light descend, or mysterious signs appear, from heaven; earthquakes, thunders and lightnings terrify the ungodly; the elements of wind and fire and water minister to the righteous; wild beasts, dogs, serpents, lions, bears and tigers are tamed by a single word from the mouths of the apostles, or turn their rage against the persecutors; dying martyrs are encompassed by wreaths of light or heavenly roses and lilies and enchanting odors, while the abyss opens to devour their enemies. The Devil himself is often introduced into these stories in the form of a black Ethiopian, and plays a considerable part. But the visionary element is the favorite one. Our Lord often appears to his servants, now as a beautiful youth, and again as a seaman, or as a shepherd, or in the form of an apostle; holy martyrs return to life to manifest themselves, at one time to their disciples, at another to their persecutors. Dreams and visions announce beforehand to apostles their approaching martyrdom, or to longing souls among the heathen the fulfillment of their desires. All this fantastic scenery has been left, for the most part, untouched by Catholic revisers, and remains, therefore in works which in other respects have been most thoroughly recast. Yet it was only in very rare cases that these romantic creations of fancy were themselves the original object in view with the writers who produced them. That object was either some dogmatic interest, or, where such retired into the background, an ascetic purpose. Many of these narratives were simply invented to extol the meritoriousness of the celibate life, or to commend the severest abstinence in the estate of matrimony. At this point Catholic revisers have been careful throughout to make regular alterations, now degrading legitimate wives to the position of concubines, and now introducing objections connected with nearness of kin or other circumstances which might justify the refusal or the repudiation of a given marriage. But where merely the praise of virginity was concerned the views of Catholics and Gnostics were nearly identical, except that the former refused to regard the maintenance of that estate as an absolute or universal moral obligation.

Recent investigations have shown that in large portions of these Acts genuine reminiscences are to be found, though not in reference to the legends themselves, yet in regard to the setting in which they are presented to us, their secular

INTRODUCTION

historical background, or their geographical and ethnographical scenery. Yet, at the same time, all efforts to derive from them any trustworthy particulars as to the actual histories of the apostles themselves, or to extract from the confused mass of legends any sound historical nucleus, have hitherto proved almost always unsuccessful. Such are in the main the characteristic points given by Lipsius in the beginning of his work mentioned before.

THE APOCRYPHAL ACTS

I.

THE ACTS OF PAUL.

LITERATURE

Harnack, *Geschichte der altchristlichen Literatur*, I, 128-131;
II, 1, 491-93.

Zahn, *Geschichte des Neutestamentlichen Kanons*, II, 2, 865-92.

Schmidt, *Die Paulusakten* (Neue Heidelberger Jahrbücher),
1897, p. 217 ff.; comp. Zahn in *Neue Kirchliche Zeitschrift*, VIII (1897), p. 933-40; Harnack, *Theologische Literaturzeitung*, 1897, no. 24.

Harnack in *Texte und Untersuchungen* (new series), IV,
3, 1899; V, 3 (1900), p. 100-106.

Ehrhard, *Die altchristliche Litteratur* (1900), p. 152 ff.

Bardenhewer, *Geschichte der altchristlichn Literatur*, I (1902),
p. 424-28.

Corssen, "Die Urgestalt der Paulusakten" (in *Zeitschrift
für die Neutestamentliche Wissenschaft*, 1903).

Hennecke, *Neutestamentliche Apokryphen*, 1904, pp. 357 ff.
and *Handbuch*, pp. 358 ff.

Schmidt, *Acta Pauli* (aus der Heidelberger Koptischen Papyrus Handschrift No. 1 herausgegeben), 2 vols.; Leipzig
1904.

Leipoldt, *Geschichte des Neutestamentlichen Kanons*, Vol. 1
(Leipzig 1907), p. 258 ff.

Bardenhewer, *Patrology* (English translation by Th. J. Shahan), St. Louis, 1908, p. 100 ff.

Schmidt, Ein neues Fragment der Heidelberger Acta Pauli in
"Sitzungsbericht der Preussischen Akademie der Wissenschaften; Berlin 1909, p. 216-220.

The Acts of Paul (*Praxeis Paulu*, or *Acta*, also *Actus Pauli*) are first mentioned by Origen, who quotes twice from them. Thus we read Hom. in John XX, 12: "if any one likes to receive that which is written in the Acts of Paul as said of the Saviour, 'I go to be crucified again.'" In a somewhat different form the same phrase occurs in the Acts of Peter. Since it is impossible to imagine that Origen should confound the Acts of Peter which were rejected as heretical with the Acts of Paul which he highly esteemed, Harnack may very well be right in supposing that the old Acts of Peter did not contain an account of Peter's martyrdom, but that this originally occurred in the Acts of Paul.

The second reference is found in *De Princip.*, I, 2, 3, where we read: "Hence that word appears to me also spoken correctly which is written in the Acts of Paul: 'This is the word, a living being;' though not expressed so well as in the Prologue to the Fourth Gospel."

Without name the Acts are also referred to by Hippolytus (*Commentary on Daniel*, III, 29, 4 ed. Bonwetsch 176) who says: "for if we believe that when Paul was condemned to the wild beasts, the lion that was loosed upon him lay down at his feet and licked him, why should we not believe what happened in the case of Daniel in the lion's den?" This seems to suppose that the writing which contained the narrative concerning Paul was regarded as trustworthy in Church circles. Besides, the parallels are so obvious that there can be no doubt as to the author of the work. That the statement of Hippolytus is taken from the Acts of Paul is clear from the statement of Nicephorus Callisti (*Church history*, II, 25 in Migne, "Patrologia Græca," Vol. CXLV, Col. 821-824, Paris 1865),[1] who relates that this incident was related in the Periodoi Pauli.

This historian of the XIV. cent. speaks of Paul's fight with the beasts at Ephesus.

Nicephorus introduces his narrative with the words that those who described the "travels of Paul" recorded also very many things which he had already done before and

---

[1] The text is also reprinted in Schmidt, *Acta Pauli*, p. 111.

suffered (before), as well as at the time when he was in Ephesus. That the "Journeys or Circuits of Paul" are identical with the "Acts or Deeds of Paul" needs no explanation.

Nicephorus then continues as follows: "When Jerome was head of the city, Paul came forth boldly. And he (Jerome) said, 'This is very good, but not the right time for such speeches.' The populace of the city, however, being enraged, had Paul put in chains and locked up in prison, till he was cast before the lions to be eaten. But Eubula and Artemilla, the wives of prominent Ephesians, who were his disciples and sought his communion at night, desired the grace of divine baptism. By means of an extraordinary divine power and angels, which had spears and illuminated the darkness of the night by the abundance of inner splendor, Paul was released from his fetters and brought them to perfection through the divine baptism, having gone to the seashore without being noticed by the prison keepers. He returned again to the prison, to be kept as food for the lions. A very big and strong lion was let loose upon him, and having run up to his feet, lay down, and though many more beasts were let loose upon him, none would touch the holy body, which was supported and strengthened by prayer. While this was going on, an awful hailstorm came and crushed the heads of many men and of the wild beasts. Jerome too was hit by a hailstone, and in consequence of this he turned with his followers to the God of Paul, and received baptism. But the lion ran away to the mountains, and Paul sailed thence to Macedonia and Greece."[2]

Eusebius (*Hist. ecclez.*, III, 25, 4), places the Acts of Paul amongst the Antilegomena, under the heading of *nothoi* or spurious, but ranks them with the Shepherd of Hermas, the Apocalypse of Peter, the Epistle of Barnabas, the Didaché, and even the Apocalypse of John and the Epistle of the Hebrews.

In the list of books given in the *Codex Claromontanus*

---

[2] Remains of a sermon of the Apostle at Athens have been discovered in John of Salisbury (about 1156) in his *Policraticus* IV, 3 (see James, *Apocrypha Anecdota in "Texts and Studies"* I, 55).

(of the VI. cent.) the order is Barnabas, Apocalypse, Acts of the Apostles, Hermas, Acts of Paul, Apocalypse of Peter. In the stichometry of Nicephorus, besides the journeys of Peter, John, Thomas, also "the journeys of Paul" are mentioned. They contained 3600 *stichoi*. That the Acts of Paul are meant thereby there can be no doubt, for the number of stichoi is almost identical with the 3560 stichoi, ascribed to the Acts of Paul in the *Codex Claromontanus*.

The *Muratorian Fragment* and the *Decretum Gelasianum* (proclaimed 496) do not mention the Acts of Paul. The latter mentions instead the *Actus Pauli et Theclæ*, which shows that long before the promulgation of the Gelasian decree the Acts of Paul and Thecla must have been detached from the main body of the "Acts." This accounts for the fact that till recently we knew considerably little of the Acts of Paul which were so highly esteemed in the Eastern Church.

The discovery of fragments of a Coptic translation of the Acts of Paul made by Prof. Carl Schmidt, has supplied us with enough material to enable us to reconstruct the original Acts. Aside from the three known portions: the Thecla narrative, the correspondence of Paul with the Corinthians, and the Martyrdom of Paul, the Coptic fragments, as far as they could be deciphered, supply enough material to show at least the connection of the narrative.

From the *Acta Pauli* published by Schmidt, we learn the following: The story opens with a deed of Paul at Antioch in Pisidia, where he raised from the dead the son of Anchares and Phila, who were evidently Jews. Being invited by Anchares to stay with him, Paul spends eight days in the house of Anchares. The Jews insist that Anchares should drive Paul from the city. But it seems that the apostle had anticipated them. Anchares openly professes Jesus as the Son of God. Now the Jews bring the apostle back to the city, abuse him, stone him and finally drive him away from the city. Anchares, who will not recompense evil with evil, retires with his wife to his house, where he fasts and prays. In the evening Paul returns again to Anchares, bids him farewell and betakes himself to Iconium.

ACTS OF PAUL

This is followed by the story of Paul and Thecla, the greater part of which is preserved.

The next scene is at Myra, where Thecla left him.[8] Here lived the dropsical Hermocrates. Having heard of the power of the God whom Paul preached, he fell down at the feet of Paul together with his wife and children, beseeching his help. The apostle promised to help him in the name of Jesus Christ. At this the dropsical man fell down, his body opened and much water came forth. Those that stood by, believed the sufferer to be dead; but the apostle lifted him up and gave him bread to eat. At this Hermocrates and his wife were baptized. But the elder son Hermippus was not pleased with the turn of affairs, as he had already been counting on the inheritance. With his friends he plotted against the life of the apostle. In the meantime the second son of Hermocrates, Dion, who carefully listened to the words of the apostle, hurt himself and died. The apostle restored him to life again. Being admonished in a vision of the danger which threatened him, he receives Hermippus who rushes upon him with his drawn sword with the same word with which Jesus met the bailiffs in Gethsemane. Hermippus suddenly grows blind. He asks his companions not to leave him in his misery and accuses himself of having persecuted innocent blood. He prays all to ask Paul to cure him from his blindness and reminds them of what Paul did for his father and brother. Paul being deeply moved, goes away. The companions carry Hermippus to the house, in which Paul is teaching. The blind man touches the feet of all who went in and asks them to intercede for him before Paul. Among these are his parents Hermocrates and Nympha who bring corn and money to be distributed among the poor because of Dion's deliverance. The parents are greatly distressed at the condition of their son. Paul and the parents pray for Hermippus; he is healed and imagines that the apostle put his hand on him. . . . From Myra Paul went to Sidon. On the way some Christians from Perge in Pamphylia join him, Thrasymachus and Aline (or Alype) Cleon and

---

[8] See Acts of Paul and Thecla, sect. 40.

Chrysa, who entertain the apostle. They rest under a tree (?) where there is a heathen altar. Paul speaks of contamination by idolatry, against which an old man protests who tries to persuade the hearers to retain the old belief, adducing many instances, where the adoption of Christianity caused the death of the converts. . . . In Sidon Paul preaches, exhorting the inhabitants to think of Sodom and Gomorrha, and admonishes them to believe because of his miracles. On this account he is imprisoned with Thrasymachus and Cleon in the temple of Apollo, and supplied with precious victuals. Paul however fasts three days and prays in the night for the help of God. At once one-half of the temple falls down. When the servants of the temple and the conspirators see this, they proclaimed it in the whole city. The inhabitants run to the temple, where they find Paul and his companions weeping "because of this temptation, which will make them a spectacle for all." At the request of the multitude they are led into the theatre. . . . (What happened here we know not. It seems that miracles were performed for the salvation of Paul, which changed the opinion of the people. For in the end the) "God is praised, who sent Paul, and a certain Theudes is baptized." Paul leaves Sidon for Tyre.

In Tyre Paul casts out some devils and two men Amphion and Chrysippus are mentioned, with whom he has to do.

(After this comes a series of mutilated fragments, but the apostle is supposed by the editor of the Coptic Acts to travel on to Jerusalem, since we come to a fragment belonging to the first half which runs as follows: "thou findest thyself in view of Jerusalem. But I trust in the Lord that thou wilt . . . Saul . . ." Since in the following the name of Peter is mentioned, it is possible that Paul meets him at Jerusalem, probably at the time of the apostolic council.)

The next fragment shows the apostle as prisoner in a mine, where, we know not. A certain Longinus is introduced, whose daughter Phrontina is condemned to be hurled from a rock. As Paul is blamed for the fate of the daughter, the father insists that the apostle should also die with her. In a vision Paul is made aware of the attempt on his life, but he goes about his work with the other prisoners as usual. On the third day Phrontina, lamented by her parents and soldiers, is carried forth on a bier to meet her death. . . . Paul raises Phrontina from the dead, and leads her through the city to the house of her father. The result is that the God who restored to life Phrontina, is now acknowledged by the multitude as the only God, the creator of heaven and earth. Paul goes to Philippi.

Here, as presently appears, Paul was put in prison because of Stratonike, the wife of Apollophanes. While at Philippi, messengers came to Paul with a letter from Corinth complaining of the teaching of Simon and Cleobius (Here follows the correspondence).

Another fragment contains a farewell scene, which reminds us of a like one, at Miletus, mentioned in the Acts of the Apostles, chap. xx. Paul says: "The grace of the Lord shall go with me, that I may finish in patience all administration, which shall come to me." When they heard this, they became sad and fasted. And Cleobius rose up, and speaking through the spirit said to them: "Brethren, the [Almighty?] will permit Paul to accomplish all and allow him to go up [to Jerusalem?]; thence he shall teach . . . in great instruction and knowledge and sowing of the word, that he will be envied, that he departs from this world." When the brethren and Paul heard this, they lifted up their voice, saying: . . . But the spirit came upon Myrte, and she said: "Brethren, . . . and look at this sign, by (?) . . . Paul namely, the servant of the Lord, shall save many at Rome, and nourish many by the word, that they shall be without number and he reveals himself more than all believers. Then shall . . . come of the Lord Jesus Christ and a great mercy shall be . . . in Rome." And this is the manner in which the Spirit spoke to Myrte. All partake then of the bread, are filled with joy and celebrate the Lord's Supper, singing psalms.— This is the substance of the Coptic fragments.

Who was the author of the Acts of Paul? Tertullian (between 220 and 240) writes in his treatise *De Baptismo*, ch. XVII: "But if any defend those things which have been rashly ascribed to Paul, under the example of Thecla, so as to give license to women to teach and baptize, let them know that the presbyter in Asia, who compiled the account, as it were, under the title of Paul, accumulating of his own store, being convicted of what he had done, and confessing that he had done it out of love to Paul, was removed from his place. For how could it seem probable that he who would not give any firm permission to a woman to learn should grant to a female to teach and baptize?" There can be no doubt that this account of Tertullian refers to the whole work and not merely to the Acts of Paul and Thecla. For in the latter little or nothing is said of deeds of the apostle. All which we now have of the Acts of Paul are only portions which were early detached from the original work. We can therefore apply the remark of Tertullian to the entire work, which was composed by a presbyter in Asia who was deposed because he used the name of the apostle. And it is interesting to know that amongst the Coptic fragments is the conclusion of the whole MS. together with the statement; "The Acts of Paul according to the Apostle," i.e. according to St. Paul himself.

The author being a presbyter of Asia, whose history Tertullian knows, we may take it for granted that the Acts were composed at least before A.D. 200, perhaps somewhere between 165 and 195, and most probably within a few years of the middle of that period. Hennecke puts the time between 160–180; Leipoldt names the year 180.

The *Acta Pauli* were no doubt intended to show the popular Christianity of the second century, of which Paul was the best exponent. The tendency of the author was to give a counterpart to the canonical Acts of the Apostles. The author who wrote "out of love to Paul" was deposed, but his work retained an honorable place in the Church literature.

A. THE ACTS OF PAUL AND THECLA.

LITERATURE

Pick. Art. "Acts of Thecla and Paul," in McClintock and Strong's *Cyclop.*, Vol. X (1881), 310–314, where the older literature is also given.

Pick, The "Acts of Paul and Thecla" in *Lutheran Quarterly*, 1888, 585–601.

Harnack, *Geschichte der altchristlichen Literatur*, I, 136 ff., II, 491–508.

Zahn, *Geschichte des neutestamentlichen Kanons*, II, 2 p. 892–910.

Von Gebhardt, "Die lateinischen Uebersetzungen der Acta Pauli et Theclæ" (in *Texte und Untersuchungen*, XXII, 2 (1902).

Lipsius, *Die apokryphen Apostelgeschichten*, II, 1 (1887), pp. 424–467.
Acta Apostolorum Apocrypha, I (1891) pp. XCIV–CVI; 235–272.

Gwynn. Art. "Thecla" in *Dict. of Christian Biography*, IV (1887), 882–896.

Wohlenberg, "Die Bedeutung der Thekla-Akten fuer die neutest. Forschung" (in *Zeitschrift fuer Kirchliche Wissenschaft und Kirchliches Leben*, IX (1888), 363–382.

Rey, *Etude sur les Acta Pauli et Theclæ, et la legende de Thecla*, Paris, 1890.

Ramsay, *The Church in the Roman Empire*, 3d ed. London, 1894, 375–428.

Conybeare, *The Apology and Acts of Apollonius and other monuments of Early Christianity*, London 1894, 49–88.

Cabrol, *La légende de Ste. Thecla*, Paris, 1895.

Hennecke, *Neutestamentliche Apokryphen*, 1904, 358 ff.
Handbuch, 1904, 359 sqq.

Schmidt, *Acta Pauli*, 1904, 145–161.

Bardenhewer, *Patrology*, p. 102 ff.

Holzhey, *Die Thekla-Akten, Ihre Verbreitung und Beurteilung in der Kirche*, Munich 1905.

One of the oldest and most interesting relics of the extant New Testament Apocrypha, is the Acts of St. Paul and Thecla. They were first edited by Grabe in his *Spicilegium*, Oxford, 1698 (2d ed., 1700); again by Tischendorf in his *Acta Apocrypha, Leipzig*, 1851; and more recently by Lipsius, who together with Bonnet, published a new edition of *Acta Apostolorum Apocrypha*, 2 Vols. 1891–1903.

Grabe's text was published from a manuscript belonging to the twelfth century. To the same time (X.-XIII. cent.) the other manuscripts belong, and it is therefore difficult to say at what time the Acta Theclæ were detached from the Acta Pauli. But this must have been done long before the so-called decree of Gelasius (496) was issued, which excludes from the list of "scriptures received by the Church" the book which is called "the Acts of Paul and Thecla." But we have yet earlier testimonies. The earliest is that of Tertullian, in his treatise *De Baptismo*, c. XVII., already alluded to. It has been taken for granted that the meaning is that a presbyter of Asia, somewhat towards the end of the first century, compiled a history of Paul and Thecla, and, instead of publishing it as a true narrative, either in his own name, or with any name at all, but in good faith, published it falsely, and therefore wickedly, under the name of Paul, as though he were himself the writer; that he was convicted of his forgery, and deposed from the priesthood.

This account has been marvelously dressed up, and some of its advocates have ventured to say that a Montanist writer of the name of Leucius was the real author of these Acts. (Tillemont, *Mémoires*, II, 446).

The next witness is Jerome, who in his *Catalogus Script. Eccl.* c:7 (written about the year 392), commenting upon the passage of Tertullian, says that the presbyter who wrote the history of Paul and Thecla was deposed for what he had done by John (*apud Johannem*) the Apostle. That Jerome relied upon Tertullian is evident from his statement; but his conduct in fathering the story of the deposition by John upon Tertullian is inexcusable, because no such statement was made by Tertullian. Tertullian speaks of an Asiatic presbyter, Jerome adds *apud Johannem*, and his copyists instead of "*apud Johannem*," write "*a Johanne.*"

Of Eastern writers who were acquainted with our Acts, we mention Basil, bishop of Seleucia (431–467), author of a "Life and Miracles of St. Thecla" (see Migne, *Pat. Gr.* 85 col. 477 ff.), Nicetas of Paphlagonia, towards the end of the ninth century, and Simeon Metaphrastes in the tenth. The only writer who treats Thecla directly, and not by way of mere passing allusion, is Methodius, the author of

ACTS OF PAUL

Symposium Decem Virginum (written about A. D. 300). Into this Symposium[1] or dialogue ten virgins are introduced as contending in the presence of Areté concerning chastity. At the end of the dialogue Thecla leads off a hymn, to which the rest, standing round as a chorus respond: "I keep myself pure for Thee, O Bridegroom, and holding a lighted torch I go to meet Thee."

In inviting Thecla to speak, Areté designates her a disciple of Paul: in her oration she speaks of those who "set little by wealth, distinction, race or marriage, and are ready to yield their bodies to wild beasts and to the fire, because of their yearning and enthusiasm for the things that are in supermundane places." After Gregorion had finished the address, Euboulios cannot suppress her admiration; she knows of other acts of Thecla, with which what they have just heard coincides, for says she: "I know her wisdom also for other noble actions, and what sort of things she succeeded in speaking, giving proof of supreme love to Christ; and how glorious she often appeared in meeting the chief conflicts of the martyrs, procuring for herself a zeal equal to her courage, and a strength of body equal to the wisdom of her counsels." After the last two virgins have finished speaking, Areté addresses them all saying: "And having in my hearing sufficiently contended by words, I pronounce you all victors and crown you: but Thecla with a larger and thicker chaplet, as the chief of you, and as having shone with greater luster than the rest." From the latter passage we can infer how greatly esteemed Thecla was already in the third century. Allusions to her we find also in the writings of Gregory Nazianzen. In his first address against Julian the Apostate,[2] he concluded a catalogue of apostles and disciples of the apostles with Thecla; he also speaks of her as a virgin who had escaped the "tyranny" of her betrothed husband and her mother (*Oratio*, XXIV.) and (*Exhortatio ad Virgines*, II)[3] connects

---

[1] English translation in Ante-Nicene Library, Vol. XIV (Edinburgh), 1869; another by Chatfield in Pick, *Hymns and Poetry of the Eastern Church*, N. Y., 1908, p. 27 ff.

[2] Migne, Patr. Gr. 35 col., 589.

[3] *Ibid.*, 35 col., 1180; 37 col., 639.

her escape with Paul's suffering hunger. Gregory of Nyssa (Hom., XIV. in *Cant. cantic.*)[4] speaks of her as Paul's virgin disciple, and (*Vita Macrinæ*) he calls her a virgin martyr. Epiphanius (*Hæres*. 79, 5) puts Thecla by the side of Elias, John the Baptist and the Virgin Mother, and praises her for sacrificing under Paul's teaching her prospects of a prosperous marriage. Chrysostom tells us how Thecla managed to see Paul. In his Homily, XXV. (in *Acta Apost.*) he says: "Hear then of the blessed Thecla, who for the sake of seeing Paul, gave up her jewels; but thou wilt not give an obolus for the sake of seeing Christ."

Isidore of Pelusium (Lib., I. epist. 260) calls her "protomartyr," and John of Damascus in an address on those who have died in the faith,[5] says, that one should pray to God not for his own soul alone, but also for that of others, as the protomartyr Thecla had done. Zeno of Verona (*De Timore*)[6] of the fourth century who joins her name with that of Daniel, Jonah, Peter gives an account of the Thecla-Antiochian martyrdom as told in the Acts, giving as it does particulars of the bulls goaded to attack her, her perils from the seals, and the fiery cloud which covered her nakedness. Ambrose joins her name with that of Agnes and with the virgin Mother, Daniel and John as the "Immaculatus chorus puritatis" (*De lapsu virginis,* c:3, 4),[7] and with Miriam, Moses' sister (epist. 63, 34 *Ad Vercellensem eccles.*);[8] and Sulpicius Severus in his account of St. Martin of Tours,[9] written about 403 narrates that Thecla together with Agnes and Mary often appeared unto him. Even Jerome[10] though as we have seen he rejects the written narrative of her life, asserts the traditional prevalence of her fame by adducing her as an example of saintliness. Churches were built in Thecla's honor. As early as 385 A. D. the "Martyri-

---

[4] *Ibid.*, 44 col., 1067.
[5] *De his qui in fide dormierunt* c:9 (Migne, Patr. Gr. 95 col., 253).
[6] *Ibid.*, Patr. Lat., II, col., 324.
[7] Migne, Patr. Lat., 16, col., 369-370.
[8] *Ibid.*, 16 col., 1198.
[9] *Dialog. de vita Martini*, II, 13, 5, p. 106, ed. Halm.
[10] *Ad. Eustoch, epist.* 22 (Migne, Patr. Lat., 22, col., 424); *Chronicum ad annum,* 377 *de Melania* (ibid., 27, col., 608).

um" of Thecla near Seleucia was visited by Sylvia of Aquitania, who in her travels gives a description of the locality with its monasteries and the church, which inclosed the "Martyrium" and states that she prayed in the "Monasterium" and read there the holy history of Thecla.[11]

From all indications it may be inferred that the work was composed at least before A. D. 200, perhaps somewhere between 165 and 195, and most probably within a few years of the middle of that period. And this will hold good of the Acts of Paul in general. Though deeply tinged with Encratism, and notwithstanding the author's deposition from his ministry, the history of Thecla was universally welcomed in Catholic circles, was frequently re-edited, and often used as a subject of homiletic discourse.

An indication of the early origin of the Acts of Thecla is the absence of quotations from the New Testament. There is not a single direct citation, yet the student cannot fail to discover many instances in which the New Testament has been used.[12]

After these preliminary remarks we now give the Acts of Paul and Thecla. The Greek text is found in Lipsius *Acta Apocrypha*, I, 235-269; the Coptic, as far as it goes and its German translation in Schmidt, *Acta Pauli*, pp. 27-53.

ACTS OF PAUL AND THECLA.

1. As Paul was going up to Iconium after his flight from Antioch, his fellow-travelers were Demas and Hermogenes,[1] the coppersmith, full of hypocrisy, and persisted in staying with Paul, as if they loved him. Paul looking only to the goodness of Christ, did them[2] no harm, but loved them ex-

---

[11] *Peregrinatio S. Silviæ Aquitanæ ad loca sancta*, ed. Gamurrini Romæ 1877, pp. 73-74.
[12] For a list of such instances see my art. in McClintock Strong, p. 313.
[1] See II Tim. IV, 10; Philem. 24, Col. IV, 14; II Tim. I, 15.
[2] "Them" omitted in the Coptic and by Grabe.

ceedingly, so that he made sweet to them all [3] the words of the Lord and the oracles of the gospel concerning the birth and resurrection of the Beloved; and he gave them an account, word for word, of the great deeds of Christ, how they were revealed to him [that Christ is born of the virgin Mary and of the seed of David].[4]

2. And a certain man, by name Onesiphorus,[5] hearing that Paul was to come to Iconium, went out to meet him with his children Simmias and Zeno, and his wife Lectra, in order that he might entertain him. For Titus had informed him what Paul was like in appearance. For he had not seen him in the flesh, but only in the spirit.

3. And he went along the royal road [6] to Lystra, and kept looking at the passers-by according to the description of Titus.[7] And he saw Paul

---

[3] "All" omitted in the Coptic, but in many Greek MSS.

[4] The words in brackets are found in the Coptic; the MSS. differ here. As a rule we use [] where the texts differ; <> means additions to the text; () denote explanatory additions of the translator.

[5] See II Tim. I, 16.

[6] This royal road was abolished in 74 A. D., see Ramsay, p. 30.

[7] In the Philopatris of Pseudo-Lucian of the 4th cent., Paul is contemptuously alluded to as "the bald-headed, hook-nosed Galilean, who trod the air into the third heaven, and learned the most beautiful things."

Malala of Antioch, of the 6th cent. describes Paul as being in person "round-shouldered, with a sprinkling of grey on his head and beard, with an aquiline nose, greyish eyes, meeting eyebrows, with a mixture of pale and red in his complexion, and an ample beard. With a genial expression of countenance, he was sensible, earnest, easily accessible, sweet, and inspired with the Holy Spirit."

Nicephorus of the 14th cent. says: "Paul was short and dwarfish in stature, and as it were, crooked in person and coming, a man small in size, bald-headed, bandy-legged, of noble mien, with eyebrows meeting, rather long-nosed, full of grace. For sometimes he seemed like a man, and sometimes he had the countenance of an angel.

4. And Paul, seeing Onesiphorus, smiled; and Onesiphorus said, " Hail, O servant of the blessed God." And he said, " Grace be with thee and thy house." And Demas and Hermogenes were jealous and showed greater hypocrisy, so that Demas said: " are we not of the blessed God, that thou hast not thus saluted us? " And Onesiphorus said, " I see not in you the fruit of righteousness; but if such you be, come also into my house and refresh yourselves."

5. And Paul having gone into the house of Onesiphorus, there was great joy, and bending of knees, and breaking of bread, and the word about self-control and the resurrection, Paul saying: " Blessed are the pure in heart, for they shall see God;[8] blessed are they that have kept the flesh chaste, for they shall become a temple of God;[9] blessed are they that control themselves, for God shall speak with them; blessed are they that have kept aloof from this world, for they shall please

---

slightly bent. His face was pale, his aspect winning. He was bald-headed, and his eyes were bright. His nose was prominent and aquiline, his beard thick and tolerably long, and both this and his head were sprinkled with white hairs."

Luther imagined; " St. Paulus war ein armes, dürres Männlein, wie Magister Philippus " (Melanchthon).

[8] Matt. V, 8.
[9] 9 Comp. I Cor. VI, 18, 19.

God;[10] blessed are they that have wives as not having them, for they shall receive God for their portion;[11] blessed are they that have the fear of God, for they shall become angels of God.

6. "Blessed are they that tremble at the word of God, for they shall be comforted;[12] blessed are they that have received the wisdom of Jesus Christ, for they shall be called the sons of the Most High; blessed are they that have kept the baptism, for they shall be refreshed by the Father and the Son; blessed are they who have come to a knowledge of Christ, for they shall be in the light; blessed are they that through love of God have come out from conformity with the world,[13] for they shall judge angels, and shall be blessed at the right hand of the Father;[14] blessed are the merciful for they shall obtain mercy,[15] and shall not see the bitter day of judgment; blessed are the bodies of the virgins, for they shall be well pleasing to God, and shall not lose the reward [16] of their chastity. For the word of the Father shall become to them a work of salvation against the day of the Son, and they shall rest [17] for ever and ever."

7. And while Paul was thus speaking in the midst of the congregation in the house of Onesiph-

---

[10] Comp. Hebr. XI, 5.
[11] I Cor. VII, 29, comp. Rom. VIII, 17.
[12] Matt. V, 4.
[13] I Cor. VII, 31.
[14] I Cor. VI, 3; comp. Matt. XXV, 34.
[15] Matt. V, 7.
[16] Heb. XI, 5; comp. Matt. X, 42.
[17] Comp. Matt. XI, 29.

ACTS OF PAUL

orus, a certain virgin named Thecla, the daughter of Theoclia, betrothed to a man named Thamyris, sitting at the window close by, listened day and night to the discourse of virginity and prayer, as proclaimed by Paul. And she did not look away from the window, but paid earnest heed to the faith [rejoicing exceedingly]. And when she saw many women and virgins going in beside Paul, she also had an eager desire to be deemed worthy to hear the words of Christ. For she had not yet seen Paul's figure, but heard his word only.

8. As she did not move from the window, her mother sent to Thamyris. And he came gladly, as if already receiving her in marriage. And Thamyris said to Theoclia, " Where, then, is my Thecla <that I may see her>" ?[18] And Theoclia answered, " I have a strange story to tell thee, Thamyris. For three days and three nights Thecla does not rise from the window, neither to eat, nor to drink; but looking earnestly as if upon some pleasant sight, she is devoted to a foreigner teaching deceitful and artful discourses, that I wonder how a virgin of her great modesty exposes herself to such painful vexations.

9. " Thamyris! this man will overturn the city of the Iconians, and thy Thecla too, besides; for all the women and the young men go in beside him to be taught by him, who says one must fear only one God and live in chastity. Moreover, also, my

---

[18] So the Coptic.

daughter, tied to the window like a spider, lays hold of what is said by him with a strange eagerness and awful emotion. For the virgin looks eagerly at what is said by him, and has been captivated. But do thou go near and speak to her, for she has been betrothed to thee."

10. And Thamyris going near, and kissing her, but at the same time also being afraid of her overpowering emotion, said, "Thecla, my betrothed, why thus? And what sort of feeling holds thee overpowered? Come back to thy Thamyris, and be ashamed." Moreover, also, her mother said the same things: "Why dost thou sit thus looking down, my child, and answering nothing, but like a mad woman?" And they <that were in the house>[19] wept bitterly, Thamyris for the loss of a wife, Theoclia of a child, and the maidservants of a mistress. And there was a great outpouring of lamentation in the house. And while these things were thus going on, Thecla did not turn round, but kept attending earnestly to the word of Paul.

11. And Thamyris, starting up, went forth into the street, and watched all going in to Paul and coming out. And he saw two men bitterly quarreling with each other, and he said to them, "Men, who are you, and tell me who is this among you, leading astray the souls of young men, and deceiving virgins, so that they do not marry, but remain as they are? I promise you money enough if you

---

[19] So the Coptic.

tell me about him; for I am the first man of this city."

12. And Demas and Hermogenes said to him, "Who he is we know not. But he deprives the husbands of wives and maidens of husbands, saying, 'there is for you a resurrection in no other way, except ye remain chaste and pollute not the flesh.'"

13. And Thamyris said to them, "Come into my house and refresh yourselves." And they went to a sumptuous supper, and much wine, and great wealth and a splendid table. And Thamyris made them drink, from his love to Thecla, and his wish to get her as a wife <on the day appointed by her mother Theoclia>.[20] And during the supper Thamyris said, "Ye men, tell me, what is his teaching, that I also may know, for I am no little distressed about Thecla, because she thus loves the stranger, and I am prevented from marrying."

14. And Demas and Hermogenes said <as with one mouth>[21] "Bring him before the Governor Castellius, because he persuades the multitude to embrace the new teaching of the Christians, and he will destroy him, and thou shalt have Thecla as thy wife. And we shall teach thee about the resurrection, that it has already taken place in the children [22] [and we rise again, after having come to the true knowledge of God]."

---

[20] So the Latin and Syriac.
[21] So the Coptic.
[22] II Tim. II, 18.

15. And when Thamyris heard these things he rose up early in the morning, and, filled with rage and anger, he went into the house of Onesiphorus with archons and lictors, and a great crowd with batons and said [to Paul],[23] "Thou hast deceived the city of the Iconians, and especially my betrothed bride, so that she will not have me! Let us go to the Governor Castellius!" And the whole crowd cried, "Away with the sorcerer! for he has misled all our wives," and the masses were also incited.

16. And Thamyris standing before the tribunal, said with a great shout, "O proconsul, this man — we know not whence he is — who makes virgins averse to marriage, let him say before thee why he teaches thus." But Demas and Hermogenes said to Thamyris, "Say that he is a Christian and he will die at once." But the proconsul stayed his intention, and called Paul saying, "Who art thou, and what dost thou teach? for they bring no small accusation against thee."

17. And Paul, lifting up his voice, said, "If I to-day must tell any of my teachings, then listen, O proconsul: the living God, the God of vengeance, [the jealous God],[24] the God who has need of nothing, who seeks the salvation of men, has sent me that I may reclaim them from corruption and uncleanness and from all pleasure, and from death, that they may sin no more. On this account God sent his

---

[23] Not in the Coptic.
[24] Not in the Coptic; omitted also in the Syriac and in some MSS.

Son, whose gospel I preach and teach, that in him men have hope; who alone has had compassion upon a world led astray, that men may be no longer under judgment, but may have faith and fear of God and knowledge of honesty and love of truth. If, therefore, I teach what has been revealed to me by God, what wrong am I doing, O proconsul?" When the proconsul heard this, he ordered Paul to be bound and sent to prison, until he had time to hear him more attentively.

18. And Thecla, by night, took off her bracelet and gave it to the gatekeeper; and the door being opened to her, she went into the prison. To the jailer she gave a silver mirror, and was thus enabled to go in beside Paul, and sitting at his feet, she heard the great deeds of God. And Paul was afraid of nothing, but trusted in God. And her faith also increased and she kissed his bonds.

19. And when Thecla was missed by her friends and Thamyris, they were running up and down the streets, as if she had been lost, and one of the gatekeeper's fellow-slaves informed them that she had gone out by night. And they examined the gatekeeper, who said to them, "She has gone to the foreigner into the prison." And having gone, they found her, as it were, enchained by affection. And having gone forth thence, they incited the people, and informed the governor what had happened.

20. And he ordered Paul to be brought before the tribunal; but Thecla was wallowing on the place where Paul had sat whilst in prison. And the Gov-

ernor ordered her also to be brought to [the tribunal], and she came with an exceedingly great joy. And when Paul had been led forth, the crowd vehemently cried out, "He is a sorcerer, away with him!"[25] But the proconsul gladly heard Paul upon the holy works of Christ.[26] And having called a council he summoned Thecla and said, "Why dost thou not marry Thamyris, according to the law of the Iconians?" But she stood looking earnestly at Paul. And when she gave no answer, Theoclia, her mother, cried out saying: "Burn the wicked one; burn her in the midst of the theatre who will not marry, that all the women that have been taught by this man may be afraid."

21. And the proconsul was greatly moved; and having scourged Paul, he cast him out of the city. But Thecla he condemned to be burned. And immediately the governor arose and went away to the theatre. And the whole multitude went out to witness the spectacle. But as a lamb in the wilderness looks around for the shepherd, so Thecla kept searching for Paul. And having looked upon the crowd, she saw the Lord sitting in the likeness of Paul, and said, "As if I were unable to endure, Paul has come to look after me." And she gazed upon him with great earnestness, but he went up into heaven.

22. And the boys and girls brought wood and straw, in order that Thecla might be burned. And

---

[25] Luke XXIII, 18.
[26] The Coptic: upon his holy works.

when she came in naked, the governor wept and admired the power that was in her. And the executioners arranged the wood and told her to go up on the pile. And she, having made the sign of the cross, went up on the pile. And they lighted the fire. And though a great fire was blazing, it did not touch her. For God, having compassion upon her, made an underground rumbling and a cloud full of water and hail overshadowed (the theater) from above, and all that was in the cavity of it was poured out, so that many <of the lookers-on> were in danger of death. And the fire was put out and Thecla saved.

23. And Paul was fasting with Onesiphorus and his wife, and his children, in a new tomb, on the way which led from Iconium to Daphne. And when many days were past in fasting, the children said to Paul: "We are hungry." And they had nothing to buy bread, for Onesiphorus had left the things of this world, and followed Paul, with all his house. And Paul, having taken off his cloak, said, "Go, my child, sell this and buy some loaves and bring them." And when the child was buying he saw Thecla their neighbor, and was astonished and said, "Thecla, whither art thou going?" And she said, "I have been saved from the fire, and am following Paul." And the child said, "Come, I shall take thee to him; for he is distressed about thee and prays and is fasting already six days."

24. And when she had come to the tomb, where Paul was kneeling and praying, "Father of

<Jesus>[27] Christ, let not the fire touch Thecla, but stand by her, for she is thine"; she, standing behind him, cried out, "O Father, who hast made the heaven and the earth, Thou the Father of thy beloved Son Jesus Christ [28] I praise thee that thou hast saved me from the fire,[29] that I may see Paul again." [30] And Paul rising up, saw her, and said, "O God, that knowest the heart, Father of [our Lord] [31] Jesus Christ; I praise thee, that thou hast speedily heard my prayer."

25. And there was great love in the tomb, for Paul and Onesiphorus and the others all rejoiced. And they had five loaves, and herbs, and water, and they rejoiced in the holy works of Christ. And Thecla said to Paul, "I will cut my hair off, and I shall follow thee whithersoever thou goest." But he said, "Times are evil, and thou art beautiful. I am afraid lest another temptation come upon thee worse than the first, and that thou withstand it not, but become mad after men." And Thecla said, "Only give me the seal in Christ, and no temptation shall touch me." And Paul said, "Thecla, be patient, thou shalt receive the water [baptism]." [32]

26. And Paul sent away Onesiphorus and all his house to Iconium; and having taken Thecla, went into Antioch. And as soon as they had arrived a

---

[27] So the Coptic.
[28] The Coptic: Father of thy holy Son.
[29] "From the Fire" omitted by the Coptic; Latin, Syriac.
[30] So the Coptic.
[31] Omitted in the Coptic.
[32] So the Coptic.

certain Syrian, Alexander by name, an influential citizen of Antioch, seeing Thecla, became enamoured of her, and tried to gain over Paul by gifts and presents. But Paul said, "I know not the woman of which thou speakest, nor is she mine." But he, being of great power, openly embraced her in the street. But she would not endure it, but looked about for Paul. And she cried out bitterly, saying, "Do not force the stranger; do not force the maiden of God. I am one of the chief persons of the Iconians, and because I would not marry Thamyris I have been cast out of the city." And taking hold of Alexander, she tore his cloak, and pulled off his crown, and made him a laughing-stock.

27. And he, on the one hand loving her, and on the other ashamed of what had happened, led her before the proconsul; and as she confessed that she had done these things, he condemned her to the wild beasts <Alexander arranging the games>.[33] The women of the city cried out beside the tribunal, "Evil judgment! impious judgment!" And Thecla [34] asked the proconsul to be let alone until she shall fight with the wild beasts. And a rich woman [of royal descent] [35] named Tryphæna, whose daughter [36] was dead, took her into keeping and had her for a consolation.

---

[33] Not in the Greek, but in the Coptic.
[34] Coptic: She.
[35] Not in the Coptic.
[36] Some MSS. "whose daughter, named Falconilla."

28. And when the beasts were exhibited, they bound her to a fierce lioness, and Queen Tryphæna followed her. And the lioness, with Thecla sitting upon her, licked her feet; and all the multitude was astonished. And the charge on her inscription was "Sacrilegious." And the women and children cried out again and again,[37] "O God,[38] outrageous things take place in this city." And after the exhibition Tryphæna received her again. For her dead daughter had said to her in a dream, "Mother, receive this stranger, the forsaken Thecla in my place, that she may pray for me and I come to the place of the just."

29. And when after the exhibition, Tryphæna had received her, she was grieved on the one hand because she had to fight on the following day with the wild beasts, on the other hand she <grieved> very much over her daughter Falconilla, and said: "Thecla, my second child, come, pray for my child, that she may live [in eternity]; [39] for this I saw in my sleep." And without hesitation she lifted up her voice, and said, "My God, thou Son of the Most High, who art in heaven [40] grant her wish that her daughter Falconilla may live in eternity." And when Thecla had thus spoken, Tryphæna grieved very much, considering that such beauty is to be thrown to the wild beasts.

---

[37] "Again and again" not in the Coptic.
[38] Not in the Coptic.
[39] Not in the Coptic.
[40] Coptic: O God of heavens, Son of the Most High.

30. And when it was dawn Alexander came to her, for it was he who arranged the exhibition of wild beasts — and said, "The proconsul has taken his seat, and the crowd is clamoring; get ready, I will take her that is to fight with the wild beasts." And Tryphæna cried aloud, so that he even fled, saying; "A second mourning for my Falconilla has come upon my house, and there is no one to help; neither child, for she is dead, nor kinsman, for I am a widow. God of Thecla, my child, help Thecla."

31. And the proconsul sent soldiers to bring Thecla. Tryphæna departed not from her, but took her by the hand and led her away, saying, "My daughter Falconilla I took away to the tomb; but thee, Thecla, I take to the wild-beast fight." And Thecla wept bitterly, and sighed to the Lord, "O Lord God, in whom I trust, to whom I have fled for refuge, who didst deliver me from the fire, reward Tryphæna, who has had compassion on thy servant, and because she kept me pure."

32. And there arose a tumult: the wild beasts howled, the people and the women, sitting near by crying, the one saying, "Away with the sacrilegious person!" The others saying, "O that the city would be destroyed on account of this iniquity! Kill us all, proconsul; miserable spectacle, awful judgment!"

33. And Thecla having been taken from the hands of Tryphæna, was stripped, and received an apron and was thrown into the arena. And lions

and bears were let loose upon her. And a fierce lioness having run up to her feet, lay down. But the multitude of the women cried aloud. And a bear ran upon her; but the lioness went to meet it and tore the bear to pieces. And again a lion that had been trained against men, which belonged to Alexander, ran upon her. And the lioness, encountering the lion, was killed along with him. And the women cried the more, since also the lioness, her protector, was dead.

34. Then they send in many beasts, she standing and stretching forth her hands, and praying. And when she had finished her prayer, she turned around and saw a large ditch full of water, and said, "Now it is time to wash myself." And she threw herself in, saying, "In the name of Jesus Christ I baptize myself on my last day." When the women saw [41] it, and the multitude, they wept and said, "Do not throw thyself into the water!" so that also the governor shed tears, because the seals were to devour such beauty. She then threw herself into the water in the name of Jesus Christ; but the seals having seen the glare of lightning, floated about dead. And there was round her a cloud of fire, so that the beasts could neither touch her, nor could she be seen naked.

35. But the women lamented, when other more fierce animals were let loose, and some threw green herbs, others nard, others cassia, others amomum,

---

[41] Coptic: heard.

so that there was an abundance of perfumes. And all the wild beasts were as hypnotized and touched her not. And Alexander said to the proconsul, "I have some terrible bulls, to which we will bind her that is to fight with the beasts." And the proconsul said in a sullen manner, "Do what thou wilt." And they bound her by the feet between the bulls, and put red-hot irons under their privy parts, so that they, being rendered more furious, might kill her. They rushed about, therefore; but the burning flame consumed the ropes, and she was as if she had not been bound.

36. And Tryphæna fainted standing beside the arena, so that the servants said, "Queen Tryphæna is dead." And the proconsul put a stop to the games, and the whole city was in dismay. And Alexander fell down to the feet of the proconsul and cried, "Have mercy upon me and upon the city, and give the woman free, lest the city be also destroyed. For if Cæsar hear of these things, he will possibly destroy the city also along with us, because his kinswoman Tryphæna [the Queen], has died beside the circus gate."

37. And the proconsul summoned Thecla out of the midst of the beasts, and said to her, "Who art thou? and what is there about thee, that no one of the wild beasts touch thee?" She answered, "I am a servant of the living God; and as to what there is about me, I have believed in the Son of God, in whom he is well pleased, wherefore not one of the beasts has touched me. For he alone is the goal of

salvation, and the basis of immortal [42] life. For he is a refuge to the tempest-tossed, a solace to the afflicted, a shelter to the despairing; in a word: whosoever believes not in him shall not live, but be dead forever."

38. When the proconsul heard these things he ordered garments to be brought, and to be put on. And she said, "He that clothed me when I was naked among the beasts, will in the day of judgment clothe me with salvation." And taking the garments, she put them on.

And the proconsul immediately issued an edict, saying, "I release to you the God-fearing Thecla, the servant of God." And the women shouted aloud, and with one mouth praised God: "(There is) one God; who saved Thecla"— so that the whole city was shaken by their voices.

39. And Tryphæna having received the good news, went with the multitude to meet Thecla. Having embraced her, she said, "Now I believe that the dead are raised! Now I believe that my child lives; come within,[43] and all that is mine I shall assign to thee." And Thecla went in along with her, and rested eight days, instructing her in the word of God, so that even some of the maidservants believed. And there was great joy in the house.

40. And Thecla kept seeking Paul. And she was told that he was in Myra. And taking young men and maidens, she girded herself; and having

---

[42] Coptic: eternal.
[43] The Coptic: come within, my daughter, Thecla.

sewed the tunic so as to make a man's cloak, she came to Myra, where she found Paul speaking the word of God. And he was astonished at seeing her and her companions, thinking that some new trial was coming upon her. And perceiving this, she said to him, "I have received baptism, O Paul; for He who wrought along with thee for the gospel has wrought in me also for baptism."

41. And Paul, taking her, led her to the house of Hermias and heard everything from her, so that Paul greatly wondered and those who heard were strengthened and prayed for Tryphæna. And Thecla rose up and said to Paul, "I am going to Iconium." Paul answered, "Go and teach the word of God." And Tryphæna sent her much clothing and gold, so that she could leave many things to Paul for the service of the poor.

42. And having come to Iconium, she went into the house of Onesiphorus, and fell upon the place where Paul used to sit and taught the word of God and she cried and said, "My God [44] and God of this house, where the light did shine upon me, Jesus Christ,[45] Son of God, my help in prison, my help before the proconsuls, my help in the fire, my help among the wild beasts, thou alone art God, and to thee be glory for ever. Amen."

43. And she found Thamyris dead, but her mother alive. And calling her mother, she said, "Theoclia, my mother, canst thou believe that the

---

[44] Coptic: Our God.
[45] Coptic: O Christ.

Lord liveth in heaven? For whether thou desirest wealth, the Lord will give it to thee through me; or thy child, behold, I am standing beside thee."

And having thus testified, she went to Seleucia and enlightened many by the word of God; then she rested in a glorious sleep.

NOTE.— In some MSS. we read after Seleucia "and dwelt in a cave seventy-two years, living upon herbs and water. And she enlightened many by the word of God. And certain men of the city, being Greeks by religion, and physicians by profession, sent to her insolent young men to destroy (or corrupt) her. For they said: She is a virgin, and serves Artemis, and from this she has virtue in healing. And by the providence of God she entered into the rock alive, and went under ground. And she departed to Rome, to see Paul, and found that he had fallen asleep. And after staying there no long time, she rested in a glorious sleep; and she is buried about two or three stadia from the tomb of her master Paul.

"She was cast, then, into the fire when seventeen years old, and among the wild beasts when eighteen. And she was an ascetic in the cave, as has been said, seventy-two years, so that all the years of her life were ninety. And having accomplished many cures, she rests in the place of the saints, having fallen asleep on the twenty-fourth of the month of September in Christ Jesus our Lord, to whom be glory and strength for ever and ever. Amen."

In a more expanded form the end of Thecla is thus described in Grabe's text as given by Lipsius, l. c. p. 271 ff.: "And a cloud of light guided her. And having come into Seleucia, she went forth outside of the city one stadium. And she was afraid of them also, for they worshipped idols. And it guided her to the mountain called Calaman or Rhodeon; and having found there a cave, she went into it. And she was there many years, and underwent many and grievous trials by the devil, and bore them nobly, being assisted by Christ. And some of the well-born women, having learned about the virgin Thecla, went to her, and

ACTS OF PAUL

learned the miracles of God. And many of them bade adieu to the world, and lived an ascetic life with her. And a good report was spread everywhere concerning her, and cures were done by her. All the city, therefore, and country round, having known this, brought their sick to the mountain; and before they came near the door they were speedily released from whatever disease they were afflicted by; and the unclean spirits went out shrieking, and all received their own in health, glorifying God, who had given such grace to the virgin Thecla. The physicians, therefore, of the city of Seleucia were thought nothing of, having lost their trade, and no one any longer had regard to them. Being filled with envy and hatred they plotted against the servant of Christ, what they should do to her. The devil then suggested to them a wicked device; and one day being assembled, and having taken counsel, they consult with each other, saying: this holy virgin has influence upon the great goddess Artemis; and if she ask anything of her, she hears her being a virgin herself, and all the gods love her. Come, then, let us take men of disorderly lives, and make them drunk with much wine, and let us give them much money, and say to them, If you can corrupt and defile her, we shall give you even more money. The physicians therefore said to themselves, that if they should be able to defile her, neither the gods nor Artemis would listen to her in the case of the sick. They therefore acted accordingly, and the wicked fellows went up to the mountain, and rushed upon the cave like lions and knocked at the door. And the holy martyr Thecla opened, emboldened by the God in whom she trusted; for she knew of their plot beforehand. And she said to them: 'What do you want my children?' And they said: 'Is there one here called Thecla?' And she said: 'What do you want with her?' They say to her: 'We want to sleep with her.' The blessed Thecla says to them: 'I am a poor old woman, a servant of my Lord Jesus Christ; and even though you want to do something unseemly to me, you cannot.' They say to her: 'By all means, shall we do to thee what we want.' And having said this, they laid fast hold of her, and wished to insult her. But she said to them with mildness: 'Wait my children, that you may see the glory of the Lord.' And being laid hold of by them, she looked up into heaven, and said: 'God, terrible and incomparable, and glorious to Thine adversaries, who didst deliver me out of the fire, who didst not give me up to Thamyris, who didst not give me up to Alexander, who didst deliver me from the wild beasts, who didst save me in the abyss, who hast everywhere worked with me, and glorified Thy name in me, now also deliver me from these lawless men, and let them not insult my virginity, which for Thy name's sake I have preserved till now, because I love Thee, and desire Thee, and adore Thee, the Father, and the Son, and the Holy Ghost for ever. Amen.' And there came a voice out of the heaven, saying: 'Fear not, Thecla, my true servant, for I am with thee. Look and see where an opening has been made before thee, for there shall be for thee an everlasting house, and there shalt thou obtain shelter.' And looking up around, the blessed Thecla saw the rock opened as far as to allow a man to enter, and she did according to what had been said to her, and courageously fleeing from the lawless ones entered into the rock; and the rock was straightway shut together, so that not even a joining appeared. And they, beholding the extraordinary wonder, became as it were distracted; and they were not able to detain the servant of God, but only caught hold of her dress, and were able to tear off a certain part; and that by the permission of God for the faith of those seeing the venerable place, and for a blessing in the generations afterwards to those that believe in our Lord Jesus Christ out of a pure heart.

"Thus, then suffered the first martyr of God, and apostle, and virgin, Thecla, who came from Iconium when eighteen years of age. With her journeying, and the going round, and the retirement in the mountain she lived yet seventy-two years more. And when the Lord took her, she was ninety years old. And thus is her consummation. And her holy commemoration is celebrated on the twenty-fourth of the month of September, to the glory of the Father, and the Son, and the Holy Ghost, now and ever, and to ages of ages. Amen."

B. Paul's Correspondence with the Corinthians.

The discovery of the Acta Pauli in the Coptic has fully confirmed the view expressed by La Croze and Zahn, that the apocryphal correspondence with the Corinthians originally formed a part of the Acta Pauli, together with the Acta Theclæ and the "martyrium" of Paul.

Zahn, *Geschichte des neutest. Kanons,* II, p. 592 ff , 606 ff.
Harnack, *Geschichte der altchristlichen Literatur,* I, 37 ff.; II, 1 p. 493 ff., 506 ff.
Vetter, "Der apokryphe dritte Korintherbrief" (in *Theol. Quartalschrift,* 1890, 610–639).
"Der apokryphe dritte Korintherbrief" (in *Literarische Rundschau,* 1892, 193-198), and under the same title, Tübingen, 1894, 13–17.
"Eine rabbinische Quelle des apokryphen dritten Korintherbriefes" (in *Theologische Quartalschrift,* 1895, 622–633).
Berger-Carriere, "La correspondence apocryphe de S. Paul et des Corinthiens" (in *Revue de theol. et de philos.,* XXIII (1891); see Harnack in *Theologische Literaturzeitung,* 1892, 2–9; Zahn in *Theolog. Literaturblatt,* 1892, 185–187.
Bratke, "Ein zweiter lateinischer Text des apokryphen Briefwechsels zwischen dem Apostel Paulus und den Korinthern" (in *Theolog. Literaturzeitung,* 1892, 585–588).
Muretow, "Ueber den apokryphen Briefwechsel des Apostels Paulus mit den Korinthern" (in *Theolog. Bote,* 1896, July-August).
Berendts, "Zur Christlogie des apokryphen, 3. Korintherbriefes" (in *Abhandlungen Alexander von Oettingen gewidmet*), Munich 1898, 1–28.
Ehrhard, *Die altchristliche Literatur,* 1900, 119 f.
Bardenhewer, *Geschichte der altkirchlichen Literatur,* 1902, Vol. I, 463 f.
Hennecke, *Neutestamentliche Apokryphen,* 1904, 357 ff.

Hennecke, *Handbuch zu den neutest. Apokryphen*, 1904, 358 ff., 388 ff.

Schmidt, *Acta Pauli*, 1904, 73 ff.

Harnack, "Untersuchungen ueber den apokryphen Briefwechsel der Korinther mit dem Apostel Paulus" (in *Sitzungsberichte der Preussischen Akademie der Wissenschaften*, January 12, 1905).

Harnack, "Die apokryphen Briefe des Paulus an die Laodicener und Korinther" (in *Kleine Texte fuer theologische Vorlesungen und Uebungen*, ed. Lietzmann, part 12, Bonn, 1905).

Zahn, *Einleitung in des Neue Testament*, 3d ed. Vol. I (1906), pp. 178, 193, 380, 386.

Leipoldt, *Geschichte des neutestamentlichen Kanons*, I (1907), 213 ff.

Bardenhewer, *Patrology*, p. 111 ff.

De Bruyne, "Une nouveau manuscript de la 3, lettre de S. Paule aux Corinthiens" in *Revue Bénédictine*, 25 Année (1908), no. 4.

In 1823 Prof. Rinck published at Heidelberg: *das Sendschreiben der Korinther an den Apostel Paulus und das dritte Sendschreiben Pauli an die Korinther*, for which he perused eight manuscripts. His researches made it clear that the correspondence in the Armenian Bible-manuscripts belonged to the body of the Pauline epistles, i.e., was originally counted in the Armenian Church as belonging to the biblical canon, because it stood as third epistle to the Corinthians after the second epistle to the Corinthians and before that to the Galatians. From other indications, Rinck also inferred that the reception of the third Corinthian into the Canon belonged to a time when the Armenian version of the Bible was made and that this was due probably to the influence of the Syriac Bible, in which the epistle must have occupied the same position. In the commentary of Ephræm Syrus[1] on the Pauline epistles, the third Corinthian is

---

[1] *Opera Ephræmi*, III, p. 116 ff. Venice, 1836; German translation in Zahn, *Kanon*, II, 2,595 ff.
Vetter, *Theolog. Quartalschrift*, 1890, p. 627 ff.

treated like the other letters of Paul and in the same order which it has in the Armenian Bible manuscripts. And the same Ephræm in his commentary on Tatian's Diatessaron,[2] quotes the 5th verse in Paul's answer as a genuine word of Paul, and before Ephræm his countryman Aphraates besides the fifth quoted also the tenth.[3] Besides in the Armenian, the third epistle to the Corinthians has also been discovered in two Latin MSS., one probably belonging to the 10th cent. and the other to the 13th. In the former the third Corinthian stands after the epistle to the Hebrews, and has the heading: "incipiunt scripta Corinthiorum ad apostolum Paulum" and "incipit resciptum Pauli apostoli ad Corinthios"; the inscription reads: "explicit epistula ad Corinthios tertia." Then follows the so-called letter to the Laodiceans. In the 13th cent. MS. the Corinthian correspondence stands at the end with the following headings: "Petitio Corinthiorum a Paulo apostolo" and "Epistola tertia ad Corinthios quæ authentica non est." At the end the copyist added: "hanc repperi ego in veteri quodam libro, qu [æ] tertia ad Corinthios inscribitur, quamv [is in ca] none non habeatur." Schmidt thinks that the third epistle existed not only in the Syriac version, but also in Greek Bibles which were in use among Greek-speaking congregations in Syria and Palestine. The Greek no doubt formed the basis of the Latin, and since the correspondence as is now proven, formed a part of the Acts of Paul, we can very well understand the existence of Latin versions of the Acts.

The Coptic version though fragmentary, is an important witness and is a proof that the original text is preserved the purest in the 13th century Latin MS. of Laon found by E. Bratke. This MS. is unhappily also deficient; but with the help of the other Latin MS. edited by Berger-Carriere, the Armenian of Rink, and Ephræm's commentary (ed. Kanajanz-Hübschmann), a translation is made possible.

In the Coptic the correspondence is thus prefaced: "The Corinthians were in great distress on account of Paul, that

---

[2] Mösinger, *Evangelii concordantis expositio*, 1876, p. 16.
[3] See *Homilien des Aphraates*, übersetzt von Bert (*Texte und Untersuchungen*, III, p. 389, hom. 23, p. 105).

he would die before his time. For men, Simon and Cleobius, had come to Corinth who said: 'there is no resurrection of the flesh, but of the spirit, and that the body of man is not created by God nor the world, that God does not know the world, nor has Jesus Christ been crucified, but only in appearance, and that he was not born of Mary nor of the seed of David.' In a word, they proclaimed (?) many things in Corinth, deceiving [many others and deceiving] themselves. When therefore the Corinthians heard that Paul was at Philippi, they sent a letter to Paul to Macedonia by the hand of Threptus and Eutychus, the deacons. The letter however was of this nature."

[A. LETTER OF THE CORINTHIANS TO THE APOSTLE PAUL.]

I

1. Stephanus and his fellow-presbyters Daphnus and Eubulus and Theophilus and Zeno to Paul, the brother in the Lord — greeting!
2. Two individuals have come to Corinth, named Simon and Cleobius, who overthrow the faith of some through pernicious words.
3. These examine yourself.
4. For we never heard such things, neither from you, nor from the other apostles.
5. But we keep what we have received from thee and from the others.
6. Since the Lord has shown us mercy, that while you are still in the flesh we should hear this [4] from you once more.
7. Come to us.[5]
8. For we believe as it has been revealed to Thence that the Lord has delivered thee from the hands of the godless.
9. What they say and teach is as follows:
10. They assert that one must not appeal to the prophets,
11. And that God is not almighty,
12. There is no resurrection of the body,
13. Man has not been made by God,

---

[4] This: not in the Coptic.
[5] Some authorities: come to us or write to us.

ACTS OF PAUL

14. Christ [6] has neither come in the flesh, nor was he born of Mary [7]

15. And the world is not the work of God, but of angels.

16. Wherefore, we beseech thee, brother, do thy diligence to come to us, that the Corinthian church [8] remain without stumbling, and the foolishness of those be confounded. Farewell in the Lord!

II

1. The deacons Threptus and Eutychus took the letter to Philippi,

2. So that Paul received it, being himself in prison because of Stratonike, the wife of Apollophanes; and he became very sad [9]

3. And exclaimed saying: "it had been better, had I died and were with the Lord than to abide in the flesh and to hear . . . such words . . . so that sorrow comes upon sorrow.

4. "And to be in prison in the face of such great distress and behold such mischief where the wiles of Satan are busy!"

5. And under much affliction Paul wrote the answer to the letter.[10]

[B. PAUL'S EPISTLE TO THE CORINTHIANS.]

1. Paul, the prisoner of Jesus Christ, to the brethren at Corinth — greeting.

2. Being in many afflictions, I marvel not, that the teachings of the evil one had such rapid success.

3. For my Lord Jesus Christ will hasten his coming, since he can no longer tolerate the wrong of those who falsify his teaching.

4. For I delivered unto you first of all what I received [11]

---

[6] In the Coptic: the Lord.
[7] Some authorities read: of the Virgin Mary.
[8] Some authorities: the city of the Corinthians.
[9] The Coptic is here defective. I followed Harnack's Greek text. Some authorities like the Armenian and Ephræm read here: so sad that he forgot his bonds and became sorry because of the words which he heard.
[10] Vs. 3-5 is greatly amplified. The Coptic is defective.
[11] One authority: from the Lord and the apostles before me.

from the apostles before me, who were always with Jesus Christ,[12]

5. That our Lord Jesus Christ was born of Mary [13] of the seed of David,[14] the Father having sent the spirit from heaven into her,

6. That he come into this world and save all flesh by his own flesh and that he raise us in the flesh from the dead, as he has presented himself to us as its type.

7. And that man is created by his Father,

8. Wherefore, also, when being lost, he was sought by him, to become alive by the adoption of sons.

9. For the almighty God,[15] maker of heaven and earth, first sent the prophets to the Jews to deliver them from their sins.

10. For he wished to save the house of Israel; therefore he took from the spirit of Christ and poured it out upon the prophets, who proclaimed the true worship [16] at many times.

11. For the wicked prince, who would be God himself, laid his hands on them and killed them and bound all flesh of man through the lust.[17]

12. But the almighty God, being just, and not wishing to cast off his creature,[18] had mercy.

13. And sent his Spirit into Mary [19]

14. Who believed with all her heart and conceived by the Holy Ghost, that Jesus could come into the world,[20]

15. That the evil one [fettered] by the same flesh, by which he wrought, be convinced.[21]

---

[12] Some: with our Lord Jesus Christ.

[13] Armenian: of the Virgin Mary.

[14] One authority: David after the flesh. Ephræm and Armenian read: David, according to the promises of the Holy Spirit.

[15] In the Armenian: God, the Father of our Lord Jesus Christ.

[16] Ephræm and Armenian: worship and the birth of Christ.

[17] One authority: lust to his will, and the consummation of the world hastened the judgment.

[18] Six lines are here wanting in the Coptic.

[19] Some authorities add: in Galilee.

[20] Harnack considers this clause as a later addition and omits it.

[21] Some authorities read: convinced, that he is not God.

16. For by his own body Jesus Christ saved all flesh,[22]

17. Presenting in his own body a temple [23] of righteousness,

18. Through which we are saved.

19. Know therefore that they who follow them are not children of righteousness, but of wrath, who despise the wisdom of God, and, not believing, assert that heaven and earth, and all that is in them, are not a work of God.[24]

20. [They are therefore children of wrath][25] they have the accursed belief of the serpent;

21. These remove from you,[26] and keep aloof from their teaching.

22. [For you are not children of disobedience, but children of the beloved Church.

23. On this account the time of the resurrection has been preached by all.][27]

24. And they who say [28] that there is no resurrection of the flesh, shall have no resurrection,

25. For they believe not that the Dead had thus risen.

26. For they know not, O Corinthians, the seed of wheat or some other grain [29] that it is cast barely into the ground, and which having been dissolved rises up again after the will of God in the same body and clothed.

27. And he dissolves not only the body which is sown, but blesses it manifold.

28. And if one will not take the parable of the seed grains [but from nobler bodies][30]

29. Let him look at Jonah, the son of Amittai, who, be-

---

[22] Armenian reads: flesh, and through faith brought it to everlasting life.

[23] Armenian and Ephræm: holy temple.

[24] Armenian and Ephræm: the work of God, the Father of the universe.

[25] So one authority, but not in the Coptic and Harnack.

[26] Harnack's reading "from us" is probably only a misprint of a letter.

[27] These two verses are not in the Coptic, are omitted also by Harnack; they are found in the Armenian.

[28] Coptic: say to you.

[29] The Coptic breaks here off.

[30] So the Armenian.

come unwilling to preach unto the Ninevites, is swallowed up by the whale.

30. And after three days and three nights God heard the prayer of Jonah out of the deepest hell, and nothing is injured in him, neither the hair nor the eyelid.

31. How much more will he raise you up, who have believed [81] in Christ Jesus,[82] as he himself was raised up.

32. And when by the bones of the prophet Elisha, one of the children of Israel that had been thrown upon them, rose from death in his body, how much more shall ye rise up on that day with a whole body, after ye have been thrown upon the body and bones and Spirit of Christ.

33. [Also Elijah, the prophet; took the son of the widow into his arms, and raised him from the dead; how much more shall Jesus Christ raise you up also on that day with a whole body, as he rose himself from the dead.][83]

34. If, however, you receive something else,[84] let no man trouble me.[85]

35. For I have these bonds on me, that I may win Christ, and I bear his marks, that I may attain unto the resurrection of the dead.

36. And whoever accepts this rule which we have received by the blessed prophets and the holy gospel, shall receive [86] a reward,[87]

37. But whosoever deviates from this, fire shall be for him and for those who preceded him therein.

38. Who are a generation of vipers,[88]

39. These resist in the power of the Lord,

40. And with you shall be peace.[89]

---

[81] One authority: raise you up, ye of little faith, and those who have believed.

[82] Armenian: in the Lord Jesus Christ.

[83] So the Armenian.

[84] One authority adds: God shall rise up against you as a witness.

[85] Armenian and Ephræm add: in future.

[86] Armenian and Ephræm: receive at the resurrection of the dead.

[87] Ephræm: reward for it and for his works.

[88] Armenian and Ephræm: vipers and basilisks.

[89] The Armenian: and the grace of the beloved First-born.

C. The Martyrdom of the Holy Apostle Paul.

Under this title Lipsius published for the first time (*Acta Apocrypha*, I, 102-117) the Greek text according to an Athos and Patmos manuscript, together with a Latin translation according to three Munich manuscripts. The Coptic (Schmidt, *Acta*, p. 83-90) is in rather a bad state, only a part is preserved.

1. Luke who had come from Gaul, and Titus who had come from Dalmatia, expected Paul at Rome. When Paul saw them, he rejoiced and rented a barn outside of Rome, where he and the brethren taught the word of truth. He became famous, and many souls were added to the Lord, so that it was noised about in Rome, and a great many from the house of the emperor came to him, and there was much joy.

A certain Patroclus, a cupbearer of the emperor, who had come too late to the barn and could not get near to Paul on account of the throng of the people, sat on a high parapet, and listened how he taught the word of God. As Satan, being bad, became jealous of the love of the brethren, Patroclus fell down from the parapet and died; speedily it was reported to Nero. Paul, however, having learned it by the Spirit, said to his hearers, " Men, dear brethren, the evil one has obtained room, that he may tempt you; go forth and ye will find a boy

---

Amen.— Another authority reads: peace, grace and love, Amen.

which had fallen down and is about dying. Lift him up and bring him hither." This they did. When the people saw him, they were frightened. Paul said to them, " Now, dear brethren, show your faith. Come, let us cry to our Lord Jesus Christ, that the boy might live and we remain unmolested." When all began to lament, the boy took breath; and having put him on a beast of burden, they sent him away alive with all those which were of the emperor's house.

2. And Nero, having heard of Patroclus's death, became very sad, and as he just came in from his bath, he ordered another one to be appointed for the wine. But his boys said, " Emperor, Patroclus is alive, and stands at the sideboard." When the emperor heard that Patroclus was alive, he was frightened and would not come in. But after having come in, and seeing Patroclus, he cried out, " Patroclus, thou livest?" He answered, "(Yea,) I am alive, Cæsar." Who said, " Who is he that made thee alive?" And the boy, being carried away by a mind of faith, said, " Christ Jesus, the King of the ages." The emperor asked in dismay, " Is he to be King of the ages and destroy all kingdoms?" Says Patroclus to him, " Yea, he destroys all kingdoms under the heaven, and he alone shall remain in all eternity, and there will be no kingdom which escapes him." And he slapped his face, and cried out, " Patroclus, thou also art fighting for that king?" He answered, " Yes, my lord and Cæsar, for he has raised me from the dead."

And Barrabas Justus the flat-footed, and Urion the Cappadocian, and Festus of Galatia, the first men of Nero, said, "And we, too, fight for him, the King of the world." After they were terribly tortured, he had them imprisoned, whom he greatly loved, and ordered that the soldiers of the great King be sought, and issued an edict that all Christians and soldiers of Christ that were found, should be executed.

3. And in the multitude Paul also was brought in fetters. Those that were imprisoned with him looked at him, so that the emperor knew that he was the leader of the soldiers. And he said to him, "Man of the great King, now my prisoner, what induced thee to come secretly into the Roman empire and to enlist soldiers in my territory?" But Paul, filled with the Holy Spirit, said in the presence of all, "Cæsar, we enlist soldiers not only in your territory, but in all lands of the earth. For thus we are commanded to exclude none who wishes to fight for my King. If it seemeth good to thee to serve him <thou wilt not regret it. Moreover, think not that> [1] riches or that which glitters in this life will save thee; but if thou becomest his subject and ask him, thou shalt be saved. For on one day he will destroy the world."

Having heard this, Nero commanded to burn all prisoners with fire, but to behead Paul in accordance with the law of the Romans. And Paul was not silent, but communicated the word to Longus the

---

[1] Following the Latin.

prefect and Cestus the centurion. And Nero being instigated by the evil one (raged) at Rome, and had many Christians executed without being judged, so that the Romans stood before the palace and cried, "It is enough, Cæsar; these men are ours; thou destroyest the strength of the Romans." Being thus convinced, he desisted <having issued an edict> not to touch any Christian till his case had been investigated.[2]

4. After the issuing of the edict, Paul was brought before him, and he insisted that he should be executed. And Paul said, "Cæsar, I live not merely for a short time unto my King; and if thou have me executed, I shall do the following: I will rise again and appear unto thee, for I am not dead, but live unto my King Christ Jesus, who shall come to judge the earth."

And Longus and Cestus said to Paul, "Whence have you this King that you believe on him, without changing your mind unto death?" And Paul answered and said, "Ye men, being ignorant and in error, change your mind and be saved from the fire which comes over the whole earth. For we fight not, as you suppose, for a King who is from the earth, but who is from heaven for the living God, who comes as judge because of the righteousness, which takes place in this world. And blessed is he who will believe on him and live in eternity when he shall come with fire to purge the earth." And

---

[2] Here endeth the Latin.

they besought him and said, "We pray thee, help us and we will release thee." But he answered <with a smiling face> [3] "I am not a deserter of Christ, but a faithful soldier of the living God. If I knew that I should die, I would do it, Longus and Cestus; but since I live to God and love myself, I go to the Lord that I may come (again) with him in the glory of his Father." And they said unto him "How can we live after thou hast been beheaded?"

5. And while they were speaking Nero sent a certain Parthenius and Pheretas to see whether Paul had already been beheaded. And they found him still alive. He summoned them beside him and said: "Believe in the living God, who will raise me, as well as all those that believe on him, from the dead." But they said, "We will now go to Nero, but when you have died and have been raised up, we will believe in thy God."

But when Longus and Cestus continued to ask [4] about their salvation, he said to them, "In the early dawn come quickly to my grave, and you will find two men at prayer, Titus and Luke; they will give you the seal in the Lord." [5]

And turning toward the east, Paul lifted up his hands to heaven and prayed much; and after having conversed in Hebrew with the fathers during prayer, he bent his neck, without speaking any more. When the lictor cut off his head, milk splashed on the dress

---

[3] So Codex Athos.
[4] Coptic: asked.
[5] Coptic: omits: in the Lord.

of the soldier. And the soldier, and all who stood near by, were astonished at this sight and glorified God, who had thus honored Paul. And they went away and reported everything to Cæsar.

6. When he heard (of it), he was much amazed, not knowing what to say. While many philosophers and the centurion were assembled with the emperor, Paul came about the ninth hour, and in the presence of all he said, " Cæsar behold, here is Paul, the soldier of God; I am not dead, but I live in my God. But upon thee, thou miserable one,[6] many evils and great punishments [6] will come, because thou hast unjustly shed the blood of the righteous, not many days hence." And after having spoken thus, Paul departed from him.[7] When Nero had heard (this), he commanded that the prisoners be released, Patroclus as well as Barsabas with his friends.

7. And as Paul had told them, Longus and Cestus the centurion, came very early to the grave of Paul, trembling. And when they came near, they found two men in prayer and Paul with them, so that they became frightened when beholding the incredible miracle, whilst Titus and Luke, being afraid at the sight of Longus and Cestus, turned to run away.

But the persecutors said to them, " We persecute you not in order to kill you, ye blessed men of God,

---

[6] Coptic omits: thou miserable one and great punishments.
[7] This clause omitted in the Coptic.

as you suppose,[8] but in order to live, that ye may do unto us [9] as Paul promised to us, whom we have just seen in prayer beside you." Upon hearing this, Titus and Luke [10] gave them joyfully the seal in the Lord, glorifying God and the Father of our Lord Jesus Christ, to whom be honor for ever and ever. Amen.[11]

The Coptic has the statement: "the Acts of Paul according to the Apostle," i.e. according to Paul himself. As the fragment which thus concludes is the story of Paul's martyrdom, we have a parallel here to the conclusion of the Pentateuch with the story of Moses' death. Probably the good people of the second century found no more difficulty in attributing the account of his own death to St. Paul than many devout Christians have in attributing Deut. XXXIV to Moses.—

---

[8] Coptic omits: ye . . . suppose.
[9] Coptic: but that ye give unto us the life.
[10] Coptic omits: Titus and Luke.
[11] Coptic: glorifying the.

II

THE ACTS OF PETER.

LITERATURE

Lipsius, *Apokryphe Apostelgeschichten*, II, 1 (1887) 96 ff., 174 ff.; Supplement 1890, p. 98 f.
Acta Apostolorum Apocrypha, I (1891), 1 pp. XXXIII–LV; 45–103.
Zahn, *Geschichte des neutest. Kanons,* II, 2 (1892), 835–855.
Harnack, *Geschichte der altchristlichen Litteratur,* II, 1 (1897), 549–560.
Patristische Miscellen (in *Texte und Untersuchungen,* new series, V, 3, 1900, p. 100–106).
Ehrhard, *Die altchristliche Litteratur,* 1900, 156 ff.
Hilgenfeld, "Die alten Actus Petri" (in *Zeitschrift für wissenschaftliche Theologie,* XI (1903).
Ficker, *Die Petrusakten. Beiträge zu ihrem Verständnis,* 1903. "Petrusakten" in Hennecke, *Neutestamentliche Apokryphen,* 1904, 383 ff.; in *Handbuch zu den neutestamentlichen Apokryphen,* 1904, 395 ff.
Schmidt, *Die alten Petrusakten,* 1903.
Leipoldt, *Geschichte des neutestamentlichen Kanons,* I (1907), 262 ff.
Flamion, "Les actes apocryphes de Pierre" (in *Revue d'histoire ecclésiastique,* Année 9, No. 3, 15 Juillet, 1908).
Bardenhewer, *Patrology,* p. 98 ff.
Nissen, "Die Pertrusakten und ein Bardesanitisther Dialog in der Aberkiosvita" (in *Zeitschrift fuer die neutestamentliche Wissenschaft, etc.,* IX (1908), parts 3 and 4.

Photius in his *Bibliotheca* (cod. 114) mentions the Acts of Peter together with those of John, Andrew, Thomas and Paul. What we now have of these Acts is contained in a

ACTS OF PETER

Latin seventh-century manuscript preserved at the Library in Vercelli, and published by Lipsius, I, pp. 5-103. These Acts are known as the *Actus Vercellenses*. A Coptic fragment was discovered by C. Schmidt, which also contains Acts of Peter. This fragment, together with a German translation, he published under the title *Die alten Petrusakten im Zusammenhang der apokryphen Apostelliteratur*, Leipzig, 1903. The deeds narrated in the Coptic take place, according to Schmidt, at Jerusalem, those in the *Actus Vercellenses* at Rome. Ficker thinks this possible, but not sufficiently established. It is possible that that which is narrated in the Coptic originally formed a part of a work which was called "Acts of Peter," and it is also possible that the Coptic narrative originally belonged to another work also called "Acts of Peter," differing from the *Actus Vercellenses*, which were intended to continue and supplement the canonical Acts of the Apostles. Ancient writers seem to have known the Acts of Peter which were used by certain communities, which the church regarded as heretical (Eusebius, *His. eccles.*, III, 3, 2.)[1] Whether these Acts were the same as the *Actus Vercellenses* cannot be said in view of the present state of the latter.

As to the author of the Acts of Peter, opinions differ. Zahn and James think that Leucius, the author of the Acts of John, is also the author of the Acts of Peter. Says James (*Texts and Studies*, V. I, p. XXIV ff): "whoever wrote the Acts of John wrote the Acts of Peter." Not so Schmidt. After examining all the testimony, he comes to the conclusion that to Leucius belongs the honor of having composed the first apostolic romance; contrary to his own expectation he paved the way for an entirely new old Christian literary production, because his example was soon followed by the author of the Acts of Paul, who was also

---

[1] Nevertheless the Acts were read by orthodox Christians, like Priscillian who recommends the reading of the Acts of the Apostles, because they recommended the purity of life. Priscillian's death was not because of heresy, but because of sorcery. Even his opponent Philastrius of Brescia recommended the reading of these Acts. See Leipoldt, loc. cit. p. 264; Schmidt, p. 43.

of Asia Minor. Standing on the shoulders of both, Pseudo-Peter wrote this romance. This will explain many things, especially the fact that Pseudo-Peter made use of the Acts of John and Paul, probably also of other sources.

According to Schmidt the Acts of Peter were composed between 200–210 A. D., at Jerusalem and Rome. Zahn pleads for Asia Minor, which would account for the author's ignorance of Roman affairs.

The Acts of Peter are valuable for our knowledge of the Ancient Catholic Church. They bring before us the Christian Church in its religious thinking, feeling and working at the end of the second century. Only a Catholic writer could present such a picture.

We first give the Coptic fragment. We then give Peter's affairs with Simon at Rome, or the *Actus Vercellenses*, which begin with Paul's abode at Rome and his taking leave of the congregation there (chaps. I–III). The next section (chaps. IV–XXXII) treats of Simon, the Magician, and the struggle which Peter had with him. Simon is overcome and the Roman congregation is re-established at Rome. The last section (chaps. XXXIII–XLI) treats of Peter's death and its causes.

With the exception of the martyrdom of Peter — which is extant in the Greek original — the greater part of the *Actus Vercellenses* is in Latin. This Latin text, which is found in MS. CVIII, 1 of the chapter library at Vercelli, follows after the Clementine Recognitions. The MS. belongs to the seventh century, but was probably copied from an earlier one, belonging, perhaps, to the fourth century.

I.

The Deed of Peter.

(P. 128).[2] But on the first day of the week, i. e., on Sunday, a multitude gathered together, and they

---

[2] This and the following numbers indicate the page in the Coptic manuscript.

ACTS OF PETER

brought many sick people to Peter, that he might cure them. And one of the multitude was bold enough to say unto Peter, "Peter, behold, before our eyes thou didst make many blind see and deaf hear and the lame walk, and hast helped the weak, and given them strength; why hast thou not helped thy virgin daughter, which grew up beautifully and (p. 129) believed on the name of God? For behold, one of her sides is wholly paralyzed, and there she is helpless in the corner. One can see those which thou hast cured; but for thy own daughter thou didst not care."

But Peter smiled and said to him, "My son, God alone knows why her body is sick. Know that God is not unable or powerless, to give his present to my daughter. But that thy soul may be convinced and those present believe the more" (p. 130) he looked at his daughter and said to her, "Arise from thy place with the help of none except Jesus alone, and walk wholly before those present and come to me." And she arose and came to him. The multitude rejoiced over that which had taken place. And Peter said to them: "Behold, your hearts are convinced that God is not powerless concerning the things which we ask of him." They rejoiced the more and glorified God. Said (p. 131) Peter to his daughter, "Return to thy place, sit down there, and be helpless again, for it is good for me and thee." And the girl did as she was bidden, and became as before. The whole multitude wept and besought Peter to make her whole.

Peter said to them: "As the Lord liveth, this is good for her and for me. For on the day on which she was born to me, I saw a vision and the Lord said to me, 'Peter, this day has been born unto thee a great (p. 132) affliction, for this (i. e. daughter) will hurt many souls, if her body remains well!' I, however, thought that the vision was chaffing me.

"When the girl was ten years old, she became a stumbling-block to many. And a very rich man, Ptolemy by name, when he saw the girl bathing with her mother, sent for her to take her for his wife; but her mother consented not. He often sent for her, for he could not wait . . .

(Pages 133-134 are wanting.)

<the men of> (135) Ptolemy brought the girl, and leaving her before the door of the house, went away.

"When I saw this, I and her mother went downstairs and found the girl, one side of her body from head to foot being paralyzed and dried up. We carried her away, praising the Lord that he had kept his servant from defilement and violation and . . . This is the reason why the girl <remains> thus to this day. But now you shall hear what happened to (p. 136) Ptolemy. He repented and lamented night and day over that which had happened to him; and because of the many tears which he shed, he became blind. Having decided to hang himself, behold, about the ninth hour of that day, whilst alone in his bedroom, he saw a great light, which illuminated the whole house, and he heard a voice saying unto him: (p. 137) 'Ptolemy, God has not given the vessels for corruption and violation; it is unseemly for thee, as thou hast believed on me, to violate my virgin, whom thou shalt know as thy sister, as if I had become one spirit to both of you — but arise, and speedily go to the house of the apostle Peter and thou shalt see my glory. He will make known the matter to thee.' And Ptolemy delayed not, but ordered his people (p. 138) to show him the way and bring him to me. When he had come to me, he told all that had happened to him in the power of Jesus Christ, our Lord. And he saw with the eyes of his flesh and with the eyes of his soul, and many hoped on Christ; he did good unto them and gave them the presence of God.

"After this Ptolemy died; he departed and went to his Lord (p. 139). <When he>, however, <made> his will, he left a piece of land in the name of my daughter, because through her he became a believer in God and was made whole. I, however, who was appointed administrator, have acted carefully. I sold the acre, and God alone knows that neither I nor my daughter have kept anything from the money of the acre, but I sent the whole sum to the poor. Know, therefore, O servant of Christ Jesus, that God (p. 140) rules (?) his people, and prepares for each what is good; we, however, think that God has forgotten us. Now then, brethren, let us mourn, be watchful and pray, and God's goodness will look upon us, and we hope for it."

And some other addresses delivered Peter before them, and glorifying the name of (p. 141) the Lord

Christ he gave of the bread to every one of them; and after having distributed it, he rose and went into the house.

[THE PRAXIS OF PETER.]

NOTE.— It is evident that the narrative given above forms a part of a larger work. This is already clear from the beginning " on the first day of the week."

A copyist detached it from the entire work for a certain purpose which he had in view. The piece was much too small to be considered as an independent whole. The postscript in the Coptic presupposes a Greek original, "*praxis Petru.*" The entire work must accordingly have had this title, and we have thus a hitherto unknown portion of the ancient Acts of Peter, first mentioned by Eusebius (*Hist. eccles.*, III, 3, 2).

Of the paralytic daughter of Peter we read in Augustine *Contra Adimantum Manichæi discipulum*, 17, 5; also Jerome *ad Jovin.*, I, 26. The *Acta Philippi* (II, 2ª p. 81) also mention this fact and it is possible that the author of the Acts of Philip perused the Acts of Peter. The story of Peter's daughter was further developed in the Acts of Nereus and Achilles,[3] where her name is given as Petronilla, and not Ptolemy but Flaccus is mentioned.

---

[3] *Acta St. Nerei et Achillei græce*, ed. A. Wirth, Leipzig, 1890 (on which see Krüger in *Theologische Litteraturzeitung*, 1891, 69 f).; *Acta St. Nerei et Achillei*, ed. Achelis (*Texte und Untersuchungen*, XI, 2 (1893). See also Schæfer, *Die Akten der heill. Nereus und Achilleus. Untersuchung* über den Original text und die Zeit seiner Entstehung (in *Römische Quartalschrift*, 8 (1894) 89-119) who claims a Latin original; the same is also the view of Hilgenfeld in *Berliner philol. Wochenschrift*, 1894, p. 1383.

ACTS OF PETER 57

2.

[Peter's Affair With Simon.[1]]

(*Actus Vercellenses.*)

(*Acta Apostolorum Apocrypha* I, pp. 45–103)

1. When Paul was at Rome and confirmed many in the faith, it also[2] happened that a certain woman named Candida, wife of Quartus the custodian, heard Paul and listened to his words and became a believer. And when she on her part had instructed her husband, who became a believer, Quartus persuaded Paul to leave the city (and to go) wherever he pleased. Paul said to him, "If such be the will of God, he will reveal it to me." And Paul fasted three days and besought the Lord to grant what were good for him, and in a vision he saw the Lord, who said to him, "Paul, arise, and in thy body be a physician to the Spaniards!" At this he related to the brethren what God had commanded (him), and without hesitation he made ready to leave the city. When Paul was preparing to leave (the city), there was a great lamentation among the brethren because

---

[1] The above title is that given by Lipsius, which we retained, though it is not the correct one. For, besides Peter's affair with Simon, the Acts also treat of Paul's leaving the Roman Congregation for Spain, and of Peter's martyrdom. A more correct title were: "Deeds of the Apostle Peter."

[2] From the word "also" it may be inferred that our section follows another narrative. Possibly the canonical Acts of the Apostles. In ch. 1, reference is evidently to Paul's imprisonment at Rome, and from Acts XXVIII, 16, we know that he had a soldier that kept him, although he dwelt in his own hired house (Acts XXVIII, 30).

they thought they would never see Paul again; yea, they even tore their garments, bearing in mind that Paul often had a quarrel with the teachers of the Jews [3] and had paid them off (with such words): Christ, on whom your fathers laid their hands, abrogated their Sabbath and their fasting and festivals and circumcision and abrogated the teaching of men and the other traditions. And the brethren adjured Paul, by the coming of our Lord Jesus Christ [4] not to stay away more than a year, saying, " We know thy love for thy brethren; forget us not, when thou comest (to Spain), and leave us not alone like children without a mother." And while they were thus beseeching him with tears, a sound was heard from heaven and a very loud voice, saying, " Paul, the servant of God, is chosen to the ministry for the time of his life; under the hands of Nero, the wicked and bad man, he will die before your eyes." And there was a great fear among the brethren because of the voice, which had come from heaven, and they were the more confirmed (in the faith).

2. And they brought bread and water as a sacrifice to Paul that he might offer prayer (over it) and distribute it among them. Among those present was also a woman, named Rufina, who also wished to receive the eucharist from the hands of Paul. And when she came forward, Paul, filled by the

---

[3] The author had undoubtedly the Acts of the Apostles in his mind.
[4] The second coming is meant. This shows that the Acts belong to a time in which the belief in the second coming of Christ, was still alive in the congregations.

ACTS OF PETER

Spirit of God, said to her: "Rufina, not as a worthy one dost thou approach the altar of God, since thou dost rise from the side not of a husband, but of a fornicator and thou dost endeavor to receive God's eucharist. Behold, Satan will trample down thy heart and expose thee before the eyes of all who believe in the Lord, that they may see and believe and know, that they have believed on the living God, the searcher of hearts. But if thou wilt repent of thy deed, he is faithful to forgive thy sins and can free thee from this sin. But if thou repentest not while thou art still in the body, the devouring fire and the outer darkness will receive thee for ever."

And directly Rufina collapsed, being paralyzed on the left side from head to foot. Nor could she speak any more, for her tongue was tied.[5] When the old believers and neophytes [6] saw this, they beat their breasts, remembering their former sins, lamented and said, "We know not whether God forgives us the former sins, which we have committed." [7]

And Paul asked for silence, and said: "Men and brethren, you who have now commenced to believe on Christ, if you continue not in your former works committed according to the tradition of your fathers, and abstain from every deceit and wrath, from all

---

[5] A drastic illustration to I Cor. XI, 27, 29.
[6] i.e. newly converted.
[7] The general notion existed that through baptism the former sins were forgiven; see Tertullian *de bapt.* I; Aristides *apol.* 4, *Hermas mand.* IV, I, 11; 2, 2; Justin *dial.*, 116, *Book of Jubilees*, XXII, 14.

cruelty and fornication and pollution and pride and jealousy and insolence and enmity,[8] Jesus the living God will forgive you what you have done ignorantly. Wherefore, ye servants of God, let every one of you put on peace, serenity, mildness, faith, charity, knowledge, wisdom, love for the brotherhood, hospitality, mercy, moderation, chastity, goodness, righteousness.[9] Then you will have in eternity for your guide the first-born of every creature and the power in peace with our Lord." When Paul had spoken thus, they asked him to pray for them. And Paul lifted up his voice and said, "Eternal God, God of heavens, God of unspeakable essence, who has established all by thy word, and hast added to thy grace a bond connected with the whole world, Father of thy holy Son Jesus Christ, we jointly beseech thee through thy Son Jesus Christ to strengthen the souls which were once unbelieving, but now believe. Once I was a blasphemer, but now I am blasphemed; once I was a persecutor, now I suffer persecution from others; once I was an enemy of Christ, now I ask to be permitted to be a friend. For I trust in his mercy and promise; (for) I believe that I am a believer and have received remission of my former sins. Therefore, I also exhort you, brethren, to believe in God the Father Almighty and put all your trust in our Lord Jesus Christ, his Son. If you be-

---

[8] This catalogue of vices is based on the Pauline epistles; see Gal. V, 19–21; Col. III, 8; Eph. IV, 31; V, 3.
[9] This list of virtues is also Pauline; see Gal. V, 22, 23; Rom. XII; Eph. IV; Col. III, 12–16.

ACTS OF PETER

lieve on him, no man will be able to pluck you out of his promise. In like manner bend your knees and commend me to the Lord, who am about to go to another nation, that his grace may go before me and my journey be prosperous, that it (the grace) may receive his holy vessels and the believers, and thanking me, who proclaimed unto them the word of the Lord, they become firmly established (in the faith)." And the brethren wept for a long time, and with Paul they besought God and said, "O Lord Jesus Christ, be thou with Paul, and bring him safely back to us, for we know our weakness, which is still in us."

3. And beseechingly a great multitude of women implored blessed Paul on their knees, and kissed his feet and conducted him to the harbor. And Dionysius and Balbus from Asia, Roman knights, illustrious men, together with a senator named Demetrius, took a hold of Paul's right hand and said, "Paul, I should like to leave the city and be always with thee, if I were not a state's officer." In like manner spoke Cleobius and Iphitus and Lysimachus and Aristeus of the house of Cæsar, and two matrons Berenice and Philostrate, together with the presbyter Narcissus,[10] after they had conducted him to the harbor. Since a storm was threatening, he

---

[10] These are not the only persons belonging to the higher ranks of Roman society, which are mentioned in the Acts. We shall meet with other names yet (see chaps. 8, 17, 23, 30, 33, 34, etc.). This proves that about the year 200 Christianity had also its adherents among the prominent and rich; see Harnack, *Mission*, p. 376 ff.

sent the brethren back to Rome (to announce) that everyone who wished to hear Paul before he left might come out. When the brethren had heard it, they went up to the city. They communicated it to the brethren who had remained in the city, and the news soon spread. Some came on horses, others walked, others came down the Tiber to the harbor, and for three days he strengthened them by (his) faith, and on the fourth day to the fifth hour. By turns they prayed with Paul, offered him their gifts, and put everything that was necessary into the ship, and gave him also two believing young men as companions, and bidding him farewell in the Lord they returned to Rome.

4. [11] After a few days there was a great commotion in the midst of the congregation, for (some) said that they had seen strange things by the hand of a man named Simon, who was at Aricia. They also added that he claimed to be the great power of God, doing nothing without God. Is he then Christ? We however believe on him, whom Paul has preached to us. For through him we saw how the dead were raised and (some) were healed from various diseases. This (the great power) seeks conflicts; we know it, for (thus far) not the least disturbance has risen among us. Perhaps he has already come to Rome. For yesterday he was asked with much acclamation (to do so), being told, " Thou art God in Italy, the saviour of the Romans;

---

[11] With this chapter begins the narrative of Peter's conflict with Simon.

hasten to Rome as quickly as possible." And he addressed the people and said with a thin voice, "On the following day about the seventh hour you shall see me fly over the gate of the city in the same dress in which I now speak to you. Wherefore, brethren, if it seemeth good to you, let us go and diligently await the end of the matter." And they all went out and came to the gate. About the seventh hour, there suddenly appeared afar off a dust-cloud in the sky, looking like a smoke shining with a glare of fire. And when it reached the gate, it suddenly disappeared. Then it appeared standing in the midst of the people, and all gazed at it and knew that it was he, whom they had seen the day before. And the brethren were exceedingly discomposed, especially as Paul was not at Rome, nor Timothy and Barnabas, whom Paul had sent to Macedonia, nor anyone who could strengthen us in the faith, especially the neophytes. And as Simon's authority grew more and more, and some of those among whom he labored, in their daily conversations, called Paul a sorcerer and a juggler, all of the great multitude which had been confirmed in the faith were led astray, excepting the presbyter Narcissus and two women in the hospice of the Bithynians, and four others, who could not leave the house; and day and night they prayed the Lord that Paul might either return as soon as possible or some one else (come) to visit his servants whom the devil by his wickedness had perverted.

5. While they were sorrowing and fasting, God

was even then preparing Peter at Jerusalem for the future. After the twelve years had passed, according to the direction of the Lord to Peter, Christ showed to him the following vision, saying, "Peter, Simon, whom thou hast driven out of Judea, after thou hast exposed him as a magician, has forestalled thee (and indeed) at Rome. And in short, all who believed on me he has perverted by the cunning and energy of Satan, whose power he proves to be. But delay not. Go to-morrow (to Cæsarea), and there thou will find a ship, ready to sail to Italy. And within a few days I will show thee my grace which is to distinguish thee before all." Admonished by this vision, Peter delayed not to mention it to the brethren and said, "I must go up to Rome, to subdue the enemy and opponent of the Lord and of our brethren." And he went down to Cæsarea and quickly entered the ship which was ready to sail without providing (himself) with provisions. But the steersman, named Theon, looked at Peter and said, "What we have belongs to thee. For what grace had we in receiving a man in precarious circumstances, who is like ourselves, without sharing with him what we have? If only we have a safe journey." Peter thanked him for his offer. And he fasted in the ship, being dejected and yet again comforted, because God regarded him as a servant worthy of his service. A few days afterward the steersman got up at breakfast time. And when he asked Peter to eat with him, he said, "Whoever thou art, I know thee too little; thou art either a

God or a man. But as much as I can see, I think that thou art a servant of God. As I directed my ship in the middle of the night, I fell asleep. It seemed to me as if a human voice from heaven said to me, Theon, Theon! Twice it called me by name, and said to me, 'Amongst all the passengers treat Peter in the most honorable way. For with his help, thou and the rest will safely make your journey.'" Peter, however, thinking that God wished to show his providence to all those who were in the ship, commenced at once to speak to Theon of the great deeds of God, and how the Lord had chosen him among the apostles and for what cause he went to Italy. Daily he spoke to him of the word of God. After they had become better acquainted, and Peter had found out that Theon was one with him in the faith and (that he would become) a worthy servant (of God), the ship was detained by the calm of the Adriatic Sea. Theon spoke of the calm to Peter, and said, "If thou thinkest me worthy to be baptized in the sign of the Lord, thou hast now a chance." For all others in the ship were asleep, being drunk. Peter let himself down by a rope and baptized Theon in the name of the Father and of the Son and of the Holy Ghost. The other ascended out of the water rejoicing; Peter also had become more cheerful, because God had deemed Theon worthy of his name. And it happened that in the same place in which Theon was baptized, a young man, radiant in splendor, appeared, and said to them, "Peace (be) with you!" And both

Peter and Theon immediately ascended, entered the cabin and Peter took bread and gave thanks to the Lord, who had deemed him worthy of his holy service and that a young man had appeared unto them, saying, "Peace (be) with you." (Peter said) "Best and only Holy One, for thou didst appear unto us, O God Jesus Christ, in thy name I have spoken, and he was signed with thy holy sign. Therefore also I give to him in thy name thy eucharist, that he may for ever be thy servant, perfect without blemish." When they were eating and rejoicing in the Lord suddenly a moderate wind but not a violent one, arose at the stern of the ship which lasted six days and six nights, till they came to Puteoli.

6. Having landed at Puteoli, Theon left the ship and went to the inn, where he usually stayed, to make preparations for the reception of Peter. The inn-keeper's name was Ariston, a God-fearing man, and to him he went for the sake of the name (of Christ). And when he had come to the inn and found Ariston, Theon said to him, "God, who found thee worthy to serve him, has also made known unto me his grace through his holy servant, Peter, who has just arrived with me from Judæa, being bidden by our Lord to go to Italy." When Ariston heard this, he fell upon Theon's neck, embraced him and asked him to bring him to the ship and show Peter unto him. For Ariston said, "since Paul had gone to Spain, there was not one among the brethren who could strengthen me. Be-

sides, a certain Jew, named Simon, had broken into the city. By means of his magical sayings and his wickedness he had wholly perverted the entire fraternity, so that I also fled from Rome hoping for the arrival of Peter. For Paul had spoken of him, and I saw many things in a vision. Now I fully believe in my Lord, that he will again establish his ministry. That all misleading be extinguished from his servants. For our Lord Jesus Christ is faithful, that he can renew again our thoughts." When Theon heard this from the weeping Ariston, his confidence grew still more, and he was still more strengthened in his faith, seeing that he believed in the living God. When they came to the ship, Peter noticed them, and, filled with the Spirit, he smiled, so that Ariston fell upon his face to the feet of Peter, and said, "Brother and sir, who makest known the sacred secrets and teachest the right way, which is in the Lord Jesus Christ, our God, through thee he has shown us his coming. All whom Paul has given to us, we have lost through the energy of Satan. But now I trust in the Lord, who bade thee his messenger to hasten to us, that he has deemed us worthy, to make us see through thee his great and wonderful deeds. I therefore ask of thee, come quickly to the city. For the brethren who gave offence, whom I saw fall into the snares of the devil, I left and fled hither, saying to them, Brethren, stand in the faith; for it is necessary that within the next two months the mercy of our Lord bring you his servant. I saw a vision, namely, Paul speaking to me, and saying, Ariston, flee from the city. Having heard this, I believed without wavering, went from the city in the Lord, and, though the flesh which I bear is weak, yet I came hither, stood daily by the shore, and asked the sailors, Has Peter come with you? And now since the grace of the Lord is given us richly, I beseech thee to go up to Rome without delay, lest the teaching of the wicked fellow increases still more." When Ariston had thus spoken amidst tears, Peter gave him his hand and lifted him up from the ground, speaking himself with tears and sighs: "He who tempts the world by his angels got ahead of us; but he who has the power to deliver his servants from all temptation will destroy his misleadings and put them under the feet of those who believe on Christ, whom we preach." And when they entered by the gate Theon asked Peter and said, "During the long sea voyage thou hast never refreshed thyself on the ship, and now wilt thou go from the ship on such a rough road? No, stay, refresh thyself, and then go. From here to Rome the road is paved and I fear thou might hurt thyself." But Peter answered and said to them, "But if it happened that about my neck and that of the enemy of the Lord a millstone were hanged (as my Lord said to us, if any had offended one of the brethren), and we be drowned in the depths of the sea? But not only will it be so that a millstone (be hanged about the neck), but what is worse, (I) the opponent of this persecutor of his servants shall be consumed far away from those who have believed on the Lord Jesus Christ." In no way could Theon persuade him to remain a day longer. Whereupon Theon gave everything that was in the ship to those to whom it belonged, and followed Peter to Rome, who accompanied Ariston to the house of the presbyter Narcissus.

7. Soon it became known among the scattered brethren of the city that Peter had come (to Rome) on account of Simon, to prove that he is a seducer and persecutor of the good. And the whole multitude came together to see the apostle of the Lord, how he would confirm (the congregation) in Christ. When they gathered on the first of the Sabbaths to meet Peter, he began to speak with a loud voice: "Ye men who are here, hoping in Christ, ye who suffered temptation a little while, learn why God sent his Son into the world, or why he begot (him) by the Virgin Mary. (Had he done this) without having in view some mercy or provision? For he meant to annul every offense and every ignorance and every activity of the devil, his instigations and powers, by means of which he once had the upper hand, ere our God shone forth in the world. Since with their many and manifold weaknesses they run into death by their ignorance, Almighty God had compassion and sent his Son into the world, of which I am a witness. And he walked on the waters, of which I am also a witness as well as of that which he wrought in the world by signs and wonders which he performed. I confess, dearest brethren, that I was present; I denied our Lord Jesus

Christ, not once, but thrice; for those who ensnared me were wicked dogs, just as they (also deceived) the prophets of the Lord. But the Lord laid it not to my charge; he turned to me and had mercy on the weakness of my flesh, so that I wept bitterly; and I mourned for my little faith, having been deceived by the devil and not heeding the word of my Lord. And now, I tell you, men (and) brethren, who are convened in the name of Jesus Christ, Satan the deceiver sends his arrows also upon you, that you leave the (right) way. But fall not off, brethren, nor fail in your mind, but strengthen yourselves, stand fast and doubt not. For if Satan has offended me, whom the Lord esteemed so highly, that I denied the light of my hope, causing me to fall and persuading me to flee as if I believed in a man, what think ye (will happen to you), which have just become converted? Do you imagine that he will not confound you for the sake of making you enemies of the kingdom of God and to bring you by the worst error into perdition? For every one whom he deprives of the hope in our Lord Jesus Christ is a child of perdition for all eternity. Repent, therefore, brethren, whom the Lord has chosen, and be firmly established in the Almighty Lord, the Father of our Lord Jesus Christ, whom no one has ever seen nor can see except he who believes on him. Know also whence the temptation has come for you. For (I came) not for the sake of convincing you with words, that he whom I preach is the Christ, but by reason of miraculous deeds and powers I exhort you by faith in Jesus Christ, let no one wait for another (Saviour) besides him who is despised and whom the Jews have reviled, this crucified Nazarene, who died and rose again on the third day."

8. The brethren (reflected) and asked Peter to overcome Simon's claim that he was the power of God. Simon was staying at the house of the senator Marcellus, whom he had won over by his magical speech. "Believe us, brother Peter" they said, "none among men was so wise as this Marcellus. All widows, who hoped in Christ, took their refuge in him; all orphans were fed by him. Will you know more, brother? All the poor called Marcellus their patron; his house was called the house of the pilgrims and poor. To him the emperor said, 'I will give you no office, lest you rob the provinces and give (the plunder) to the Christians.' To which Marcellus replied, 'Yet everything that is mine is thine.' Said Cæsar to him, 'It were mine if you kept it for me; but now, it is not mine, since you give it to whom you please, and who knows to what low people?' This, brother Peter, we know and report to thee, now that the so great benevolence of the man has been turned into blasphemy. For had he not been changed we certainly should not have left the holy faith in God our Lord. Now this Marcellus is furious and repents of his good deeds and says, 'So much wealth have I spent for such a long time, in the foolish belief that I spent it for the knowledge of God.'

(In his rage he even goes) so far that, when a pilgrim comes to the door of his house, he beats him with a stick or has him beaten, and says, 'O, if I had not spent so much money on those impostors!' And many more blasphemies does he utter. But if you have something of the compassion of our Lord in you and the goodness of his precepts, help this man in his error; for he has shown goodness to a great many of God's servants." When Peter perceived this, he was very much moved, and said, "O, the manifold arts and temptations of the devil! O, the cunnings and devices of the evil one! Treasuring up unto himself the great fire against the day of wrath, destruction of simple men, a ravening wolf, devouring and destroying eternal life! Thou didst entice the first man to evil lust, and by thy former wickedness and bodily bond thou hast bound him (to thee). Thou art the fruit of bitterness, which is entirely bitter, for thou infusest various desires. Thou hast forced my school-fellow and co-apostle Judas to act wickedly, that he betrayed our Lord Jesus Christ; it is necessary that thou be punished. Thou didst harden the heart of Herod and kindle Pharaoh and didst make him fight against Moses, the holy servant of God; thou didst embolden Caiaphas to deliver our Lord Jesus Christ to the unfriendly multitude; and now thou art still firing thy poisonous arrows at innocent souls. Thou wicked foe of all, thou shalt be extinguished as a curse from his Church (namely, from the Church), of the Son of the holy, almighty God, and as a firebrand thrown from the fireplace, by the servants of our Lord Jesus Christ. Let thy blackness turn against thee and against thy sons, the worst seed; let thy wickedness turn against thee; and against thee thy threats, and thy temptations against thee and thy angels, thou beginning of iniquity, abyss of darkness! Let the darkness which thou hast be with thee and thy vessels, which thou ownest. Depart, therefore, from those who are about to believe in God; depart from the servants of Christ and from those who will serve in his army. Keep for thee thy garments of darkness; without cause thou knockest at strange doors which belong not to thee, but to Christ Jesus, who keeps them. For thou, ravening wolf, wilt rob the sheep, which belong not to thee, but to Christ Jesus, who keeps them with the greatest diligence."

9. When Peter had thus spoken with great sorrow of his soul, many more believers were added (to the congregation). And the brethren asked Peter that he should cope with Simon and not suffer that he disturb the people any longer. And without delay Peter left the meeting (synagogue), and went to the house of Marcellus, where Simon was. And a great multitude followed him. When he came to the door, he summoned the keeper and said to him, " Go, tell Simon, ' Peter, on whose account thou didst leave Judea, awaits thee at the door!'" The keeper answered and said to Peter, "I know not, sir, whether thou art Peter. But I have instructions: Knowing that thou didst arrive yester-

day in the city, he said to me, 'Whether he comes in the day or at night, or at whatever hour, say that I am not at home.'" But Peter said to the young man, "Thou hast done well in telling me this, although thou hast been forced by him (not to say it to me)." And Peter, turning around to the people which followed him, said," You are about to see a great and wonderful sign." And Peter saw a big dog, chained by a big chain, and he went and loosened him. The dog, being loosed, became endowed with a human voice, and said to Peter, "What wilt thou to have me to do, servant of the unspeakable living God?" To which Peter said, "Go inside and tell Simon in the presence of the people, Peter sends word to thee to come outside. For on thy account have I come to Rome, thou wicked one and destroyer of simple souls." And the dog ran away at once, and went into the midst of the people, which were with Simon, and, lifting his forefeet, he said with a very loud voice, "Thou, Simon, Peter, who stands at the door, bids thee to come outside before all; for on thy account have I come to Rome, thou wicked one and destroyer of simple souls." When Simon heard this and saw the incredible occurrence, he had no words with which he otherwise deceived those present, while the others were confounded.

10. When Marcellus had seen this, he ran outside and fell down before Peter, and said, "Peter, thou holy servant of the holy God, I embrace thy feet; I have committed many sins; resent not my

ACTS OF PETER

sins, if thou hast some true faith in Christ, whom thou preachest; if thou rememberest the commandments, to hate none, to do no evil to anyone, as I have learned from thy fellow-apostle Paul; mention not my sins, but pray for me to the Lord, the holy Son of God, whom I angered in persecuting his servants. Pray, therefore, for me, like a good advocate of God, that I may not be given over with the sins of Simon to the everlasting fire. For by his persuasion it came about, that I erected to him a statue [12] with the following inscription: (Dedicated) to Simon, the juvenile god. If I knew, Peter, that thou could be gained over with money, I would give (thee) all my property. Despising, I would give it to thee, to save my soul. If I had sons, I would esteem (them) for nothing, but only believe in the living God. I confess, however, that he only seduced me because he said that he is the power of God. Nevertheless I will tell thee, sweetest Peter: I was not worthy to hear thee, servant of God, and I was not firmly established in the belief in God which is in Christ: wherefore I flinched. I pray thee, therefore, be not angry at what I am about to say. Christ our Lord, whom thou preachest in truth, said to thy fellow-apostles in thy presence, 'If ye have faith as a grain of mustard seed, ye shall say unto this mountain, Re-

---

[12] Justin Martyr *Apol.* I, 26, 56, also speaks of such a statue. This subject has been treated by Lugano (in *Nuovo Bulletino di archeologia cristiana*, VI, 1900, pp. 29–66) in his essay: "Le memorie leggendarie di Simon Mago e della sua volata."

move hence to yonder place and it shall remove.' [13] But this Simon called thee, Peter, an unbeliever, because thou didst doubt on the waters.[14] And I heard that he also said this: Those who are with me, understood me not.[15] If, therefore, ye, upon whom he laid his hands,[16] whom he even has chosen, with whom he even performed miraculous deeds — if ye doubted, therefore I also am sorry, and relying upon his testimony, I flee to thy intercession. Receive me, who has fallen away from our Lord and his promise. But I believe that by repenting he will have mercy on me. For the Almighty is faithful to forgive my sins." And Peter said with a loud voice, " Glory and praise be unto our Lord, Almighty God, Father of our Lord Jesus Christ. To thee be praise and honor for ever and ever. Amen. Since thou hast now also fully strengthened us and hast fully established us in thee before the eyes of all who see it, holy Lord, confirm Marcellus and give him and his house thy peace to-day. But all that are lost or erring, thou alone canst lead them rightly. We worship thee, O Lord, the Shepherd of the sheep once scattered, but now they will be brought together through thee. So receive Marcellus also as one of thy sheep, and suffer not that he walk about any longer in error

---

[13] Matt. XVII, 20; XXI, 21; Mark XI, 23.
[14] Comp. Matt. XIV, 31.
[15] The subject is Christ, not Simon. The saying is extra-canonical, and belongs to the many mentioned in Pick, *Paralipomena*, p. 66. Whence the author of the Acts has it, we know not.
[16] Of this the canonical gospels know nothing.

or in ignorance; but receive him among the number of thy sheep. Yea, Lord, receive him, since he beseeches thee with sorrow and with tears."

11. Having thus spoken, and having embraced Marcellus, Peter turned to the multitude which stood beside him, when he perceived one laughing, in whom was a very bad devil. Peter said to him, " Whoever thou art which hast been laughing, show thyself in public." When the young man heard this, he ran into the court of the house, cried with a loud voice, threw himself against the wall, and said, " Peter, there is a good contention between Simon and the dog, which thou didst send inside. For Simon says to the dog, Say I am not here. But the dog tells him more things than thou didst command. And when he has fulfilled thy behest, he will die at thy feet." And Peter said, " Demon, whoever thou art, in the name of our Lord Jesus Christ, depart from this young man without hurting him. Show thyself to all present." When the young man heard this, he rushed forward took hold of a large marble statue, which stood in the court of the house, and demolished it by kicks. It was a statue of Cæsar. When Marcellus saw this, he slapped his forehead and said to Peter, " A great crime has been committed; for should Cæsar hear of it through one of his spies, he will greatly punish us." Peter answered, " I see that thou art not so, as a short time ago, when thou didst say to be ready to spend everything for the salvation of thy soul. But if thou art in earnest with thy repentance and

believest in Christ with all thy heart, take the water flowing down into thy hands and beseeching the Lord, sprinkle it in his name on the pieces of the statue, and it shall be whole as before." Marcellus doubted not, but believed with his whole heart, and before taking the water he lifted up his hands and said, "I believe in thee, Lord Jesus Christ. For thy apostle Peter has examined me whether I have the right faith in thy holy name. Wherefore I take water in my hands and sprinkle this statue in thy name, that the statue become whole again as before. If it is thy will, O Lord, that I live and receive no punishment from Cæsar, let this statue be whole as before." And he sprinkled water on the stones, and the statue became whole. Peter was proud therefore, that he hesitated not to petition the Lord; but Marcellus also rejoiced in the Spirit, that such a sign — the first one — took place under his hands. He believed therefore, with all his heart on the name of Jesus Christ, the Son of God, by whom all things impossible become possible.

12. And Simon being inside, spoke thus to the dog: "Tell Peter that I am not in." But the dog said to him in the presence of Marcellus, "Thou most wicked and impudent, worst enemy of all who live and believe in Christ Jesus. A dumb animal, which received a human voice, has been sent to thee to convince thee and to prove that thou art a juggler and deceiver. It required so many hours for thee to say, Say I am not here! Thou hast not been ashamed to lift up thy weak and useless voice

against Peter, the servant and apostle of Christ, as if thou couldst be hidden from him who told me to speak to thy face. And this, not on thy account, but on account of those whom thou didst deceive and bring into perdition. Thou shalt therefore be accursed, thou enemy and destroyer of the way of Christ's truth, who shall punish thy iniquities which thou didst do with the imperishable fire, and thou shalt be in outer darkness." Having thus spoken these words, the dog ran away. And the multitude followed, so that Simon remained alone. And the dog came to Peter, who was with the crowd (which had come), to see the face of Peter; and the dog reported of his affair with Simon. To the messenger and apostle of the true God the dog said as follows: " Peter, thou shalt have a hard fight with Simon, the enemy of Christ, and with his adherents; but many whom he deceived thou wilt convert to the faith. For this thou shalt receive a reward for thy work from God." Having thus spoken, the dog fell at the feet of Peter and expired.[17] When the multitude with great astonishment saw the talking dog, many fell down at the feet of Peter, but others said: "Show us another miracle that we may believe thee as a servant of the living God; for Simon too did many wonders in our presence, and on that account we followed him."

13. And Peter turning around saw a smoked tunny hanging by a window which he took, saying

---

[17] In the Acts of Thomas, ch. 41, we read the same of the speaking ass.

to the people, "When you see this swimming in the water like a fish, will you be able to believe on him whom I preach?" And all said with one voice, "Indeed we shall believe thee." So he went to the pond near by, saying, "In thy name, O Jesus Christ, on whom they believe not yet — (Tunny) in the presence of all these, live and swim like a fish." And he cast the tunny into the pond, and it became alive and began to swim. When the multitude saw the swimming fish — and he let him swim not only in (that) hour, but lest they said that it is a deception, he made him swim longer, thus bringing the people together from all parts and showing that the smoked tunny had again become a fish, the success was such that many threw pieces of bread into the water, thus seeing the fish fully. Very many who had witnessed this, followed Peter, and believed on the Lord, and met day and night in the house of Narcissus the presbyter. And Peter spoke to them of the prophetical writings and of the things done by our Lord Jesus Christ in word and deed.

14. Marcellus, however, increased daily (more and more in the faith), seeing the signs which Peter did by the grace of Jesus Christ, which was given to him. And Marcellus attacked Simon, who sat in the dining-room of his house. Revilingly he said to him, "O thou most malevolent and most pestilential of men, destroyer of my soul and of my house, who didst intend to lead me away from the Lord Christ, my Saviour." And he laid his hand

ACTS OF PETER 81

on him, and ordered that he be thrown out of his house. And the servants having obtained permission, treated him in the most shameful way; some struck him in the face, some beat him with a rod, some flung stones at him, some emptied vessels containing dirt over his head (those especially), who for his sake had left their master and were imprisoned; other servants whose master he had influenced against them reviled and said to him, " Now we return to thee the worthy reward, according to the will of God, who had mercy upon us and upon our lord." And Simon, thus treated, left the house and went to the house in which Peter stayed. Standing at the door of the house of the presbyter Narcissus, he cried, " Behold, here am I, Peter; come down, Peter, and I will prove that thou didst believe in a Jewish man and the son of a carpenter."

15. When Peter heard these things, he sent to him a woman with her suckling and said to her, " Go forth speedily and thou shalt see one seeking me. As for thee, speak not, but keep silent and listen to what the child which thou holdest will say to him." And the woman went down. And her babe was seven months old. Assuming a manly voice, it said to Simon, " O thou horrible before God and men; O destroyer of truth and worst seed of corruption; O unfaithful fruit of nature! Only a little while, an everlasting punishment awaits thee. Son of an impudent father, never taking root in good (soil), but in poison; unfaithful generation, destitute of all hope: when the dog accused thee,

thou wast not confounded. I, a child, am forced by God to speak and still thou blushest not. But against thy will, on the coming Sabbath day, another shall lead thee to the Julian forum that thou mayest be shown what thou art. Leave, therefore, the door by which the saints enter in. For no more shalt thou corrupt innocent souls whom thou didst destroy and lead away from Christ. Thy whole evil nature will therefore be manifested, and thy machinations will be spoiled. Now I say to thee the last word: Jesus Christ says to thee, Grow speechless by my name, and leave Rome till the coming Sabbath."

At once he became speechless, and being constrained he left Rome till the next Sabbath and remained in a stable. The woman returned to Peter with the babe, and told Peter and the other brethren what the child had said to Simon. And they praised the Lord, who had shown such things to men.

16. When the night came, Peter saw Jesus clothed with a shining garment, smiling. Peter was yet awake, and (Christ) said to him, "the greatest part of the brethren has already come back through me, and through him by whom thou hast made signs in my name. But on the coming Sabbath thou shalt have a contest of faith, and many more Gentiles and Jews shall be converted in my name to me, who was reviled, despised and spit upon. For I shall show myself unto thee, when thou askest for signs and wonders, and thou shalt

convert many, but thou wilt have an opponent in Simon through the works of his father. But all his doings shall be manifested as sorcery and magical deception. And now delay not and thou shalt confirm in my name all those whom I shall send to thee." When it was day, he told the brethren how the Lord had appeared unto him and what he commanded him.

"Believe me, men and brethren, I have driven this Simon from Judea; by means of his magical sayings he did much mischief. In Judea he stayed in the house of a woman called Eubola, highly esteemed in this world and having much gold and pearls. With two like him Simon sneaked in; none of the servants saw the two but only Simon; they used their magic art, carried off all the gold of the woman, and were not seen. When Eubola had found out what had taken place, she had the servants tortured, and said, You made use of the opportunity (when) the man of God (came to me), and robbed me, because you saw that he came to honor a plain woman; his name is the name of the Lord. And I fasted three days and prayed that this event become known, and in a vision I see Italicus and Antulus, whom I had instructed in the name of the Lord, and a boy naked and bound giving unto me a wheaten bread and saying, Peter hold out yet for two days, and thou shalt see the great deeds of God. For (thou shalt see) that by means of magical art and trickery Simon and his two fellows have stolen the things from the house of Eubola. At the ninth hour of the third day thou shalt see them at the gate which leads to Neapolis, trying to sell to a goldsmith, Agrippinus by name, a golden satyriscus weighing two pounds, and containing a precious stone. But thou must not touch him, in order not to pollute thyself; but let some of the lady's servants accompany thee, and having shown them the shop of the goldsmith, leave them. This event will make many believe in the Lord. For what they did steal in their cunning and wickedness shall be made manifest.

"Upon hearing this, I went to Eubola, whom I found sitting in a rent garment and with disheveled hair and in grief. I said to her, Eubola, rise (and desist) from thy grief; put thy face in order, arrange thy hair, and put on a dress which is suitable for thee, and pray to the Lord Jesus Christ, who judges every soul. For he is the son of the invisible God, in whom thou must be saved, if thou wilt only heartily repent of thy former sins; and receive strength from him. For the Lord wishes to inform thee through me that thou shalt get back all that thou hast lost. And having received it, see to it that he may find thee as such a one who renounces the present world and finds an everlasting comfort. Wherefore listen: let some of thy (servants) watch at the gate which leads to Neapolis. Day after tomorrow, about the ninth hour, they shall notice two young men who will offer for sale a golden satyriscus set in stones and weighing two pounds — for thus I was shown in a vision — to a certain

Agrippinus, a man of piety and believing on the Lord Jesus Christ. Through him it will be shown to thee to believe on the living God and not in Simon the magician, the deceitful demon who would have thee sorrowing and thy innocent servants tortured, who deceived thee with flattering words, but only with words, and only spoke with the mouth of piety, whereas he is wholly impious. For when thou didst imagine to have a good day and didst put up an idol and adorned it, and didst exhibit all thy ornaments on a costly table, he (came) with two young men, whom none of you did see; they uttered their magical saying, robbed thy jewels, and were not seen. But this trickery cannot last. For my God has revealed it to me that thou mayest not be deceived and perish in hell; and whatever impiety and opposition thou hast shown toward God, who is all truth and a righteous judge of the living and the dead <he shall pardon thee>, and men have no other hope of life except by him, through whom that which thou hast lost has been saved for thee. And now save thy soul. And she fell down to my feet and said, Man, who thou art, I know not. It is true that I received that man as a servant of God, and whatever he asked of me for the care of the poor I spent much through his hands, besides what I richly gave to him. But what have I ever done to him that he brought such great misery over my house? Peter said to her, We must not believe in words, but in works and deeds. Therefore let us bring about what has been commenced. Thus I left her, and with two stewards of Eubola I went to Agrippinus and said to him, See that thou recognizest these. For to-morrow two young men shall come to thee, offering for sale a golden satyriscus set in stones, which belongs to their mistress. Receive them under the pretense of examining and praising the work of the artist. These will come in — and the rest God will bring about for a proof. On the following day the stewards of the matron arrived about the ninth hour, and those young men were about to sell to Agrippinus the golden satyriscus. They were seized at once and the matter was reported to the matron. And she went to the governor, her mind being troubled, and with a very loud voice she told him of what had happened. When the governor, Pompey, noticed her, who had never appeared in public, and perceived how troubled she was in her mind, he arose from his judgment seat and went to the pretorium and had them brought before him and carefully examined. Being tortured, they confessed that they were in the service of Simon, who had induced them with money. They also confessed that all which belonged to Eubola was hidden in a cave under the ground on the other side of the gate together with many other things. When Pompey heard this, he arose to go to the gate, the two having been bound with double bonds. And behold, Simon came to the gate to seek them, because they were so slow, when he beheld the great multitude and the two in bonds. He at once understood the case, took to flight, and was never since seen in Judea. Eubola, after she got her property, gave it for the service of the poor; she believed in the Lord Jesus Christ and was strengthened, despised and renounced this world, supported the widows and orphans, clothed the poor, and after a long time fell asleep. This, most beloved brethren, took place in Judea, and he who was called the angel of Satan was driven away thence.

18. "Dearest and most beloved brethren, let us fast and pray to the Lord. He who drove him away thence is powerful enough to extirpate him hence. May he give us his power to oppose him and his magical sayings, and to demonstrate that he is the angel of Satan. For on the Sabbath our Lord will bring him against his will to the Julian forum. Let us therefore bend our knees before Christ, who hears us, though we have not cried (to him); who sees us, though he is not seen with these (our) eyes, but he is among us; if we wish, he will not forsake us. Let us therefore purify our souls from every evil temptation, and God will not leave us; and if we only beckon him with the eyes, he is with us."

19. When Peter had spoken thus, Marcellus came near, and said, "Peter, I have purified my whole house for thee from every vestige of Simon, and have blotted out (every vestige) of his shameful dust. I took water and with his other servants, which belong to him, I called upon the holy name of Jesus Christ, and sprinkled my whole house and every dining-room and every colonnade as far as

the door, and said, I know, O Lord Jesus Christ, that thou art pure and undefiled from every impurity, so that mine enemy and opponent is driven away from before thy glance. And now, most blessed, I have invited to my purified house the widows and elders to come to thee, that they pray wtih us. And each will receive for the sake of the ministry (of Christ) a piece of gold, that in truth they may be called servants of Christ. Everything else, however, is already prepared for the service (of God). Now I pray thee, most blessed Peter, to seal their petitions, and beautify their prayers (which they offer) for me (by thy presence). Let us therefore go; we will also take along Narcissus and all the brethren which are here." Peter consented to his simplicity, and in order to do his will, he goes with him and the other brethren.

20. When Peter had entered, he saw one of the old women deprived of her eyesight, whom her daughter led by the hand and conducted into the house of Marcellus. And Peter said to her, " Come here, mother; from this day Jesus gives you his right hand; through him we have a light which no man can approach unto, which darkness cannot cover. Through me he says to thee, Open the eyes, be seeing and walk alone." And the widow noticed at once how Peter put his hand upon her. When Peter came into the dining-room he saw that the gospel was read. And closing it he said, " Men, ye who believe on Christ and hope in him, you shall know how the holy writing of our Lord must

be explained. What we have written down according to his grace, though it may seem to you ever so little, yet what it contains is comprehensive (enough) to be understood by humanity. It is necessary that we first know God's will or his goodness, since deceit was once spread and many thousands of men were drawn in perdition, wherefore the Lord was moved by compassion to show himself in another form and to appear in the image of man, whom neither the Jews nor we can view in a worthy manner. For each of us saw (him) as his capacity permitted to see (him). Now, however, I will explain to you that which has been read to you. And our Lord wished to let me see his majesty on the holy mountain; [18] but when I with the sons of Zebedee saw his brightness, I fell at his feet as dead, closed my eyes and heard his voice in a manner which I cannot describe; I imagined I had been deprived of my eyesight by his splendor. I recovered a little and said within me, Perhaps the Lord has brought me hither to deprive me of my eyesight. And I said, If such be thy will, O Lord, I shall not contradict. And he took me by the hand and lifted me up. And when I arose, I saw him again as one whom I could not comprehend. How the merciful God, most beloved brethren, has borne our infirmities and took upon him our transgressions, as the prophet says: 'He bears our griefs; and has sorrows for us; yet we did esteem him

---

[18] II Pet. I, 16, 18; comp. Matt. XVII, 1 seq.

stricken and afflicted.'[19] Whereas 'he is in the Father and the Father in him';[20] in him also is the fulness of all majesty, who has shown us all his benefits. He ate and drank on our account, though he was neither hungry nor thirsty; he suffered and bore revilings for us, he died and rose for us. He also defended and strengthened me through his greatness when I sinned; he will also comfort you, that you love him, this Great and Small One, this Beautiful and Ugly One, this Young Man and Old Man, appearing in time, yet utterly invisible in eternity; whom a human hand has not grasped, but is now held by his servants; whom flesh has not seen and now sees; who has not been heard, but is known now, the word which is heard, and now he has suffered as ourselves; never chastised, but now chastised; who was before the world and is now perceived in time, great beginning of all dominion and delivered to the princes; glorious, but low among us; homely looking, yet attractive. This Jesus you have, brethren, (as) the door, the light, the way, the bread, the water, the life, the resurrection, the recreation, the pearl, the treasure, the seed, the satiety, the grain of mustard seed, the vine, the plow, the grace, the faith, the word: he is everything, and there is none greater than he; to him be praise in all eternity. Amen."[21]

---

[19] Isa. LIII, 4.
[20] John X, 38; XVII, 21; Col. I, 19; II, 9.
[21] Justin Martyr also gives a list of different names of Christ, but they are all taken from the Old Testament (*Dial.* c. 34, 59, 61, 100, 113, 126, 128). It is true that our

21. When the ninth hour had passed, they arose to pray. And behold, blind widows from the company of the old women who were present without Peter knowing it, and who were disbelieving cried out suddenly and said to Peter, "We sit together, O Peter, hoping and believing on Jesus Christ. As thou didst give the eyesight to one of our company, we ask, Peter, give us also of his compassion and love." But Peter said to them, "If you believe on Christ, if he is confirmed in you, see with the mind what you cannot see with the eyes; and your ears are closed, but within your mind they may be opened. These eyes will be closed again, which see nothing else than men and cattle, and dumb animals and stone and wood; but not all eyes see Jesus Christ. But now, O Lord, let thy sweet and holy name help them; touch their eyes, for thou art mighty, that they may see with their eyes." After they had prayed, the dining-room in which they were, became as bright as lightning; but such a (brightness) as is usually in the clouds. And it was not such a light as is during the day (but), indescribable, incomprehensible, as no man can describe it, a light which illuminated us so far that its wonderfulness made us dizzy, and we cried to the Lord and said, "Lord, have mercy upon thy servants! What we can bear, O Lord, grant unto us;

---

author uses the O. T. also, but he mainly uses the New Test. Some of the predicates of Christ mentioned here are not found in the New Test. Christ is never called "grace," "faith."

for this we can neither see nor bear." Whilst we were prostrated, those widows stood erect, for they were blind. The bright light, however, which appeared unto us, entered into their eyes and they became seeing. Peter said to them, " Tell what you have seen." They said, " We saw an old man whose appearance we cannot describe unto thee "; some, however (said), " We saw a young man "; others said, " We saw a boy tenderly touching our eyes; thus our eyes were opened." Wherefore Peter praised the Lord, and said, " Thou alone art the Lord God, to praise whom we need so many lips, able to thank thee for thy mercy. Therefore, brethren, as I told you before in a few words, greater is the constancy of God than our thoughts, as we have learned from the old widows, how they saw the Lord in different forms."

22. And he exhorted (the brethren) altogether that they might understand the Lord with all their strength, and with Marcellus and the other brethren he began to minister to the virgins of the Lord, and to rest till morning. Marcellus said to them, " Ye holy, undefiled virgins of the Lord, hearken: You know where you (may) abide. For that which is mine, is it not yours? Depart not, but refresh yourselves, for on the Sabbath which will commence to-morrow, Simon will contend with Peter, the holy one of the Lord. As the Lord has always been with him, may the Lord Christ be on his side, as for his apostle, for Peter has refused to eat anything, but fasted continually to be enabled to overcome the

bad enemy and persecutor of the truth of the Lord. For my servants have come and reported how they saw platforms erected in the forum and heard the multitude say, To-morrow at the break of the day two Jews must contend here concerning the discourses of God. Therefore let us watch till to-morrow morning and beseechingly ask our Lord Jesus Christ to hear our prayers in behalf of Peter." And Marcellus slept for a little while, and awaking said to Peter: "O Peter, apostle of Christ, let us boldly carry out our resolution. In my sleep I saw thee sitting in an elevated place, and before (thee) a great multitude, and a very ugly woman, according to her appearance an Ethiopian,[22] no Egyptian, but very black, clad in filthy rags, but with an iron chain about the neck and a chain on her hands and feet; she danced. When thou didst see her, thou didst say to me with a loud voice, Marcellus, this is the whole power of Simon and of his god, which dances: behead her. And I said to thee, Brother Peter, I am a senator of a noble race, and I have never contaminated my hands, not even a sparrow

---

[22] The notion of the devil as of an Ethiopian widely prevailed (in Egypt?). In the Arabic life of Schnudi we read: "Puis il (the devil) prit la forme d'un nègre abyssinien, d'une haute taille et d'une horrible figure" (*Mission archéologique française au Caire*, IV, 1 p. 444). In the *Vie de Paul de Tamoueh ibidem* IV, 2, p. 766): "il se transfigura, il devint un grand Ethiopien, ses yeux étaient pleins de sang, tout son corps plein d'épines et il sentait mauvais comme un bouc.' In the middle ages this trait still prevailed. It is said of French Manichæans of the XI. cent.: "Adorabant diabolum, qui primo eis in Æthiopis, deinde angeli lucis figuratione apparet" (Gieseler, *Kirchengeschichte*, II, 1⁴, p. 410, note 3).

have I ever killed. Upon hearing this, thou didst cry the louder, Come, our true sword, Jesus Christ, and cut off not only the head of the demon, but break also all his members in the presence of all these, whom I have tested in thy service. And at once a man like thee, O Peter (came) with a sword in his hand and knocked her down. And I looked at both of you, at thee and at him who knocked down that demon, and you were both alike to my astonishment. After I awoke I communicated to thee these signs of Christ." Upon hearing this, Peter was the more encouraged, because Marcellus had seen these things, for the Lord everywhere takes care of his own. Rejoicing and strengthened by these words, he rose to go to the forum.

23. And the brethren and all those which were at Rome came together, and for the pieces of gold (which they had received) each occupied a seat. Senators and prefects and officers also met. But when Peter came, he stood in the midst. All cried aloud, " Show us, O Peter, who thy God is, or which majesty there is which gave thee confidence. Be not disaffected to the Romans, they are lovers of the gods. We have the proofs of Simon, let us have yours also; show us, both of you, whom we must believe." And when they spake thus, Simon also came. Dismayed he stood by the side of Peter, glancing especially at him. After a long silence Peter said, " Ye Roman men, ye shall be our true judges. I say that I believe on the living and true God, of whom I will give you proofs, already

known to me, and of which many among you (can already) testify. You see that this one is silent, because he has been refuted and because I have driven him from Judea on account of the frauds perpetrated upon Eubola, a highly respected but single woman, by means of his magic. From thence he was driven away by me and came hither, believing that he can remain unknown among you; and now, here he stands face to face. Say on, Simon, didst thou not fall at my feet and those of Paul, when in Jerusalem thou didst perceive the miraculous cures which took place by our hands, and saidst, I pray you, take as much money of me as you wish, that (I too) may by laying on of hands perform such deeds. And when we heard this from thee, we cursed thee: do you think that we try to possess money? And now you fear nothing?[23] My name is Peter, because the Lord Christ had the grace to call me 'to be ready for every cause.'[24] For I believe in the living God, through whom I shall destroy thy magic arts. Let him perform in your presence the wonderful things which he did. And will you not believe me what I just told you concerning him?" And Simon said, "Thou hast the impudence to speak of Jesus the Nazarene, the son of a carpenter, himself a carpenter,[25] whose family is of Judea. Listen Peter:

---

[23] Comp. Acts of the Apostles VIII, 18-20.
[24] This is a Latin play of words. (Petrus and paratus). The reference is evidently to Matt. XVI, 17-19.
[25] Celsus also calls Christ a carpenter (*Origen. contra Celsum* VI, 34). But in ch. 36, Origen says that in the

The Romans have understanding; they are no fools." And turning to the people, he said, "Men of Rome, is a God born? is he crucified? Whoever has a master, is no God." And when he spoke this, many said, "Thou art right, Simon."

24. And Peter said, "Cursed be thy words against Christ. Thou didst speak so impudently whereas the prophet says of him, 'Who shall declare his generation?'[26] And another prophet says: 'And we have seen him, and he had no former comeliness.'[27] And: 'in the last days a child shall be born of the Holy Spirit; his mother knows not a man, and no one also says that he is his father.'[28] And again he says: 'she has brought forth and has not brought forth.'[29] And again: 'is it a very little thing to offer you a battle? Behold, in the womb a virgin shall conceive.'[30] And another prophet says to honor the father: 'We neither heard her voice, nor did a midwife come.'[31] Another prophet says, 'he came not out of the womb of a woman, but de-

---

gospels nothing of this kind is said of Jesus. He seems to have overlooked Mark VI, 3.

[26] Isa. LIII, 8.

[27] The author erroneously ascribes to "another prophet" what also belongs to Isaiah (LIII. 2).

[28] Lipsius refers this to Orac. Sibyll. VIII, 457 ff.

[29] According to Tert. *de carne Christi,* c. 23, the author of this saying is Ezekiel; as a word of scripture it is also quoted by Clem. Alex. *Stromata* VII, 16, 94; Epiphan. *hæres.* XXX, 30. The quotations are found in Resch, *Agrapha,* p. 305 sq.

[30] See Isa. VII, 13 (LXX).

[31] In the *Ascensio Jesaiæ* XI, 14, we read: "she has not borne a child, nor has a midwife gone up (to her), nor have we heard the cries of pain."

scended from a heavenly place,'[32] and 'a stone was cut out without hands and has broken all kingdoms,'[33] and 'the stone which the builders refused is become the head stone of the corner,'[34] and he calls it 'the tried precious'[35] stone. And again the prophet says of him: 'I saw him come with the clouds of heaven like the Son of man.'[36] And what more shall I say? Ye men of Rome, if ye knew the prophetical writings, I would explain to you all. It was necessary that through them it should be (spoken) in mystery (and) the Kingdom of God be completed. But this shall be opened unto you afterward. Now (I turn) to thee, Simon: do now one (of the signs) whereby thou didst deceive them before, and I shall frustrate it through my Lord Jesus Christ." Simon took courage and said, "If the prefect permits."

25. The prefect, however, wished to show (both) his patience, that he might not appear as acting unjustly. And the prefect summoned one of his slaves and thus spoke to Simon: "Take him, kill (him)." To Peter he said, "And do thou revive him." And to the people the prefect said, "It is for you to decide which of these is accepted before God, he who kills, or he who revives." And Simon whispered something into the ear of

---

[32] Lipsius states "unde verba sint nescio" (i.e. I know not whence these words), Resch, l. c. p. 278 refers to John I, 13.—
[33] Dan. II, 34.
[34] Ps. CXVIII, 22; comp. Matt. XXI, 42.
[35] Isa. XXVIII, 16; I Pet. II. 4, 6.
[36] Dan. VII, 13; Matt. XXIV, 30; XXVI, 64.

the slave, and without speaking aloud he brought it about that the slave became silent and died. But when the people began to murmur, one of the widows which had been cared for by Marcellus cried out, "Peter, servant of God, my son is dead, the only one which I had." The people made room for her, and they brought her to Peter. And she fell down at his feet and said, "I had only one son; by the labor of his hands he provided for me;[37] he lifted me up, he carried me. Now he is dead, who will give me a hand?" Peter said to her, "In the presence of these witnesses go and bring thy son, that they may be able to see and believe that he was raised up by the power of God; the other shall see it and perish." And Peter said to the young men, "We need young men, especially such as shall believe." And at once thirty young men offered themselves to carry the widow and to fetch her dead son. When the widow had recovered, the young men lifted her up. But she cried and said, "Behold (my) son, the servant of Christ has sent for thee," and she tore her hair and scratched her face. And the young men which had come looked at the nose of the boy, whether he were really dead. When they perceived that he was dead, they comforted his mother and said, "If thou really believest in the God of Peter, we will lift him up and bring him to Peter that he may revive him and restore him to thee."

---

[37] Comp. Luke VII, 11 sq.

ACTS OF PETER

26. While the young men were thus speaking, the prefect in the forum looked at Peter and said, "What sayest thou, Peter? Behold, the lad is dead; the emperor liked him, and I spared him not. I had indeed other and many young men; but I trusted in thee and thy Lord whom thou proclaimest, if indeed ye are sure and true: therefore I desired him to die." And Peter said, "God is neither tempted nor disparaged. But the Most Beloved (and) he who is to be worshipped with the whole heart, will hear those which are worthy. Since, however, my God and Lord Jesus Christ is now tempted among you, although he did so many signs and miracles through me to turn you from your sins, revive now, O Lord, in the presence of all, him whom Simon killed by his touch, through my voice in thy power." And Peter said to the master of the lad, "Go, take hold of him by the right hand, and you shall have him alive and walk with you." And the prefect Agrippa ran and came to the lad, took his hand, and woke him up. And when the multitude saw this, they cried, "There is only one God, the God of Peter."

27. Meanwhile the widow's son is also brought on a bier by the young men. The people made room, and they brought him to Peter. Peter, however, lifted up his eyes toward heaven, stretched forth his hands and said, "Holy Father of thy Son Jesus Christ, who hast given us power to ask and to obtain through thee, and to despise everything that is in this world and follow thee only, who art seen

in a few and wishest to be known in many: shine round, O Lord, enlighten, appear, revive the son of the aged widow, who is helpless without her son. And I take the word of my Lord Christ and say to thee, young man, arise and walk [38] with thy mother, as long as thou canst be of use to her. Afterward thou shalt be called to a higher ministry and serve as deacon and bishop." And the dead rose immediately, and the multitude saw and were amazed, and the people cried, " Thou, God Saviour, thou, God of Peter, invisible God and Saviour." And they spoke with one another and wondered at the power of a man who with his word called upon his Lord, and they took (what had taken place) for their sanctification.

28. When the news had spread through the entire city, the mother of a senator came, and making her way through the multitude she fell down at Peter's feet and said, " I heard many people say that thou art the minister of the merciful God and that thou dost impart his mercy to all who desire this light. Impart, therefore, also to (my) son the light, since I have learned that thou art not ill-disposed toward any one: since a matron beseeches thee, turn not away." Peter said to her, " Wilt thou believe in my God, through whom thy son shall rise?" And the mother, weeping, said with a loud voice, " I believe; Peter, I believe." The whole multitude cried out, " Give the mother

---

[38] Luke V, 23; VII, 14.

her son." And Peter said, "Let him be brought hither into the presence of all." And Peter, turning to the people, said, "Ye men of Rome, I, too, am one of you! I have human flesh and I am a sinner, but I have obtained mercy. Do not imagine that what I do, I do in my own power; I do it in the power of my Lord Jesus Christ who is the judge of the quick and the dead. I believe on him, I have been sent by him, and (therefore) I dare to call upon him (and) to raise the dead. Go, therefore, thou also O Woman, and have thy son brought hither and have him raised." And the woman made her way through the multitude, ran into the street with great joy, believed with her heart, and, coming to the house, she made her young men carry him, and came back to the forum. And she told the young men to cover their heads and go before the bier and carry everything that she intended to spend for the body of her son in front of the bier, that Peter, seeing this, might have pity on the body and on her. Whilst all were weeping, she came to the multitude, followed by a multitude of senators and matrons, who were to see God's wonderful deeds. And Nicostratus, who had died was very noble and much liked in the senate. They brought him and placed him before Peter. And Peter asked them to be silent, and said with a very loud voice, "Ye Romans, let a righteous judgment now take place between me and Simon, and judge ye who of us believes in the living God, this or I. Let him raise up the body which is before us and believe (then) him like an angel of God. If he is not able, I will call upon my God. I will give the son alive to his mother, and (then) believe, that he is a sorcerer and deceiver, who enjoys your hospitality." When they heard this, it seemed right to them what Peter had said. They encouraged Simon, saying, "Show thyself publicly what thou canst do: either thou convincest (Peter) or thou shalt be convinced. Why dost thou stand still? Commence."

When Simon perceived that they all pushed him, he stood in silence. When the people had become more quiet and looked at him, Simon cried and said, "Ye Romans, when ye see that the dead is raised, will you cast Peter out of the city?" And the whole multitude said, "We shall not only cast him out, but also burn him at once." Simon came to the head of the dead, bowed, and said three times, "Rise," and he showed the people how the dead had lifted up his head and moved it, and opened the eyes and lightly bowed to Simon. And immediately they began to gather wood to burn Peter. But Peter, having received the power of Christ, lifted up his voice and said to those who cried against him, "Now I see, Romans — what I dared not to say — that you are foolish and silly, so long as your eyes and your ears, and your senses are blinded. So far has your mind become darkened that you perceive not that you are bewitched, since you seemingly believe that a dead man rose who has not risen. It were sufficient for me, ye

Romans, to keep silent and to die in silence and to leave you in the illusions of this world. But the punishment of the fire which is not quenched is before mine eyes; if it therefore seems good to you, let the dead speak, let him rise; if he is alive, let him untie the band from the chin, let him call his mother and say to you, Bawlers, why cry ye? Let him beckon to you with his hand. If therefore, you wish to see that he is dead and you are bound, let this one step back from the bier, and you shall see him as you did see him when you brought him," And the prefect Agrippa could no longer restrain himself, but rose and with his own hand he chased Simon away. And the dead looked as before. And the people got into a rage and, converted from the magical spell of Simon, began to cry, " Hear, O Cæsar, should the dead not rise, let Simon be burned instead of Peter, because he has really deceived us." But Peter stretched forth his hand and said, " Ye Romans, be patient. I say not that in case the boy is not raised, that Simon should be burned; when I say so, you will do it." And the people cried, " Even if you should not wish it, Peter, we shall do it." Peter said to them, " If you continue thereat, the boy shall not rise. We know not to recompense evil for evil, but we have learned to love our enemies, and to pray for them that persecute us. For should he even repent, it is better. For God will not remember the evil. Let him, therefore, come to the light of Christ. But if he cannot, let him inherit the portion of his father, the devil. But let not your hands be contaminated. Having thus spoken to the people, he came to the boy, and before raising him he said to his mother, "These young men, whom thou hast set free in honor of thy son, can as free men (also) obey their living master. For I know that the souls of some (among them) will be wounded, should they see thy risen son and they serve again (as slaves). But let them all be free and receive their subsistence as before — for thy son shall rise again — and let them be with him." And Peter looked at her for some time awaiting the answer. And the mother of the boy said, "How can I do otherwise? Wherefore I will declare before the prefect that they should possess all that which I had to spend on the corpse of my son." Peter said to her, "Let the rest be divided among the widows." And Peter rejoiced in his soul, and said in the spirit, "O Lord, who art merciful, Jesus Christ, manifest thyself to thy Peter, who calls upon thee, as thou didst always show mercy and goodness, in the presence of all these who have been set free, that they may be able to serve. Now let Nicostratus arise." And Peter touched the side of the lad, and said, "Arise." And the lad arose, took up his garment, and sat and untied the chin, asked for the other garments, came down from the bier, and said to Peter, "I ask thee, man, let us go to our Lord Christ, whom I heard speak to thee; he said unto thee, pointing at me, Bring him hither, for he belongs to me." When Peter heard this he was still more strengthened in the spirit by the help of the Lord, and said to the People, "Ye Romans, thus the dead are awakened, thus they speak, thus they walk rising; they live so long as it pleases God. But now (I turn to you) who came to see the spectacle: if you do not repent from these your sins, and from all your gods which you made, and from all uncleanness and evil lust <you shall forever be lost; repent therefore and> [39] receive the communion of Christ in faith (that) you may obtain life for eternity."

29. From that hour on they worshipped him like a god upon their faces, and the sick, which they had at home (they brought) to be cured by him. And when the prefect perceived that such a great multitude adhered to Peter, he asked him to depart. And Peter bade the people to come into the house of Marcellus. And the mother of the lad asked Peter to come to her house. And Peter had charged Marcellus (to see to it) that on Sunday he be enabled to see the widows, as Marcellus had promised, that he might minister unto them with his own hand. And the lad who had been raised said, "I leave not Peter." But his mother returned joyfully and cheerfully to her house. And on the day after the Sabbath she came into the house of Marcellus and brought two thousand pieces of gold, and said to Peter, "Divide these among the virgins of Christ, who minister to Him." But the lad who had been raised, perceiving that he had

---

[39] The text is deficient; the words within <> are by Lipsius.

not yet given anything to anyone, ran to his house, opened a chest and brought four thousand pieces of gold, and said to Peter, "See, I also, who have been raised, offer the double gift of myself from now on as a living sacrifice unto God."

[MARTYRDOM OF THE HOLY APOSTLE PETER.] [1]

30. (1) And on Sunday Peter spoke to the brethren and encouraged [2] them in the belief on Christ. And many senators and knights and wealthy women (and) matrons were present,[3] and they were strengthened in the faith. There was also present a very rich woman, named Chryse, because all her vessels were of gold — since her birth [4] she neither used a vessel of silver nor of glass, but only of gold. She said to Peter, "Peter,[5] servant of God, in a dream [6] he stood by me whom thou callest God,[7] and said to me, Chryse,[8] bring ten

---

[1] Besides the Latin Lipsius gives here also a Greek text with the heading as given above. The Greek is based on a Patmos MS. belonging to the 9th cent., and on a MS. belonging to the monastery Batopedi on mount Athos, belonging to the time between the 10th and 11th cent. The former commences with ch. 33, the latter with ch. 30. For both MSS. see Lipsius Prolegomena, pp. LII–LIV. As the Greek text seems to come nearer to the original, we follow it, noting, however, the variations in the Latin. The number in parenthesis indicates the chapter in the Greek text.

[2] Lat.: entreated them to persevere in the belief on our Lord Jesus Christ.

[3] Lat.: came.

[4] Lat. omits: since her birth.

[5] Lat. omits: the second Peter.

[6] Lat. omits: in a dream.

[7] Lat.: My God stood by me.

[8] Lat.: without Chryse.

thousand pieces of gold to my servant Peter; thou owest these to him. I have brought them,⁹ fearing that some evil may come from him whom I saw and who went to heaven." ¹⁰ And having said this, and laid down the money, she went away. And Peter, seeing this, praised God, that the poor should now be provided for. Some of those present said to him, " Peter, is it not wrong to have accepted this money from her? All Rome ¹¹ speaks of her fornications, and (it is reported) that she is not satisfied with one husband; ¹² she uses even her own slaves. Have thou therefore ¹³ nothing to do with the golden table, but let everything be sent back to her, that came from her." ¹⁴ When Peter heard this, he laughed and said to the brethren, " As to her conduct, ¹⁵ I know nothing of it; since I have received this money I received it not without reason,¹⁶ she brought it to me as a debtor ¹⁷ of Christ and gives it ¹⁸ to the servants of Christ. For he has provided for them." ¹⁹

31. (2) And they also brought the suffering to

---

⁹ Lat. omits: I have brought them.
¹⁰ Lat.: saw, looking down from heaven.
¹¹ Lat. omits: all Rome.
¹² Lat.: she left no man alone.
¹³ Lat. for "therefore": if it seems good to thee.
¹⁴ Lat. erroneously: give her nothing from the table of our Lord Jesus Christ, but let his fire be sent on her.
¹⁵ Lat. omits: to the brethren, as to her conduct.
¹⁶ Lat. omits: since . . . reason.
¹⁷ Lat.: I received this money from a debtor.
¹⁸ Lat.: I give it.
¹⁹ Comp. The Talmudic story given in Pick, *Paralipomena,* p. 111 f.

him on the Sabbath and asked (him) [20] to treat them. And many [21] lame and podagrous were healed, and such as had fever and other diseases, and believed on the name of Jesus Christ, and very many [22] were gained on that day for the grace of the Lord. When some days had passed Simon the Magician promised the people to convince Peter of not believing in the true God, but in a fallacious one. As he performed many tricks, those among the disciples which were steadfast laughed at him.[23] In the dining halls he made some spirits appear, which had the semblance of life, but in reality did not live. And what more shall I say unto you? Having spoken a great deal of magic, he seemingly cured the lame and blind for a time, and dead persons, too, he made suddenly alive and made them move about, as well as Stratonicus.[24] In all this Peter followed him and refuted him before those

---

[20] Lat. omits: asked —
[21] Lat. omits: many.—
[22] Lat. omits: very many.—
[23] Lat. reads: "he seduced not" for "laughed at him."
[24] Lat.: Nicostratus. In the Recognitions of Clement II, 9 and Clementine Homilies, IV, 4, Simon speaks of his miraculous deeds, which resemble those mentioned in the Acts of Peter. But the author of the Recognitions is not deceived by them. For though he regards them as true, he says nevertheless (III, 59): "he who is of the evil one, the signs that he works do good to no one; but those which the good man worketh are profitable to men." To Simon Magus can be applied the words of the presbyter by Irenæus I, 15, 6, with reference to the Gnostic Marcus:

"Thou idol-framer, Mark, and portent-gazer,
Skill'd in the astrologer's and wizard's art,
Strengthening thereby the words of thy false lore,
Dazzling with signs whome'er thou lead'st astray,
Strange handywork of God-defying power,

who saw it. And as he cut a poor figure, and was ridiculed by the Romans and lost their confidence since he promised to do something and could not do it (it came about) that he said to them, "Romans, you now think that Peter has overcome me, as if he were mightier (than I), and pay now more attention to him. You are mistaken.[25] For to-morrow I shall leave you godless and impious ones [26] and take refuge with God above, whose power I am, though having become weak. If, therefore, you have fallen, behold I stand. I ascend to the father,[27] and shall say to him, Me, thy son which stands, they meant to make sit down;[28] however, I had no deal with them, but returned to myself."[29]

32. (3) And on the following day a still larger multitude gathered on the *via sacra*,[30] (i. e., holy street) to see him fly. And Peter also went to the place to see the spectacle and to refute him. For

---

    Such to perform thy father Satan still
    Affords thee might, by an angelic Power
    Azazel:— thee, by the destroyer mark'd
    Chosen forerunner of the impious craft."

[Quoted from Lightfoot, *The Apostolic Fathers* (ed. Harmer, London, 1893), p. 553; the original text is given on p. 539 f.]

[25] Lat.: he deceived you.
[26] Lat. omits: "leave you . . . ones."
[27] Lat. Father of all.
[28] Lat. say to him: "thy sons have done wrong to me."
[29] Lat. however I returned to thee.
[30] On the Sacra Via and the place of Simon's fall, see De Rossi, "Della memoria topografica del sito ove cadde Simone il mago sulla via sacra," in *Bulletti-to di archeologia cristiana*, V, 1867, p. 70 ff.; Lugano, "Le memorie leggendarie di Simon mago e della suo volata" in *Nuovo Bullettino di archeologia cristiana*, VI, 1900, p. 60 ff.

when he came to Rome, he confused the people by his flying. But Peter, who rebuked him, was not yet at Rome which he misled and deceived, so that some were driven out of their senses.[81] And standing on an elevated place [82] he began to speak upon seeing Peter: "Peter, now, when I am about to ascend in the presence of all who see it, I say to thee, if thy God is almighty,[83] whom the Jews have killed, who stoned you, who were chosen by him, let him show that his belief is of God; [84] let it be manifested by this (event), whether it is worthy of God.[85] For I ascend [86] and will show myself to this people, who I am." And, behold, he was lifted up,[87] and they saw him ascending over Rome and over its temples and hills. And the believers looked at Peter.[88] And beholding the wonderful spectacle,[89] Peter cried to the Lord Jesus Christ, "If thou allowest him to do what he has undertaken, all who believed on thee shall be offended, and the

---

[81] The words: "For when he came . . . senses" are omitted in the Latin.

[82] The Latin omits this topographical notice; according to the "Passio Petri et Pauli" 51 (*Acta Apocrypha,* I, p. 162), Nero ordered a lofty tower to be made in the Campus Martius, from whence Simon took his flight. In another Passio Petri et Pauli 10 (*Acta Apocrypha,* I, p. 230), the elevated place is called "mons Capitolinus."

[83] Lat.: God can do anything.

[84] Lat.: Let it be seen what thy belief is.

[85] Lat. omits: let it be manifested . . . God.

[86] Lat.: I go to him (or to God, according to Lipsius' emendation).

[87] Lat.: lifted up suddenly.

[88] Lat. omits: and the believers looked at Peter.

[89] Lat.: And Peter saw it and wondered at such a spectacle.

signs and wonders [40] which thou hast shown to them through me will not be believed. Make haste, O Lord, show thy mercy and [41] make that he fall down, become enervated, and die not, but be prevented from doing damage and break his shank in three places." And he fell down [42] and broke his shank in three places. And they cast stones upon him, and each went to his home having all faith in Peter.[43] And one of Simon's friends, Gemellus by name, from whom Simon had received much — he had a Greek wife [44] — quickly [45] ran away from the street, saw him with the broken shank, and said,[46] "Simon, if God's power is broken, shall not that God, whose power thou art, be darkened?" [47] And Gemellus also followed Peter, and said to him, "I also, wish to be one of those who believe on Christ." And Peter said, "How could I be spiteful, my brother? [48] Come and stay with us." And Simon, being in misery, found some who carried him by night [49] on a stretcher from Rome to Aricia.

---

[40] Lat. omits: and wonders.

[41] Lat. reads: and show to all who adhere to me thy power, and I pray not that he die, but become somewhat hurt in his members.

[42] Lat.: and he suddenly fell to the ground.

[43] Lat.: And they stoned him, all believing and praising the Lord.

[44] Lat. omits: he had a Greek wife.

[45] Lat. omits: quickly.

[46] Lat.: said to him smiling.

[47] Lat.: art thou God's power? Who has broken thy shank? Is it not that God himself, whose power thou claimest to be?

[48] Lat.: brother.

[49] Lat. omits: by night.

There he remained and stayed [50] with a man (named) Castor, who on account of his sorcery [51] had been driven from Rome to Terracina. Being operated,[52] Simon,[53] the angel of the devil, found there the end of his life.

33. (4) [54] Now Peter remained in Rome, and rejoiced with the brethren in the Lord, returning thanks day and night for the multitude which was daily [55] added to the holy name by the grace of the Lord.[56] And the four [57] concubines of the prefect Agrippa [58] also came to Peter, Agrippina, Nicaria, Euphemia and Doris.[59] And they heard the preaching concerning chastity and all sayings of the Lord, and repented and agreed among themselves to abstain from cohabitation with Agrippa, but were troubled by him. When Agrippa became embarrassed [60] and distressed [61] — for he loved

---

[50] Lat. adds: a few days.
[51] Lat. omits: on account of his sorcery.
[52] Lat. adds: by two physicians.
[53] Lat. omits: Simon.
[54] Here begins the second manuscript, which has preserved the Greek text of the martyrdom of Peter. (Codex Patmius, 48). Here also commences a paraphrasing Latin translation of the martyrdom of Peter, known under the title: "Martyrium beati Petri apostoli a Lino episcopo conscriptum" and published in *Acta apost. apocrypha*, I, 1-22. It is independent of the translation of the *Act. Vercellenses*. We call it Linus-martyrdom.
[55] Lat. omits: daily.
[56] Lat. omits: by the grace of the Lord.
[57] Lat. omits: four.
[58] Lat. omits: Agrippa.
[59] Lat. omits: the four names; the Linus-martyrdom (p. 2) has the four names, but writes Eucharia for Nicaria, and Dionis for Doris.
[60] Lat.: and as he troubled them, they made excuses and thus embarrassed him.
[61] Lat.: and becoming angry.

them very much — he had them watched and secretly observed, whither they went, and he found out that they went to Peter. When they came (back),[62] he said to them, "that Christian[63] has taught you not to have any communion with me. Know, then, that I will destroy you and burn that one alive."[64] But they were ready to endure anything by the hand of Agrippa, but would no more suffer themselves to satisfy his lust; they had become strong in the power of Jesus.[65]

34. (5) And a very beautiful woman, the wife of Albinus,[66] a friend of the emperor, named Xanthippe,[67] also came to Peter with the other matrons, and kept away from Albinus. Being in love with Xanthippe, he became enraged and wondered why she did no more share the couch with him, and, mad, like a beast, he intended to kill Peter.[68] For he perceived that he was the cause of the separation from the bed.[69] But many other[70] women delighted in the preaching concerning chastity and separated from their husbands, and men removed the couches of their wives,[71] because they wished to serve God in chastity and purity. And there was

---

[62] Lat. omits: When they came back, and reads: Agrippa said.
[63] Lat.: Peter instead of: that Christian.
[64] Lat.: Know, then, that I will destroy you and him.
[65] Lat.: The Lord strengthened them — for: they had . . Jesus.
[66] Lat.: Albinus, a very famous man.
[67] The Linus-martyrium reads Xandips.
[68] Lat.: He sought how to destroy Peter.
[69] Lat. omits this sentence.
[70] Lat.: other honest women.
[71] Lat.: and men from their wives.

a great commotion in Rome,[72] and Albinus told Agrippa what had happened to him, and said, "Either thou avengest me of Peter, who has alienated my wife from me,[73] or I shall avenge myself." And Agrippa said, "I suffered the same, for he has alienated my concubines."[74] And Albinus said to him,[75] "Why art thou waiting?[76] Let us seize him and kill him as an inquisitive man, that we may get our wives back, and avenge those also, which cannot kill him, whose wives he has also alienated."

35. (6) And as they took counsel together, Xanthippe heard of the advice which her husband had given to Agrippa, and she sent word to Peter, and asked him to leave Rome. And the other brethren, together with Marcellus, requested him to leave (the city).[77] But [78] Peter said to them, "Shall we run away, brethren?" And they said, "Nay; only <go away> since thou canst still

---

[72] Lat. omits: in Rome. The translation of this whole sentence reads in the Latin: But when a great tumult had been made by Albinus, he told the prefect of his wife, and said to him.

[73] Lat.: Who has persuaded my wife to become a Christian.

[74] Lat. omits: for he has . . . concubines.

[75] Lat.: to the prefect.

[76] Lat: Why doest thou not protect thyself and the rest? Let us therefore kill him, that we get our wives back — the rest is omitted.

[77] Lat.: And Xanthippe arranged a colloquy, and she sent word to Peter and asked him to leave Rome, that for the time being the evil one may have no room. The same the other brethren also said to him.

[78] From here till toward the end of Chapter 36, there is a gap in the Latin.

serve the Lord." He obeyed the brethren, and went away alone, saying, "Let none of you go with me; I will go alone, after having changed my garment." When he went outside of the gate, he saw the Lord come into Rome. And seeing Him, he said, "Lord, whither art thou going?" And the Lord said to him, "I go to Rome to be crucified." And Peter said to Him, "Lord, shalt thou be crucified again?" And He said, "Yea, Peter, again I shall be crucified." This was to be done to Peter.

36. (7) He went again to the brethren and told them of the vision which he had. And their souls were sorrowing, and they wept and said, "We adjure thee, Peter, have regard for us, the younger ones." And Peter said, "If it be the Lord's will, it will be, even if we will not. The Lord is mighty to strengthen you in his faith, and he will establish you in it and increase it in you whom He has planted, that you may also plant others through him. I will not object, so long as the Lord will keep me alive; and again if He will take me away, I shall be glad and rejoice."

While Peter was speaking thus and the brethren wept, four soldiers seized him and brought him to Agrippa. And being sick [79] he ordered to crucify him because of atheism. And the whole multitude of the brethren came together, rich and poor, widows and orphans, low and powerful; they

---

[79] The Linus-martyrium, p. 10: love-sick.

wished to see Peter and tear him away. And the people cried unceasingly as with one voice, "What, has Peter sinned, Agrippa? What evil has he done to you? Tell it to the Romans." And others said "<We must be afraid> lest the Lord destroy us also, should he die." And when Peter had come to the place, he appeased the multitude and said, "Ye men,[80] who are in the service of Christ; ye men, who hope in Christ, remember the signs and wonders, which ye saw took place by me; think of the compassion of God,[81] how he performed cures for your sakes. Wait[82] for him, till He comes and rewards every man according to his works. And now, be not angry with Agrippa,[83] for he is a servant of the power of his father.[84] And that which happens takes place as the Lord has told me that it should happen.[85] And why do I delay, and go not to the cross?"

37. (8) And when he had come to the cross, he began to say,[86] "O name of the cross, hidden mystery;[87] O unspeakable mercy, which is ex-

---

[80] Here commences the Coptic text of the martyrdom of Peter, published by O. V. Lemm in the *Bulletin de l'Academie imperiale des sciences de St. Petersbourg*, Nouvelle serie, III (XXXV), 1894, p. 240-284. It comprises the Greek text of Lipsius I, p. 90, line 11 to p. 102, line 6.

[81] The Coptic: of Christ.

[82] Here begins the Latin.

[83] Coptic adds: for my sake.

[84] Lat. adds: and his tradition.— The Coptic: for he serves the work of his father.

[85] Lat.: and that which happened to me, my Lord has shown to me before.

[86] Lat. omits: and when . . . say.

[87] Lat.: every mystery of the cross is dark. Lipsius corrects "every" (omne) and reads: O nomen.

pressed in the name of the cross; O nature of man, which cannot be separated; O ineffable and inseparable love, which cannot be shown by impure lips;[88] I now apprehend thee,[89] who is standing at the end of his earthly career. I will make thee known, as thou art.[90] I will not hide from me the mystery of the cross once closed and hidden to my soul.[91] Ye, who hope in Christ,[92] think not this to be a cross which is visible; for entirely different from that which is visible is this (suffering) in conformity with the suffering of Christ. And now especially, since you, who can hear, can (hear it) from me, who is in the last and parting hour of his life, listen: Keep your souls from everything which you can perceive with the senses, from all that seems to be, and is not in reality.[93] Close these your eyes, shut these your ears;[94] <keep from you>[95] the things (which are without). And you shall perceive what took place with Christ and the whole mystery of your salvation.[96] But the hour (has come) for thee, Peter, to deliver thy body to the

---

[88] Coptic omits: O ineffable . . . lips.

[89] Coptic: thee with power.

[90] Lat. omits: I will . . . art.

[91] Lat. translates: I conceal not that I once desired to enjoy the mystery of the cross.— The Coptic: the mystery of the cross which is hidden in my soul from the beginning.

[92] The Coptic: Christ, let the cross not be to you only that as which it appears.

[93] Lat. and Linus-mart. omit: and is not in reality.

[94] The Coptic: the ears of your flesh.

[95] So the Coptic and adopted by Lipsius.

[96] Linus-mart.: And ye shall know, that the mystery of salvation is brought about in Christ through the cross.— The Coptic: And know what took place with Christ and perceive the whole mystery of your salvation.

bailiffs.[97] Take it, whose business it is.[98] Of you, executioners, I ask to [99] crucify me with the head downward, and not otherwise.[100] And the reason I shall explain to the hearers."[101]

38. (9) Having done as he wished, he began again: [102] "Ye men, whose calling it is to hear, listen what I, being suspended, am about to tell you just now. Understand the mystery of the whole creation and the beginning of all things, as it was. For the first man whose image I bear, thrown downward with the head, showed a generation which did not formerly exist; [103] for it was dead, having no motion. Having been drawn down [104] who cast his origin upon the earth, he established the whole of the arrangement,[105] suspended it after the manner of the calling, whereby he showed the right as the left and the left as the right, and changed all signs of nature, to behold the ugly as beautiful and the really bad as good. On this the Lord says in a mystery: [106] "Unless ye make the right as the left, and the left as the right, and the top as the bottom and the front as the backward,

---

[97] Lat.: The hour has come to deliver my body.
[98] Coptic: take now what belongs to you.
[99] Lat. omits: of you . . . to.
[100] Lat. omits: and not otherwise.
[101] Coptic adds: when they shall crucify me.
[102] Lat. omits: again.
[103] Coptic: revealed first the generation, which had no existence.
[104] Lat. omits: showed a generation . . . drawn down.
[105] Lat. omits: he established . . . arrangement.
[106] So also Linus-mart.; the Latin: The Lord himself says.

ye shall not know the Kingdom (cf heaven)." [107] This intelligence I brought to you, and the manner of my suspension is the illustration of that man who was first made. Ye, my beloved, who now hear it and shall hear it,[108] you must desist from the first error and return again. For it was fitting to come to the cross of Christ, who is the extended word, the one and only one, concerning which the Spirit [109] says: For what else is Christ than the Word, sound of God? [110] That this wood standing erect, on which I am crucified, be Word; the sound, however, is the crossbeam (namely, the) nature of man; and the nail which on the erect wood holds the crossbeam in the middle is the conversion and repentance of man.

39. (10) " Since [111] thou hast made this known and revealed unto me, O Word (of life), which has now been called by me wood of life,[112] I thank thee, not with these lips which are nailed, neither with this tongue, through which comes forth truth and falsehood, also not with this wood, which is produced by the skill of earthly nature, but I thank thee, O King,[113] with that voice which is heard

---

[107] This saying is found also elsewhere; see Pick, *Paralipomena*, p. 65.— Linus-mart.: Kingdom of God; the Coptic: ye shall not come into the Kingdom of God.

[108] Copt.: hear it afterward.

[109] Lat.: holy Spirit.

[110] The source of this saying is unknown. Perhaps we should read "cross" for "Christ." The Coptic reads: the interpretation of the cross is the word, the voice of God.

[111] Lat.: since, O Lord.

[112] Lat.: revealed unto me that it is word of life, which is now called by me wood.

[113] Lat. omits: O King.

through silence,[114] which is not heard by all, which comes not through the organs of the body, which enters not in the world and sounds not upon earth, which is also not written in books, which is also not heard by the one, nor by the other,[115] but with this (voice), Jesus Christ,[116] I thank thee: with the silence of the [117] voice which the Spirit meets within me, who loves thee, speaks with thee, and sees thee. Thou art knowable only according to the Spirit. Thou art to me, father, mother, brother, friend, servant, steward. Thou (art) all, and all (is) in thee; and thou (art) the existence, and there is nothing that is, besides thee. To him, brethren, flee you also, and learn that your existence is in him alone, and you shall then obtain that of which he said to you: "Eye hath not seen, nor ear heard, neither have entered into the heart of man." [118] We now ask (of thee) undefiled Jesus,[119] what thou hast promised us [120] to give; we praise thee, we thank thee, we confess thee, in glorifying thee, though we are weak, because thou alone art God,[121] and none other, to whom be glory [122] now and for ever, Amen."

---

[114] Lat. omits: which is heard through silence.
[115] Lat. omits: which is also . . . other.
[116] Lat.: Lord Jesus Christ.
[117] Lat.: Thy voice.
[118] Lat.: of sinful man.— This word which Paul quotes, I Cor. II, 9, as word of Scripture, as does also Clem. Alex. (see Pick, *Paralipomena*, p. 72, No. 33), is here quoted as saying of Christ.
[119] Lat. omits: undefiled Jesus, so also the Coptic.
[120] Lat. omits: us.
[121] Lat.: Lord.
[122] Lat.: honor, glory and power.

ACTS OF PETER

40. (11) When the surrounding multitude cried aloud [123] the Amen, Peter, during this Amen, gave up his ghost to the Lord.[124]. When Marcellus saw that the blessed Peter had given up his ghost, without communicating with anyone, which were also impossible, he took him down from the cross with his own hands, and bathed him in milk and wine. And he broke seven pounds of mastic and other fifty pounds of myrrh and clove and spice and anointed his body, and filled a very costly trough of stone with Attic honey and buried him in his own tomb. And Peter came to Marcellus by night, and said, "Marcellus didst thou not hear the Lord say, 'Let the dead be buried by their own dead?'" When Marcellus said, "Yea," Peter said to him, "What thou didst spend on the dead is lost. For, though living, thou didst care like a dead for the dead." When Marcellus awoke, he narrated the appearance of Peter [125] to the brethren, and he was with those who had been strengthened by Peter in the faith on Christ, strengthening himself now the more till the arrival of Paul at Rome.[126]

41. (12) When Nero heard that Peter had departed this life, he blamed the prefect Agrippa that he had been killed, without having obtained his consent. For he had the intention to punish him the more severely, because Peter had instructed

---

[123] Coptic: aloud with Peter.
[124] Lat. omits: Peter, during . . . Lord.
[125] Lat.: Peter, the apostle of Christ.
[126] Lat. omits: and he was . . . Rome.

some of his servants and alienated them from him. Therefore he was angry, and for a long time he spoke not with Agrippa.[127] He sought to destroy all brethren whom Peter had instructed.[128] And in the night [129] he sees one [130] striking him, and saying: "Nero,[131] thou art not able now to persecute or destroy [132] the servants of Christ. Keep therefore thy hands from them."[133] And in consequence of such a vision [134] Nero became much afraid, and let the disciples [135] alone at that time, in which Peter had also left the life.[136] For the rest the brethren continued with one accord, rejoicing and glorying in the Lord, and praised the God and Saviour of our Lord Jesus Christ with the Holy Spirit, to whom be glory in all eternities. Amen.[137]

---

[127] Lat. omits: And for a long . . . Agrippa.
[128] Lat. omits: brethren . . . instructed.
[129] Lat.: And whilst he was thus thinking.
[130] Lat.: an angel of God.
[131] Lat.: Nero, listen.
[132] Lat. omits: or destroy.
[133] Lat.: from my servants, if you will not feel, that you have despised me.
[134] Lat. and Coptic omit: and in . . . vision.
[135] Lat.: disciples of God and of Christ.
[136] Coptic: life in the peace of God. Amen.— The Coptic ends here.
[137] For the last sentence the Latin reads: Peace be with all brethren, with the readers as well as with the hearers. The affair of the Apostle Peter is ended with peace (and of Simon). Amen.— The words "and of Simon" are added by the copyist. The Manuscript of Vercelli adds besides: "Finished is the epistle of the holy Peter with the magician Simon. What the port is for the sailor, the last line is for the writer."

III.

THE ACTS OF JOHN.

Thilo, *Fragmenta actuum S. Joannis a Leucio Charino co*-scriptorum*, part I, Halle, 1847.

Tischendorf, *Acta apostolorum apocrypha*, Lipsiæ, 1851, p. 266-276.

Zahn, *Acta Joannis*, Erlangen, 1880.

Lipsius, *Apokryphe Apostelgeschichten*, Braunschweig, I (1883), p. 348-542; II, 2 (1884), 425 ff.

Zahn, *Geschichte des neutest. Kanons*, II. 2 (1892), 856-865.

Harnack, *Geschichte der altchristlichen Litteratur*, I (1893), 124-127; II, 1 (1897), 541-543.

Corssen, "Monarchianische Prologe zu den vier Evangelien" (in *Texte und Untersuchungen*, 15, 1 (1896), 72-134) deals not directly with the Acts of John, but tries to show that the fourth gospel was composed in opposition to the Acts of John, a view which was opposed by Jülicher (*Göttinger Gelehrte Anzeigen*, 1896, 841-851); H. Holtzmann (*Theol. Litt.-Zeitung*, 1897, 331-335), and others.

James, *Apocrypha anecdota*, II (1897), p. IX-XXVIII, 1-24.

Bonnet, *Acta apostolorum apocrypha*, 2, 1 (1898), p. XXVI-XXXII, 151-216.

Zahn, "Die Wanderungen des Apostels Johannes" (in *Neue Kirchliche Zeitschrift*, 10 (1899), 191-218.
Forschungen zur Geschichte des neutest. Kanons, 6 (1900), 14-18.

Hilgenfeld, "Das Johannesbild des Lykomedes" (in *Zeitschrift fuer wissensch. Theologie*, 42 (1899), 624-627.
"Der gnostische und der kanonische Johannes über das Leben Jesu" (*ibid.* 43 (1900), 1-61).

Ehrhard, *Die altchristliche Literatur*, I (1900), 158-160.

Bardenhewer, *Geschichte der altchristlichen Literatur*, I (1902), 437–442.

Schmidt, *Die Alten Petrusakten*, 1903 (see *Johannes-Akten* in the index).

Schimmelpfeng-Hennecke in Hennecke, *Neutestamentliche Apokryphen*, 1904, 423–459; also in Hennecke, *Handbuch zu den Neutest. Apokryphen*, 1904, 492–543.

Leipoldt, *Geschichte des Neutest. Kanons*, I (1907), 262 ff.

Bardenhewer, *Patrology*, p. 105 f.

The Acts of John, which have been made use of by the author of the Acts of Peter and Thomas, belong to the second century, perhaps to 150–180 A. D. According to Nicephorus, the Acts of John comprised twenty-five hundred stichoi, or lines, or about the same space as our present Matthew-Gospel occupies. Unless there is a mistake, we have about two-thirds of the whole, and it may be said that of all the Gnostic Acts these seem to have left the greatest traces on Church tradition. As author the name of Leucius is generally connected with the Acts of John, for he seems to have been a companion and an attendant on that apostle (comp. c. 18 ff., 60–62, 73, 111, 115). Several traditions concerning John, which are mentioned by very early writers, agree so closely with what we know to have been told in the Gnostic Acts as to favor the idea that these Acts may have been the original source of these traditions. But this account cannot be given of all the stories told about this apostle. For instance, the beautiful story of John and the robber appears to have been derived by Clement of Alexandria (*Quis dives salv.*, 42) from some different source; for later Christian writers, who show independent knowledge of other things contained in the Leucian Acts, appear to have known for this story no other authority than Clement.

The Leucian Acts came under discussion at the Second Council of Nicæa, in 787. They had been appealed to by the Iconoclasts. In order to discredit their authority, passages [1] from these Acts were read to the council to exhibit

---

[1] The fragments were collected by Thilo, l. c.; see also Zahn *Acta*, p. 211 f.; 223; Bonnet, p. XXXI, who mentions

ACTS OF JOHN

their heretical character. The Docetism of the Acts comes out very plainly from this evidence. John is related as informing his disciples among other things that when he tried to lay hold on our Lord it had sometimes appeared to him to find solid substance, but not at other times. This passage is evidently alluded to by Clement of Alexandria (*Hypotyposes* on I John, 1, 1), who states that he read "in the traditions" that when John handled the body of our Lord it offered no resistance, but yielded place to the apostle's hand. This is one of the reasons for thinking it possible that these Acts may be as old as Clement of Alexandria. But it is probable that the Acts of John were in circulation before the time of Clement. Zahn dates the Leucian Acts of John as early as 130; Lipsius places them thirty years later. Like the Acts of Paul, those of John no doubt originated in Asia Minor.

The Acts as we now have them, are not complete. They commence with c. 18, and narrate, roughly speaking: 1, arrival and first abode at Ephesus (c. 18–55); 2, return to Ephesus, and second abode (Drusiana narrative, c. 58–86); 3, the life of Jesus and his trance (c. 87–105); 4, the end of John (c. 106–115). For this matter, besides the manuscripts, together with the acts of the second Nicene Council, Bonnet made use of a number of manuscripts, which he mentions in the preface. Besides these manuscripts, use has been made of the work of Abdias, the reputed author of a collection of apocryphal acts of the Apostles. This Abdias claimed to have been the first bishop of Babylon, is said to have written the deeds of the apostles in Hebrew, which his disciple Eutropius translated into Greek and the historian Africanus divided into 10 books. The work was edited by Wolfgang Lazius, Basel, 1551, and often reprinted. The fifth book of *Abdiæ Episc. Babyloniæ Historia Certaminis Apostolorum* treats of John, and contains matter which seems to belong to the original Leucian Acts, and is of greater importance for the reconstruction of the text than the life of John, composed

---

manuscripts and other works relating to the council-acts. The same list is also given under the text on p. 151; Hennecke, *Handbuch*, p. 499–501.

in the first half of the fifth century by a certain Prochorus (Acts of Apostles, VI, 5), a supposed disciple of John. Prochorus no doubt perused the Leucian Acts, as can be seen from a comparison of two manuscripts *Q* (cod. Paris. gr. 1468 of the XI cent.) and *V*. (Vat. gr. 654; XII or XIII cent.). The narrative of Prochorus is, a Catholic revision of the Johannine legend. It was first published by Michael Neander in an appendix to the third edition of his Græco-Latin edition of Luther's smaller catechism, Basel, 1567 (p. 526–663), and is now accessible in Zahn's edition (*Acta Joannis*, 1–105).

The beginning of the Acts, c. 1–14, which describes John's journey from Ephesus to Rome and banishment to Patmos, which Bonnet puts at the beginning, and c. 15–17, which describe John's return from Patmos, and which Bonnet puts below the text, may contain some original matter, though nothing certain can be ascertained for the present. These chapters were formerly published by Tischendorf (p. 262–272). For the benefit of the reader we give these chapters as they are given by Bonnet (p. 151–160).

ACTS OF THE HOLY APOSTLE AND EVANGELIST JOHN THE THEOLOGIAN.

1. When Agrippa, King of the Jews, who advised for peace, was stoned and put to death, Vespasian Caesar, coming with a great army, invested Jerusalem; some prisoners of war he took and slew, others he destroyed by famine in the siege; most he banished and at length scattered them. And having destroyed the temple, and put the holy vessels on board a ship, he sent them to Rome, to make for himself a temple of peace, and adorned it with the spoils of war.

2. And when Vespasian was dead, his son Do-

mitian, having got possession of the Kingdom, along with other wrongful acts, set himself also to make a persecution against the righteous men. For having learned that the city was filled with Jews, remembering the edicts given by his father about them, he purposed casting them all out of the city of the Romans. And some of the Jews took courage, and gave Domitian a writing, in which the following was written:

3. "O Domitian, Cæsar and King of all the world, as many of us as are Jews entreat thee, as suppliants we beseech of thy power not to banish us from thy divine and benignant face; for we are obedient to thee, and the customs, and the laws, and practices, and policy, doing wrong in nothing, but being of the same mind with the Romans. But there is a new and strange nation, neither agreeing with our customs nor consenting to the religious observances of the Jews, uncircumcised, inhuman, lawless, subverting whole houses, proclaiming a man as God, all assembling together under a strange name, that of Christian. These men reject God, paying no heed to the law given by Him, proclaim to be the Son of God a man born of ourselves, Jesus by name, whose parents and brothers and all his family are connected with the Hebrews; whom on account of his great blasphemy and his wicked foolery we gave up to the cross. And they add another blasphemous lie to their first one: him that was nailed up and buried, they glorify as having risen from the dead; besides, they also falsely as-

sert that he has been taken up in clouds into the heavens."

4. At this the King, being affected with rage, ordered the senate to publish a decree that they should put to death all those who confessed themselves to be Christians. Those, then, who were found in the time of his rage, and who reaped the fruit of patience, and were crowned in the triumphant contest against the works of the devil, received the repose of incorruption.

5. And the fame of the teaching of John was spread abroad in Rome; and it came to the ears of Domitian, that there was a certain Hebrew in Ephesus, John by name,[1] who spread a report about the empire of the Romans, saying that it would quickly be rooted out, and that the Kingdom of the Romans would be given over to another. And Domitian, troubled by what was said, sent a centurion with soldiers to seize John and bring him. And having gone to Ephesus, they asked where John lived. And having come up to his gate, they

---

[1] According to cod. Vatic. 654 (XI, or XII, cent.) the Ephesians sent the following report to the emperor after the destruction of the Artemis-Temple: "To the imperator Cæsar Augustus, the glorious, the triumphator. Be it known to thee, that a certain man, named John, of Jewish descent and a Galilean according to his religion, has come into Asia, even into thy devoted city of Ephesus. He has excited all and turned them away from the religion of the fathers, and made them follow him, so that a strange name and a strange people originated. And unless you destroy him quickly, you will lose the people and the country." When the Emperor Hadrian heard this, he sent swift-footed soldiers to fetch the apostle.— This report differs from the contents in ch. 3 given above.

found him standing before the door; and, thinking that he was the porter, they inquired of him where John lived. And he answered and said: I am he. And they, despising his common, and low, and poor appearance, were filled with threats, and said: Tell us the truth. And when he declared again that he was the man they sought, the neighbors moreover bearing witness to it, they said he was to go with them at once to the king in Rome. And urging them to take provisions for the journey, he turned and took a few dates, and straightway went forth.[2]

6. And the soldiers, having taken the public conveyances, travelled fast, having seated him in the midst of them. And when they came to the first change, it being the hour of breakfast, they entreated him to be of good cheer, and to take bread, and eat with them. And John said: I rejoice in soul indeed, but I care not for any food. And they started, and were carried along quickly. But when it was evening they stopped at a certain inn; and as, besides, it was the hour for supper, the centurion and the soldiers being most kindly disposed, en-

---

[2] The Vatican recension tells us that when the soldiers had come to Ephesus and asked for John the Galilean, they "were shown our cell. And when they entered they found the theologian and asked him: Art thou John the Galilean? He said: I am he. But when they saw the virtue of the man and his modest and quiet demeanor, as well as his noble countenance, they were afraid, and respectfully said to him: 'The King of the Romans wants thee; come, go with us.' Upon hearing this, John gets up quickly, takes his pallium, together with about two handfuls of dates, and says to them: 'Come, let us go.'"

treated John to make use of what was set before them. But he said that he was very tired and in want of sleep more than any food. And as he did this every day, all the soldiers were struck with amazement, and were afraid lest John should die, and involve them in danger. But the Holy Spirit showed him to them as more cheerful. And on the seventh day, it being the Lord's day, he said to them: Now it is time for me also to partake of food. And having washed his hands and face, he prayed, and brought out the linen cloth, and took one of the dates and ate in the presence of all.

7. And when they had ridden a long time they came to the end of their journey, John thus fasting. And they brought him before the king and said: Worshipful King, we bring to thee John, a god, not a man; for, from the hour in which we apprehended him, to the present, he has not tasted bread. At this Domitian being amazed, stretched out his mouth on account of the wonder, wishing to salute him with a kiss; but John bent down his head, and he kissed his breast. And Domitian said, "Why hast thou done this? Didst thou not think me worthy to kiss thee?" And John said to him: It is right to adore the hand of God first of all, and in this way to kiss the mouth of the king; for it is written in the holy books: "The heart of the King is in the hand of God."[8]

---

[8] Prov. XXI, 1.— The Vatican recension narrates that John kissed the King's head and breast. The King says to him: "Why did you kiss me; I am only a man, and thou teachest,

8. And the King said to him: Art thou John, who said that my Kingdom would speedily be uprooted, and that another King, Jesus, was going to reign instead of me? And John answered and said to him: Thou also shalt reign for many years given to thee by God, and after thee very many others; and when the times of the things upon earth have been fulfilled, out of heaven shall come a King, eternal, true, Judge of living and dead, to whom every nation and tribe shall confess, through whom every earthly power and dominion shall be brought to nothing, and every mouth speaking strange things shall be shut. This is the mighty Lord and King of all breath and flesh, the Word and Son of the living One, who is Jesus Christ.

9. At this Domitian said to him: What is the proof of these things? I am not persuaded by words only; words are a sight of the unseen. What canst thou show in earth or heaven by the power of him who is destined to reign, as thou sayest? For he will do it, if he is the Son of God. And immediately John asked for a deadly poison. And the King having ordered poison to be given to him,

---

as I hear, that all men worship and adore a heavenly God." John replied: "Because it is written, 'the heart of the King is in the hand of God' and again, 'the hand of the Lord is over the King's head.' For this reason I kissed thy breast and head." The King being pleased with John's answer, said to him, "I heard concerning thee that thou didst excite all people, especially that of the Ephesians, by deceptions and magical arts. Thou also preachest a strange God and adorest him instead of the true gods, which we worship. Meanwhile I will try and find out whether the God, whom thou preachest, will help thee."

they brought it on the instant. John therefore having taken it, put it into a large cup, and filled it with water, and mixed it, and cried out with a loud voice, and said: In thy name, Jesus Christ, Son of God, I drink the cup which Thou wilt sweeten, and the poison in it do Thou mingle with the Holy Spirit, and make it become a draught of life and salvation for the healing of soul and body, for digestion and harmless assimilation, for faith not to be repented of, for an undeniable testimony of death as the cup of thanksgiving.[4]

10. And when he had drunk the cup, those standing beside Domitian expected that he was going to fall to the ground in convulsions. And when John stood, cheerful, and talked with them safe, Domitian was enraged against those who had given him the poison, as having spared John. And they swore by the fortune and health of the King, and said that there could not be a stronger poison than this. And John perceiving what they were whispering to one another, said to the King: Do not take it ill, O King, but let a trial be made, and thou shalt learn the power of the poison. Let some condemned criminal be brought from the prison. And

---

[4] According to the Vatican recension the King orders a magician, an excellent worker of the devil, to come, and says to him: Prepare for me such a deadly poison, that he who touches it, dies within an hour. The magician does as he is bidden and brings the poison to the King. The King says: "Let it be given to John the Galilean." The magician fills the cup and gives it to John. He takes the poison, makes the sign of the cross over it, calls upon the Lord Jesus Christ and drinks it as with great pleasure.

when he had come, John put water into the cup, and swirled it round, and gave it with all the dregs to the condemned criminal. And he, having taken it and drunk, immediately fell down and died.[5]

11. And when all wondered at the signs that had been done, and when Domitian, seized by fear, intended to retire and go to his palace, John said to him: O, Domitian, King of the Romans, didst thou contrive this, that, thou being present and bearing witness, I might to-day become a murderer? What is to be done about the dead body which is lying? And he ordered it to be taken and thrown away. But John, going up to the dead body, said, O God, Maker of the heavens, Lord and Master of angels, of glories, of powers, in the name of Jesus Christ, Thine only begotten Son, give to this man who has died for this occasion a renewal of life, and restore him his soul, that Domitian may learn that the Word of God is much more powerful than poison, and is the ruler of life. And having taken him by the hand, he raised him up alive.[6]

---

[5] The Vatican recension narrates: The King and the magician and all standing beside the King are amazed at the non-effect of the poison. The King is enraged against the magician, as having spared John. But John saith to him: "The poison is deadly; but Christ, my God, who said: if those who believe on him shall drink something deadly, it shall not hurt them, has made this also and all arts of the devil and his servants of no effect. But if thou, O King, wilt know the truth of those words, let some condemned criminal, etc., etc.

[6] The Vatican recension reads: When the king and all beside him saw this, they were greatly afraid. Saith John: "Since I am the cause of the death of this man, it is my duty to revive him by prayer." Having stood there for one

12. And when all were glorifying God, and wondered at the faith of John, Domitian said to him: I issued a decree of the senate, that all such persons should be summarily dealt with, without trial; but since I find from thee that they are innocent, and that their religion is rather beneficial, I banish thee to an island, that I may not seem myself to do away with my own decrees. He asked then that the condemned criminal should be released; and when he was released, John said: Depart, give thanks to God, who has this day delivered thee from prison and from death.[7]

13. And while they were standing a certain home-born slave of Domitian's, of those in the bedchamber, was suddenly seized by the unclean spirit, and lay dead, and it was announced to the King. And the King was moved, and entreated John to help her. And John said: It is not in man to do this; but since thou knowest how to reign, but dost not know from whom thou hast received it, learn who has the power over both thee and thy kingdom. And he prayed thus: O Lord, the God of every Kingdom, and Master of every creature, give

---

hour in prayer, he raised the dead in the presence of the King and those who were with him.

[7] The Vatican recension reads: When the King and those with him saw this they feared the God of heaven and many believed on God and on the apostle. When the King saw that he had a plausible reason against us, he said to the apostle: "Since we have accepted the accusation against thee and the royal edicts demand that the accused shall not go unpunished, we command that thou be taken for a time to an isle called Patmos. John said to him: "Do as you please."

to this maiden the breath of life. And having praised, he raised her up. And Domitian, astonished at all the wonders sent him away to an island, appointing for him a set time.

14. And straightway John sailed to Patmos, where also he was deemed worthy to see the revelation of the end. And when Domitian was dead, Nerva succeeded to the Kingdom, and recalled all who had been banished; and having kept the Kingdom for a year, he made Trajan his successor in the Kingdom. And when he was king over the Romans, John went to Ephesus, and regulated all the teaching of the Church, holding many conferences, and reminding them of what the Lord had said to them, and what duty he had assigned to each. And when he was old and changed he ordered Polycarp to be bishop over the church.[8]

---

[8] The following Bonnet has below the text

14. Having spent three years in Patmos. . . . After the king of the Romans had died during the time of the banishment of John, the apostle, finding no ship in the isle which left for the shore, took a small boat of cork, put it into the water, entered the boat, and permitted me also to go with him. And he made it sail opposite the city of Miletus. When the sea sees the apostle and beloved disciple of the Lord, like a good maid it spreads it back under him and hastens in all piety to bring him to the shore.

15. Having left the sea on a certain point, about 8 miles from the city of Miletus, he found there a little village. And he went in and sat himself on a rock; as was his custom to do among all nations which he taught, so he did here also. And he enlightened all the inhabitants of the place by his teaching.

16. From here he went to the city of the Ephesians. On his way he came also to Miletus. Having performed there many miracles according to the grace of the Holy Spirit, he made also many of the inhabitants there disciples of Christ and citizens of heaven. Some evil-doers arose and caused

Arrival at Ephesus and Work There.

Lycomedes and Cleopatra.[1]

(Acta pp. 160-165.)

18. John hastened to Ephesus, induced by a vision. On this account Daemonicus and his relative Aristodemus and the very rich Cleobius and the wife of Marcellus detained him hardly a day at Miletus to rest with him. When they had left early in the morning, and had almost gone about four miles, a voice from heaven was heard: "John, thou art to procure, for thy Lord at Ephesus the glory which thou knowest, thou and all thy brethren with thee, and some of those who shall believe there through thee." And John rejoicing considered within himself what it might be that were to happen to him at Ephesus, and said, "Lord, behold I go according to Thy will. Thy will be done."

19. When we came near the city, Lycomedes

---

the apostle many temptations. They even gave him a deadly cup to drink, but could do nothing against him. For he drank the poison at once without being hurt, and joyfully continued on his way.

17. The men of that village, however, where the apostle had left the sea, built a small house of prayer in honor of the theologian, placing in the midst the rock on which the apostle sat and instructed them to worship and to praise Christ our true God. That rock ceased not to send forth from time to time a fragrant balm in testimony for all believers. When we entered into Ephesus all the people went forth to meet the apostle.

[1] The headings are not in the original, but by the translator, for the convenience of the reader.

the commander in chief of the Ephesians, a wealthy man, met us, fell down before John, and asked him for help, with these words, "Thy name is John; the Lord whom thou preachest, sent thee for the benefit of my wife, which is paralyzed already seven days and lies past recovery. But give the glory to thy God and treat her out of compassion for us." Whilst I was reflecting what to do, a certain man came to me and said, "Desist, Lycomedes, from the evil thought which militates against thee, yield not to it! For out of compassion for my servant Cleopatra, I sent to thee a man from Miletus, named John, who will comfort her and restore her to thee cured. Delay not, therefore, servant of that God who announced thee to me, but hasten to the rattling woman." And John went at once from the gate with the brethren who were with him, and followed Lycomedes into his house. And Cleobius said to his young servants, "Go to my relative Callippus and make yourselves comfortable in his house — for I come thither with his son — that we may find everything well arranged!"

20. When Lycomedes and John had come into the house, in which was the woman, he (Lycomedes) again touched his feet, and said, "See, Lord, the lost beauty, see the youth, see the much talked of bloom of my unhappy wife, the admiration of all Ephesus! Woe to me, unhappy one! I was envied, humbled, the enemy's eye struck me. I never wronged anyone, although I could harm many. I was always anxious to experience no sor-

row or anything like it! Of what use is my care now for Cleopatra? What good was it to me, that I was called godly to this day? I suffer more than an ungodly, that I must see thee, Cleopatra, thus suffering. The sun shall not see me in his circuit, if you are no more with me. Before thee, Cleopatra, I will die. I will not spare my still young life. I will justify myself before the goddess of right, how I served her in righteousness, if judgment is to be pronounced against her unrighteous sentence. I will avenge myself on her by coming as a shade. I will say to her, thou hast forced me to leave the light of life, because thou didst rob Cleopatra. Thou art the cause of my death, by having prepared for me this fate. Thou hast forced me to blaspheme Providence by destroying my confidence."

21. And still more spoke Lycomedes to Cleopatra, went to her couch, and cried bitterly. But John drew him away and said, "Abandon these tears and thy unbecoming words! It behooves thee not, who art seeing, to be disbelieving. Know that thy partner for life will be restored to thee. Therefore join us, who have come for her sake, and pray to the God whom thou sawest, when He showed me to thee in a vision! What is the matter, Lycomedes? Wake up and open also thy soul! Cast from thee the much sleep! Ask the Lord, beseech Him for thy wife, and He will support her." But he fell to the ground and wept dejectedly. And John said with tears, "Woe to the treachery

ACTS OF JOHN 139

of the vision, woe to the new temptation prepared for me, woe to the new craft of him who devises cunnings against me! Has the voice from heaven, which came to me by the way, yielded to me this, predicted to me this, what should here take place? Will it deliver me up to such a great multitude of citizens, for the sake of Lycomedes? The man lies here lifeless, and I know not that I shall leave this house alive. What dost thou intend, Lord? Why hast thou deprived us of thy good promise? Let not, I beseech thee, Lord, let not him rejoice, who rejoices over the sorrow of others. Let him not dance, who always laughs at us! But let thy holy name and thy compassion come quickly! Waken the bodies of the two, who have fallen to my injury."

22. While John was thus crying, the city of Ephesus ran to the house of Lycomedes, supposing that he were dead. And when John saw the great multitude, he prayed to the Lord: "Now the time of refreshing and confidence is with thee, O Christ, now for us weary ones the time of help from Thee, physician, who heals for nothing. Keep my entrance here free from derision! I beseech thee, Jesus, help such a great multitude to come to Thee, the Lord of the universe. Behold the affliction, behold how they die! Of those also who came here on that account, make holy instruments for thy service, after they have seen thy gift! For thou hast said thyself, O Christ, ask and it shall be given you. We therefore beseech thee, O King, not for

gold, not for silver, not for riches, not for possession, nor for any transient, earthly goods, but for two souls through which thou wilt convert those present to thy way, to thy knowledge, to thy confidence, and to thy infallible promise. For many of them shall be saved, after they have known thy power through the resurrection of the departed. Give, therefore, hope in thee! Therefore I will go to Cleopatra and say, Arise, in the name of Jesus Christ."

23. And he went, touched her face, and said: "Cleopatra, He whom every ruler fears, and every creature, power, abyss and darkness and gloomy death and the light of the heavens and the windings of the lower world and the resurrection of the dead and the sight of the blind and the whole power of the ruler of the world, and the pride of the prince, he says, 'Rise and become not a pretext for many, who will not believe, and an affliction for souls, which hope and could be saved.'" And Cleopatra cried out at once: "I will rise, Lord, Save thy handmaiden!" After she had risen who for seven days <had been prostrated by an incurable disease>, the whole city of Ephesus was stirred by the miraculous sight. And Cleopatra asked for her husband Lycomedes. John answered, "Cleopatra, if thou hast a steadfast and firm soul, thou shalt immediately see thy husband beside thee, provided thou become not excited and confounded over that which took place, but believest in my God, who through me will give him to thee alive. Follow

me into another room, and thou shalt see him dead but rising up by the power of God."

24. And Cleopatra followed John into her room, and saw Lycomedes dead on her account. Her voice failed, she gnashed her teeth, bit her tongue, closed her eyes, and commenced to weep. And silently she looked at the apostle. And John had compassion for Cleopatra, and, perceiving that she became neither restless nor excited, he called upon the full mercy free from presumption, saying, "Lord Jesus Christ, thou seest that she collects herself; thou seest that she imposes restraint on herself; thou seest how Cleopatra's soul cries in silence. For she hides within herself the insufferable grief. And I know that she will die yet because of Lycomedes." And in a low voice she said to John, "This I have in my mind, Lord, and nothing else." And the apostle went to the litter, on which Lycomedes was, seized the hand of Cleopatra, and said, "Cleopatra, because of the people which stand by and because of thy relatives which have come, call to thy husband. 'Arise, and glorify God's name, because He gives the dead to the dead!'" And she went and spoke to her husband as she was told, and immediately she raised him. Having risen, he fell down and kissed the feet of John. And he lifted him up and said, "Man, kiss not my feet, but God's; by whose power both of you have risen!"

25. And Lycomedes said to John, "I beseech and adjure thee by the God in whose name thou hast revived us, abide with us with all thy companions."

In like manner did also Cleopatra. And John answered, "To-morrow I will be with you." And they said again to him, "We have no hope in thy God, but would be revived in vain, if thou didst not abide with us." And Cleobius, Aristodemus and Daemonicus, grieved to the very heart, said to John, "Let us abide with them, that they remain unmolested with the Lord!" So he remained with the brethren.

THE PICTURE OF JOHN.

(Acta pp. 165–167.)

26. And a great multitude gathered together for the sake of John. And while he was preaching to those present, Lycomedes, who had a talented painter as friend, hastily went to him and said, "Thou seest that I have come to thee. Come quickly to my house, and whom I shall point out, paint him without him perceiving it. And the painter gave the necessary instruments and colors to some one, and said to Lycomedes, "Point him out to me, and care not for the rest!" And Lycomedes pointed out John to the painter, and brought him into a room close by, from which the apostle of Christ could be seen. And Lycomedes ate bread with the blessed, united in faith and in the knowledge of our God; but rejoiced still more that he was to have him in that picture.

27. On the first day the painter made the outline and left; on the following day he completed the

picture and gave it to Lycomedes, who rejoiced. He took it, put it in his bedchamber, and crowned it. And John, who perceived this afterward, said to him, " My beloved child, what art thou doing, when upon leaving the bath thou goest alone into thy bedchamber? Do I not pray with thee and the other brethren? Or dost thou hide something from us?" Thus speaking, he entered into the room with him. And he saw the crowned picture of an old man, and beside it candlesticks and an altar before it. And he said to him, " Lycomedes, what does this picture mean to thee? Is the painted one of thy gods? I see that thou art still living like a heathen!" Lycomedes replied, " Only he is my God who has revived me and my wife from the dead. But if one is permitted next to God to call those gods, who are our benefactors, then it is thou, father, who art painted in the picture, whom I crown, love, and worship is him who has become my good guide."

28. And John who had never yet seen his own face, said to him, " Thou mockest me, child. Do I look thus . . . ? How wilt thou convince me that the picture is like me?" And Lycomedes brought a mirror. And when he (John) saw himself in the mirror, he said, " As the Lord Jesus Christ lives, the picture is like me,[1] child, but like

---

[1] It was this part of the Acts (ch. 27, 28, as far as like me), to which the iconoclasts had referred at the synod of Constantinople in the year 754. This induced the fathers of the second Nicene council in 787 to examine the origin of that supposed apostolic testimony and to show that it was rather taken from the pseudepigraphical journeys of the holy apostles. The heretical character of the apocryphon

the picture of my body. For if that painter, who imitated this my face in the picture, will paint me, he would now lack the colors given to thee as well as tables and opportunity (?) and access (?) and carriage and form and age and youth and everything visible.

29. "But be thou, Lycomedes, a good painter to me. Thou hast colors, which Jesus gives thee through me, who paints all for himself, who knows the shape and form and gesture and disposition and image of our souls. And the colors which I charge thee to lay on are as follows: Belief in God, knowledge, fear of God, love, communion, meekness, goodness, brotherly love, chastity, integrity, firmness, fearlessness, freedom from sorrow, honesty, and the whole chorus of colors, which represents thy soul in the picture, and supports at once thy prostrated members which rose, but appeased, delivered from plagues, heals thy wounds, arranges thy entangled hair, washes thy face, trains thy eyes, purifies thy heart, empties thy stomach, and mutilates the abdomen. In short, if all such colors are combined and mixed in thy soul, they will make it bold, intrepid, and firm, and bring it to our Lord

---

was shown from the quotation of two other fragments from the same work. The synod prohibited the copying of the abominable book and declared it worthy to be burnt. The fragment used by the iconoclasts is found in the Acts of the Nicene Synod (Harduin IV, 296; Mansi, XIII, 168; also in Acta Concilii edita a Ph. Labbe et G. Cossart, tom. VII, Parisiis a. 1671, made use of by Bonnet, who also refers (p. XXXI), to different manuscripts and the Latin translation by the librarian Anastasius). The Greek text of Harduin is reprinted by Zahn, p. 223, 224.

Jesus Christ. But what thou hast done now is childish and imperfect: thou didst paint the dead picture of a dead."

HEALING OF THE OLD WOMEN.

(Acta pp. 167-169).

30. And he ordered brother Berus, who ministered unto him to bring all the old women of all Ephesus, whilst he himself and Cleopatra and Lycomedes made the necessary preparations. And Berus came and told John, " Of the old women which live here, I only found sixty-four in a healthy state; of the rest some are paralyzed and some otherwise sick." When John had heard it, he remained silent for some time, rubbed his face, and said, " O, of the indolence of those who dwell in Ephesus! O, of the despair and weakness (in the faith) in God! O, of the devil who mocked in course of time at the believers in Ephesus! Jesus, who gives me grace and the gift to trust in Him, speaks now quietly to me: ' Have the sick women brought, come with them to the theatre, and heal them through me! For of those which will come to this spectacle are some which I will convert by such cures, that they may be of some use.' "

31. When all the people had met at Lycomedes' house on account of John, he took leave of them, saying, " All of you who wish to know the power of God, come to the theatre!" On the following day, it being yet dark, the people ran to the theatre. The

proconsul also hastened thither, and sat among the people. A captain, Andronicus, at that time one of the most prominent Ephesians, said, "John has promised impossible and incredible things. But," said he, "if he can (really do) of what I hear he boasts, let him come to the theatre naked, without having anything in his hand; let him also pronounce that magic name which I heard him call upon!"

32. Upon hearing this and moved by these words, John had the old women brought to the theatre. When they were brought there, all resting on couches, some being asleep, and after the whole city had gathered together, amidst the greatest silence John opened his mouth and spoke thus:

33. "Men of Ephesus, know ye first why I tarry in your city, or what is my confidence over against you, which is so strong that it even became known to this assembly, to all of you. I have not been sent with a human message, and I went not into a distant land with a hopeless task. I am no merchant who buys or exchanges goods, but Jesus Christ, whom I preach, will according to His mercy and goodness through me convert you entirely and deliver you from your aberration, who are domineered by unbelief and are sold into ignominious lusts. By His power I will also confound your captain in his unbelief by raising up those who are before us, whose external condition and diseases are visible to you all. And this I cannot now (attain), when they perish, and healed, they shall be raised.

34. "One thing, however, I would in the first place implant into your ear, why I have come to you, the care for your souls, that you think not that this time last to all eternity, which is rather a time of the yoke, and that you lay not up for yourselves treasures upon earth, where everything passeth away. Think also not, if you have children, to rest in them, and seek not to rob and defraud on their account! Mourn also not, ye who are poor, if you cannot serve the lusts! For even those who can do it, call you happy, when they are sick. And ye who are rich, rejoice not because you have more treasures! For their possession causes you unlimited sorrow, when you have lost them. And again, when you have them, you must be afraid that on their account some one might kill you.

35. "And thou who art of bodily beauty, and with proud confidence liftest up thy countenance, thou at least wilt only see the end of the promise, when thou comest to the grave. Thou who delightest in adultery, know that law and nature revenge themselves on thee, and above all the conscience! And thou, adulteress, which didst trespass against the law, thou knowest not whither thou wilt go. and if thou didst keep thy treasures without helping the poor, having left this body and being in the flames of the (hellish) fire, thou shalt find no one that will have mercy on thee when asking for mercy. Thou who art passionate and raging, know that thou livest like brutes; thou drunkard and

brawler, perceive that thou losest thy senses by serving a vile, filthy passion!

36. "Thou hast thy pleasure in gold and ivory, and precious stones delight thee, but seest thou what thou lovest, after the night has set in? Thou delightest in soft raiment; but being departed out of this life, will it also help thee in the place whither thou goest? Thou murderer, know that the merited punishment is doubly preserved for the time after the separation from here! In like manner ye also, ye poisoners, sorcerers, robbers, defrauders, sodomites, thieves, and all who belong to that chorus, accompanied by your works, ye shall go into the fire that never shall be quenched, to the greatest darkness, to the place of torture of the abyss, and to eternal damnation. Therefore, men of Ephesus, repent; understand this also that the kings, the rulers, the tyrants, the boasters, the victors in wars, naked depart from this world, to suffer pains in everlasting torments!"

37. Having thus spoken, John healed all the diseases by the power of God.

DESTRUCTION OF THE ARTEMIS TEMPLE

(Acta pp. 169-173.)

And the brethren from Miletus said to John, "We remained a long time at Ephesus. If it seemeth good to thee, let us also go to Smyrna. For we already hear that the wonderful works of God have there also been heard of." And Andronicus said,

"If it pleases the master, then let us go!" John said, "First let us go to the temple of Artemis! For there also in consequence of our coming we shall be able to find ministers of the Lord."

38. After two days the birthday of the idol's temple was celebrated. While all were dressed in white garments, John put on a black one and went to the temple. They laid hold of him and tried to kill him. But John said, "Men, ye are mad, by laying hold of me, the servant of the only God." And ascending a platform he spoke to them:

39. "Men of Ephesus, ye are in danger of having the character of the sea. Every discharging river and every precipitating spring, downpours and compact waves and torrents rushing from the rock, are permeated by the bitter salt which is in the sea. Thus to this day you are unchangeably hostile to true piety, and by degrees you perish in your old idolatry. How many miraculous deeds did you see me perform, how many cures! And still you are hardened in the heart and cannot look up. What now, men of Ephesus? I ventured now to come down to this idol's temple, to convince you that you are wholly without God and dead through human reasonings. Behold, here I stand. You all assert that Artemis is powerful. Pray to her, that I alone die! Or if you cannot accomplish this, I alone will call upon my God to kill you all on account of your unbelief."

40. Since they already knew him and had seen how the dead woke up, they cried aloud, "Deal not

thus with us and kill us, we beseech thee, John; we know, indeed that thou canst do it." And John answered them, "If you wish not to die, let me convince you of your idolatry, and why? That ye may desist from your old error. Be now converted above all through my God — or I will die through your goddess. For I will pray before your face to my God, and ask him to have mercy upon you."

41. After these words he prayed thus: "God, who art God above all so-called gods, who to this day has been despised at Ephesus, thou didst induce me to come to this place, which I never had in view. Thou hast abrogated every worship of the gods through conversion to thee. In thy name every idol, every demon, and every unclean spirit is banished. May the deity of this place, which has deceived so many, now also give way to thy name, and show thus thy mercy on this place! For they walk in error."

42. And with these words of John the altar of Artemis suddenly cleft into many parts, and the oblations put up in the temple suddenly fell to the ground, and what happened to be good (?) broke, also more than seven of the idols. And half of the temple fell down, so that the priest also, when the roof came down, was killed by one stroke. And the people of the Ephesians cried, "There is only one God, that of John, only one God who has compassion for us; for thou alone art God; now we have become converted, since we saw the miraculous

deeds. Have mercy upon us, God, according to
thy will, and deliver us from our great error."
And some of them were on their faces and cried;
others bent their knees and prayed. Others, again,
rent their garments and lamented; still others tried
to escape.

43. And John lifted up his hands and prayed
with uplifted soul to the Lord: " Glory be to thee,
my Jesus, true, only God, that procurest servants for
thee in manifold manner!" And after these words
he spoke to the people: " Rise up from the ground,
men of Ephesus, pray to my God, and know how
His invisible power was made manifest and his miraculous deeds took place before your eyes! Artemis herself should have helped. Her servant
should have received help from her and not
die. Where is the power of the deity? Where the
sacrifices (offered to her)? Where the birthday?
Where the festivals? Where the wreaths? Where
the great enchantment and the poisoning congenial
to it?"

44. And the people rose up from the ground and
made haste to destroy also the remainder of the
temple, crying, " We know that the God of John is
the only one, and henceforth we worship him, since
we have obtained mercy from him." And as they
came down, many of the people touched John, saying, " Help us, John, help us who die useless!
Thou seest our intention; thou seest how the multitude following thee cleaves to the hope in thy God.
We saw the way, which we have gone astray, when

wé lost it. We saw that our gods are erected in vain. We saw the great disgraceful laughing over them. But give us, we beseech thee, that help comes to us without hindrance, when we have come to our houses! Receive us, who are in anxiety!"

45. John answered them, "Men, believe that for your sakes I remained at Ephesus, although I was anxious to go to Smyrna and the other cities, that the people there become converted to Him as servants of Christ. But when I was about to leave and my mind was not yet completely composed with regard to you, I remained in prayer to my God and asked Him to leave Ephesus only after I have strengthened you. Since I have perceived that this is done, and still more, I shall not leave till I have weaned you like children from the milk of the nurse, and have set you upon a firm rock."

THE RAISING OF THE PRIEST.

(Acta pp. 173-175).

46. Thus John remained with them, and received them in the house of Andronicus. And one of those gathered there and placed the body of the Artemis priest, whose relative he was,[1] before the gate, and had quickly come in with the others, without saying anything to anyone. After John had preached to the brethren, prayed, thanked and

---

[1] According to Cod. Q̇ (Pares, græc. 1468, XIth cent.), he is a brother of the dead priest; and the raising takes place at Smyrna.

blessed everyone by laying on of hands, he said, moved by the Spirit, " Here is one, brought hither through the faith in God, who put the priest of Artemis before the gate and afterward came in, because in the desire of his soul he regarded the care for his soul as the first, and thought thus within himself: It is better to care for the living than for the body of my relative. For I know that by turning to the Lord and saving my soul John will not refuse to raise the dead." And John rose from his place and went to that which the relative of the priest had occupied with these thoughts, and, taking him by the hand, he said, " Were these not thy thoughts, as thou camest to me, child?" And he answered tremblingly, " Yea, lord!" and fell down at his feet. And John said, " Our Lord is Jesus Christ, who will prove His power on the body of thy relative by raising him."

47. And lifting up the young man, he took him by the hand, and said, " It is not a great task for a man who is lord over great mysteries to bother himself with small things. Or is it something great to drive away bodily diseases?" And still holding the young man by the hand, he said, " I say to thee, son, arise, and raise the dead without saying anything (else) than only this: The servant of God, John, says to thee, Arise!" And the young man went to his relative and said in the presence of much people these words only, and then returned with the living to John. When he saw him who had been raised, he said, " Thou that hast been raised art in-

deed not living, and art not partaker and heir of the true life. Wilt thou belong to Him by whose name and power thou hast been raised? Believe now and thou shalt live in all eternity." He immediately believed in the Lord Jesus and followed John.

THE PARRICIDE.
(*Aa. pp.* 175-179).

48. On the following day, having seen himself in a vision walking three miles outside of the gates, John hesitated not, but rose early in the morning, and went away with the brethren. And a young farmer, having been admonished by his father not to take to himself the wife of his colaborer, whilst the other threatened to kill him, was offended at his father's warning, and suddenly killed him. When John perceived what had taken place, he said to the Lord, "Lord, hast thou on this account bidden me to come here to-day?"

49. When the young man saw the hasty death, he was afraid of being seized, took the sickle from his girdle, and hastily ran to the house. When John met him, he said, "Stand still, thou most villainous demon! Whither art thou running with the sickle thirsting for blood?" The young man being confused, let the iron drop to the ground, and said to him, "I have committed a very unhappy, inhuman deed, and knowingly; therefore, I resolve to do myself a more violent and more cruel harm, to die once for all. For whilst my father always exhorted me earnestly to lead a chaste and honorable life, I

felt offended at his censure, and struck and killed him. And when I perceived what had taken place, I intended to go to the woman on whose account I had become a parricide and try to kill her and her husband, and finally myself. For I could not bear the look of her husband, whilst being executed."

50. And John said to him, "That I may not give him a chance who in thee laughs and mocks by my withdrawal and by not caring for thy danger, come with me and show me where thy father is! And in case I raise him up for thee, how will I keep thee away from the woman which became dangerous to thee?" The young man replied, "By giving me back my father alive, and by seeing and hearing him, I will give up the rest."

51. And whilst thus speaking, they came to the place where the body was of the old man, while other travelers stood by. John said to the young man, "Unhappy one, not even the age of thy father hast thou regarded?" And the other cried, tore his hair, and confessed he felt sorry. But the servant of the Lord, John, prayed, "Thou who has this day shown me the way thither, who knowest that this deed was to take place, before whom no deed in human life can be hidden, who didst grant to me every healing and salvation according to thy will, grant to me also that the old man may live, since thou seest how the murderer became his own judge! And do thou alone spare him, O Lord, although he did not spare his father, because he received from him such good advice!"

52. After these words he went to the old man and said, "My Lord shall not be powerless to extend to thee his good compassion and his mercy devoid of presumption. Arise, therefore, and give God the honor in the present work." And the old man said, "I rise up, lord." And he arose, and, having raised himself, he said, "I was delivered from a life of the most fearful pain, who had to suffer the many fearful abuses and unkindness of my son; and now, man of the living God, thou hast called me back — (and) to what purpose?" <John replied: "If> thou risest up to the same purpose, thou hadst done better to remain dead. But rise up to a higher purpose!" And he took him, brought him to the city, and preached to him of the mercy of God, so that the old men believed, before he came into the gate.

53. And when the young man saw the unexpected resurrection of his father and his own salvation, he took the sickle and cut off his privy parts. And running into the house, where he kept the adultress, he flung (them) into her face saying, "On thy account I became a parricide, and (should have also) became (a murderer) both of thee and myself. Here hast thou which is the cause of all. God have mercy upon me, that I have perceived his power."

54. He returned to John, and in the presence of the brethren narrated what he had done. But John said to him, "He who induced thee, young man, to kill thy father and to become the lover of an-

other man's wife, has also represented to thee the removal of the immoderate members as a righteous work. But thou shouldest not have destroyed the members, but the temper which proved itself evil through the members. For not the instruments are hurtful to man, but the hidden sources, by which every shameful inclination is called forth and becomes manifest. Repent, therefore, my son, such guilt, and know Satan's cunnings, and thou shalt have the God, who helps thee in every need of thy soul." And the young man continued to lead a quiet life in repentance for his former sins, that he might obtain forgiveness through God's goodness, and parted not from John.

55. While performing these deeds at Ephesus, Smyrnæans sent messengers to him, saying: "We hear that God whom thou preachest is an unenvious God, and has bidden thee not to remain in one place with partiality. Being the preacher of such a God, come to Smyrna and the other cities, that we may know thy God, and, knowing him, put our hope in him!

[Here is a gap in Bonnet's text, but codex Q. has here the following story which Bonnet gives under the text.]

JOHN AND THE PARTRIDGE.

(Aa. p. 178-179).

56. One day John was seated and a partridge flew through the air and walked in the sand before him. John looked at this with amazement. And

a priest, one of the hearers, came to John, seeing the partridge running before him, and said within himself, fretfully, "Such a great and old man rejoices over a partridge running in the sand!" But John perceived his thoughts and said to him, "It were better if thou, too, my son, would look at a partridge running in the sand, and would not contaminate thyself with disgraceful and impure acts. He who expects the repentance and conversion of all has brought thee hither for that cause. For I have no need of a partridge running in the sand. The partridge is thy soul."

57. When the old man heard this and perceived that he was not hidden, but that Christ's apostle had said everything which filled his heart, he fell to the ground and said, "Now I know that God dwelleth in thee, blessed John. And blessed he who has not tempted God in thee! He that tempts thee, tempts him who cannot be tempted." And he asked him to pray for him. And (the apostle) instructed him, gave him commandments, and dismissed him, praising the Almighty God.[1]

---

[1] In a somewhat different form we find the same story in Cassian's Collat. XXIV, 21 in *Bibl. Patr. Max.* VII, 246; reprinted in Fabricius, *Bibl. græc.* II, 774 ff.; Thilo, p. 8.

The narrative reads thus: It is handed down that the most blessed evangelist John, when once playing with a partridge, suddenly noticed a hunter coming to him. He wondered that such a famous man could find pleasure in such trifles and said to him: "Art thou not that John whose great celebrity has filled me with the greatest desire to make thy acquaintance? Why, then, hast thou pleasure in such small things?" John replied: "What is that thing which thou carriest in thy hand?" "A bow," replied the hunter. "Why then is it unstrung?" "Because," said the hunter, "were I

RETURN TO EPHESUS AND SECOND ABODE THERE.

FROM LAODICEA A SECOND TIME TO EPHESUS.[1]

(*Aa.* 179-181).

58. Some time passed without any of the brethren ever being afflicted by John. But now they were afflicted, when he said, "Brethren, it is time for me to go to Ephesus — for such is the agreement with those who remained there — that they become not light-minded, being for a long time without their pastor. But you may direct your mind to God, who leaves us not." And when the brethren heard this, they became sad that they should be separated from him. And John said, "Though I go from you, Christ is always with you. If you love him purely, you shall continually enjoy the blessing of his communion. For though he be loved, he loved those first who love him."

59. Having spoken thus, and having parted from them, he left much money to the brethren for distribution, and went to Ephesus, all brethren being sorrowing and weeping. Those that were with him from Ephesus were Andronicus and Drusiana, Lycomedes and Cleobius and their attendants.

---

to keep it always strung, it would lose its spring, and become useless." "Even so," replied John, "be not offended at this my brief relaxation, which prevents my spirit from waxing faint."

[1] This heading is found in Codex M (Venetus Marcianus græcus, 363, 12th cent.). The following narrative is also given in Greek by Zahn, *Acta Joannis*, p. 225 ff.; see also *ibidem*, p. LXXXIII.

They were joined afterward by Aristobula, who had heard that her husband Tertullus had died on the way, Aristippus with Xenophon, the chaste damsel, and many others, whom he always directed to the Lord, and who would no more leave him.

60. On the first day when we [2] came to a lonely inn and being in perplexity on account of a bed for John, we experienced a joke. There was a bedstead without covers; we spread our cloaks, which we brought, over it and requested him to lie down and to rest, whilst we slept on the floor. He had hardly lain down, when he was molested by bugs. But as they became more and more troublesome, and it being midnight already, we all heard him say to them, "I say unto you, O ye bugs, be ye kindly considerate; leave your home for this night and go to rest in a place which is far from the servants of God!" And while we laughed and talked, John fell asleep. And we conversed gently, and owing to him we remained undisturbed.

61. When it was day, I rose up first, and with me Berus and Andronicus. And in the door of the room which we had taken, was a mass of bugs. And having gone outside to have a full view of them, and having called all brethren, John was still asleep. When he woke up, we showed to him what we saw. And sitting up in bed, and seeing them, he said, "Since you have been wise to be-

---

[2] The narrator uses in the narrative the first person of the plural, thus speaking as companion of the apostle.

ware of my punishment, come back to your place!" Having spoken thus, and having risen from the bed, the bugs hastened from the door to the bed, ran from between his feet into the joints, and disappeared. And John said again, "This animal heard the voice of a man and kept quiet, without trespassing (against the command). We, however, hear God's voice, and yet in our light-mindedness we transgress his commandments. And how long yet!"

END AND RAISING OF DRUSIANA.

(*Aa. pp.* 181-193).[1]

62. After this we came to Ephesus. And when the brethren who lived there had learned that John had returned after a long time, they met in the house of Andronicus, where he also used to visit, touched his feet, put his hands to their faces, and kissed them. [Very many also rejoiced by the touch of his garment, and were healed because they had touched the garment of the holy apostle.][2]

63. And while there was great love and endless joy among the brethren, one, a servant, of Satan, coveted Drusiana, although he saw and knew that she was the wife of Andronicus. Very many also

---

[1] See also Zahn, *loc. cit.*, p. 226 f. With ch. 62 commences a parallel narrative by Abdias (*histor. apost.*, V, 4, in Fabricus, *cod. pseudepigr. Novi Test.* ed., 2, II, 542 ff.)

[2] There is a gap in the Greek text. The words in [] are from Abdias.— The following Drusiana-story has been used by the nun Roswitha of Gandersheim (10th cent.) as theme in her *Calimachus*, the best of her dramatic efforts (opp. ed. Barack, 1858, p. XXXV).

remonstrated with him, "It is impossible for thee to obtain this woman, especially also since she separated from the communion with her husband out of piety. Or dost thou alone not know that Andronicus, who was not before what he now is, namely a godly man, had locked her up in a tomb, saying, "Either I'll have thee as a wife, as I had thee before, or thou must die? And she rather preferred to die than to do the act repugnant to her. Now, if she denied out of piety to her husband and master her consent to (sexual) intercourse, yea, persuaded him to become like-minded, should she consent to thee, who wishes to commit adultery with her? Desist from thy passion, which gives thee no rest! Desist from thy scheme, which thou canst not accomplish!"

64. Though his intimate friends remonstrated with him, they could not persuade him, who was even so impudent as to send her word. When Drusiana heard of his disgraceful passion and shameless demands, she became very despondent, and after two days she was ague-struck. She said, "O, if I only had not come back to my native city where I became a stumbling-block to a man, who believes not in the worship of God! For if one were filled with God's word, he would not fall into such a passion. Therefore, O Lord, since I became accessory to a blow which struck an inexperienced soul, deliver me from this prison and take me soon to thee!" And without being understood by anyone, Drusiana, departed this life in the presence of

John — not rejoicing but sorrowing over the physical trouble of that (man).

65. And Andronicus was sad, and carried a hidden sorrow in his heart, and wept bitterly, so that John could only silence him by saying to him, " Drusiana has departed this life for a better hope." To this answered Andronicus, " Of this I am certain, John, and I have no doubt in the belief in my God. But my hopes are mostly grounded on this, that she departed this life pure."

66. After she was interred, John took Andronicus apart, and, having learned of the cause, he sorrowed more than Andronicus. And he kept silence, considering the threats of the enemy, and sat down a little. When the brethren were assembled to hear which words he would say concerning the departed, he began to speak:

67. " When the helmsman who crosses the ocean has landed with the ship and passengers in a quiet haven free from storms, he feels secure. The husbandman who gave the seed-grains to the ground, and cared for them with great pains, is only then to enjoy a rest from his labors when he has sheltered abundant corn in his barns. Whoever promised to take part in the race should only rejoice when he has obtained the price of victory. Whose name is entered on the list of prize fighting should only triumph after he received the crowns. And thus it is with all races and arts, when they disappoint not at the end, but are so carried out, as they were intended.

68. "Thus, I think, it is with the faith which every one of us practices, and which can only be decided as having been the true one when it remained the same to the end of life. For there are many obstacles which cause unrest to human reasoning: cares, children, parents, glory, poverty, flattery, youth, beauty, boasting, thirst for riches, anger, pride, frivolity, envy, passion, carelessness, licentiousness, love, slaves, money, pretense, and all the other like obstacles which exist in life; thus for the helmsman who takes his course in a quiet journey, the adverse winds and a great tempest and a mighty wave, when the heaven is serene; for the husbandman, untimely weather and blight and creeping worms appearing from the ground; for the athletes, the "almost," and for the artists, the obstacles issuing from them.

69. "The believer must above all things consider the end and carefully examine how it will come, whether energetic and sober and without impediment, or in confusion and flattering this world and bound by passions. Thus one can only praise the beauty of the body, when it is wholly uncovered; and the great general, when one has happily finished the whole campaign, as he promised, and the excellent physician, when he has succeeded in every cure, and so also a soul as filled with faith and worthy of God if it happily accomplished that which it promised, not one which made a (good) beginning, and gradually descended into the errors of life and became weak; also not the

paralyzed one, which forcedly busied itself with higher things, and was afterward drawn downward to the perishable; also not that which loved the temporal more than the eternal; neither that which exchanged the perishable <for the lasting>, also not that which honored that which was not to be honored <and loved> works of dishonor; also not that which accepted pledges from Satan, and received the serpent into its house; not one which was reviled for God's sake and afterward was ashamed, neither one which said with the mouth, Yea, but showed it not by the deed; but one which refused to be inflamed in filthy lust, to succumb to levity, to be caught by thirst after money and to be betrayed by the strength of the body and anger."

70. While John continued to preach to the brethren, so that they despised the earthly goods for the sake of the eternal ones, the lover of Drusiana, inflamed by the activity of the polymorphous Satan, to the most ardent passions, corrupted the greedy steward of Andronicus with much money. And he opened the tomb of Drusiana and left to him to accomplish on the body that which was (once) denied to him. Since he had not procured her during her lifetime, he continually dwelt in thought upon her body after she was dead, and exclaimed, "Although when living thou didst refuse to unite with me in love, after thy death I will still commit a rape on thy body." Being in such a frame of mind he obtained the opportunity to execute his impious design through the accursed stew-

ard, and both went to the tomb. Having opened the door, they began to take the graveclothes from the corpse, and said, "What good was it to thee, unhappy Drusiana? Couldst thou not have done, while alive, that for whose voluntary execution thou wouldst soon have had no more grief?"

71. Whilst they thus spoke and only the shirt remained, there appeared something wonderful, which people that do such things deserve to experience. A serpent appeared of a sudden, bit the steward, and killed him. And the serpent bit not the young man, but encircled his feet, spitting fearfully, and when he had sunk down, the beast sat on him.

72. On the following day John and Andronicus and the brethren, went at the break of day to the tomb in which Drusiana has been for three days, that we break the bread there. And when about to start, the keys were not to be found. And John said to Andronicus, "Rightly they are lost, for Drusiana is not in the tomb. Nevertheless, let us go, that thou appearest not careless, and the doors will open of themselves, since the Lord has given us already many other things."

73. When we came to the place, the doors opened at the master's behest, and at the tomb of Drusiana we saw a beautiful youth smiling. When John saw him, he exclaimed and said "Dost thou forestall us here also, noble one (beautiful one)? And why?" And he heard (his) voice saying to him, "For the sake of Drusiana,

which thou art to raise up — for I had almost found her defiled and on account of the dead lying near the tomb." And when the noble one had thus spoken to John he ascended to heaven before the eyes of all. And John turned to the other side of the tomb and saw a young man, the very prominent Ephesian Callimachus — for thus he was called — and on him a very great snake sleeping also the steward of Andronicus, named Fortunatus dead. Upon seeing both, he stood helpless and said to the brethren, "What meaneth all this? Or why did the Lord not reveal unto me what took place here, who was always concerned for me?"

74. When Andronicus saw these bodies, he jumped up and went to the tomb of Drusiana, And when he saw her in her bare shirt, he said to John, "I understand what took place, blessed servand of God. This Callimachus loved my sister. And as he could not get her, although he tried it often, he no doubt bribed this my accursed steward with much money with the intention — as one can at least perceive — to accomplish his purpose through him. For this Callimachus said to many, If she will not yield to me alive, rape shall be committed on her death. This, O master, the noble one saw and did not suffer that her earthly remains should be violated, wherefore they who endeavored this are dead. And this the voice which came to thee, Raise Drusiana! announced to thee before. For she departed this life through sorrow. And I will be convinced by him who had spoken, that this

one belongs to the deceived people. For you were advised to raise him also. Of the other I know that he deserves not the deliverance. But one thing I ask of thee. Raise Callimachus first, and he shall confess what took place."

75. And John looked at the corpse and said to the poisonous snake, "Go from him who is to serve Jesus Christ!" Then he rose and prayed thus: "God, whose name is praised by us, as it is meet; God, who overcomes each work of the lower (power); God, whose will is done, who always hears us, make thy grace now also efficacious on this youth! And if through him some dispensation is to take place, make it known to us, when he is raised!" And the young man immediately arose and rested for a whole hour.

76. Having regained his sense, John asked what his intrusion into the tomb meant. And having learned from him what Andronicus already told, how he passionately loved Drusiana, John asked furthermore whether he had accomplished his wicked design to commit rape on the solemn earthly remains. And he replied, "How could I have accomplished this when this fearful beast killed Fortunatus by a bite before my eyes — and this according to merit, for he encouraged me to such frantic act, whereas I already desisted from the ill-timed fearful frenzy — but he frightened me and put me in such a state in which thou didst see me, before I arose again? But I will tell thee another greater miracle, which seized me still more and had

almost killed me. When my soul was seized with mad passion and the incurable disease did trouble me keenly, when I had already robbed her of her graveclothes with which she was dressed, and went from the grave to put them down as thou seest, I turned back to perpetrate the abominable deed. And I saw a beautiful youth covering her with his upper garment. Rays of light fell from his face upon hers, and he turned to me also and said, Callimachus, die, that thou mayest live. Who it was, I knew not, servant of God. Since thou hast come here, I perceive that it was an angel of God. And this I truly know, that the true God is preached by thee; and I am sure of it. But I pray thee, see to it that I may be delivered from such a fate and awful venture, and bring to thy God a man who has gone astray in scandalous, abominable deceit. On my knees I ask thy help. I will become a man, (one) of those who hope in Christ, that the voice may also become true, which spake here to me, Die to live! And it is already fulfilled. For that unbeliever, immoderate, godless, is dead; I am raised by thee as a believer for the future, <moderate>, godly, that I may know the truth, which I ask of you to reveal unto me."

77.[3] And John, rejoicing, noticed the whole spectacle of the salvation of men and said, "O Lord Jesus Christ, I know not how powerful thou art, I am amazed at thy great mercy and endless

---

[3] This whole section is omitted in Codex M.

long-suffering. O what greatness descended to servitude! O unspeakable freedom, which was enslaved by us! O, inconceivable glory, which has come upon us! Thou who didst keep the grave from shame, who became the Saviour of that man who contaminated himself and didst teach him to be chaste who <meant to violate> dead bodies. Father full of mercy and compassion toward him, who regarded thee not, we praise, glorify, and honor thee and thank thee for thy great goodness and long-suffering, holy Jesus, for thou alone art God and none else, thou, against whose power all devices can do nothing now and in all eternity! Amen!"

78. After these words, John took Callimachus apart, kissed him, and said, "Glory be to our God, who had mercy upon thee, child, and deemed me worthy to praise his power, and delivered thee by a wise method from that passionate madness and intoxication and called thee to rest and renewal of life."[4]

79. When Andronicus saw that Callimachus had been raised from the dead, he and the brethren besought John to raise Drusiana also, and said, "John, let her be raised and happily complete life's short space, which she gave up out of sorrow for Callimachus, because she thought to be an offense to him! And when it pleases the Lord, he will take her to himself. And without delay John came to the

---

[4] Here and in the following Codex M is deficient.

grave seized her hand and said, "Thou who alone art God, I call upon thee, the immense, the unspeakable, the incomprehensible, to whom all worldly power is subject, before whom every might bows, before whom every pride falls down and is silent, before whose voice the demons are confounded, at whose contemplation the whole creation surrenders in quiet meditation. Thy name will be hallowed by us, and raise Drusiana that Callimachus be still more established in thee who alone canst do what is wholly impossible with man, and hast established the dispensation of salvation and resurrection, and let Drusiana come out comforted from the grave, which in consequence of the conversion of the youth has no more in herself the least impediment, to long for thee!"

80. Having spoken thus, John said, "Drusiana, arise!" And she arose and came from the tomb. And when she saw that she wore nothing but her shirt, she knew not how to explain it, how it happened. Having learned everything from Andronicus, while John was upon his face and Callimachus weepingly praised God, she also rejoiced and praised God.[5]

81. Having dressed herself and looking around, she saw Fortunatus. And she said to John, "Father, he, too, shall rise, though he tried ever so much to become my traitor." When Callimachus heard her speaking thus, he said, "No, I

---

[5] Here the text ends in Zahn, *loc. cit.*, p. 234.

pray thee, Drusiana. For the voice which I heard did not mention him, but only announced thy resurrection, and when I saw it, I believed. If he were good, God would have certainly raised him out of mercy through the blessed John. He knew that it is good if the man remains dead." And John answered him, " Child, we have not learnt to recompense evil with evil. For God has not recompensed the evil which we have done unto him, but has given us (the opportunity for) repentance. And when we knew not his name, he did not forget us, but had mercy upon us. And when we reviled him, he forsook us not, but was merciful. And when we were disbelieving, he remembered not the evil. And when we persecuted his brethren, he did not requite us, but made us repent, turn away from the sins, and called us to himself, as he called thee also, child Callimachus, and, without remembering thy former sins, made thee his servant through his long-suffering mercy. If thou wishest me not to raise Fortunatus, let Drusiana do it."

82. Without wavering in the joy of her spirit and soul, she went to the body of Fortunatus and said, " God of the æons, Jesus Christ, God of truth, thou didst permit me to see signs and wonders, thou didst give me the grace to partake of thy name. Thou didst breathe into me thy spirit with thy polymorphous face, and didst show unto me much compassion. With thy rich goodness, thou hast protected me when my former husband, Andronicus, did violence to me, and didst give me afterward

ACTS OF JOHN

thy servant Andronicus for a brother. Until now thou hast kept me, thy maiden, pure. Me, the dead, thou didst raise through thy servant John, To me, which had risen, thou didst show without offense him who was offended (at me). Thou didst give me perfect rest in thee, and didst deliver me from the hidden illusion. I love thee with all my heart. I beseech thee, Christ, not to dismiss thy Drusiana without being heard, who asketh of thee the resurrection of Fortunatus, though he tried ever so much to become my traitor."

83. And she took the hand of the dead and said, "Rise, Fortunatus, in the name of our Lord Jesus Christ!" And Fortunatus rose up. And beholding John in the tomb and Andronicus and Drusiana risen from the dead and Callimachus believing, he said, "O how far has the power of these awful people spread! I wish I were not raised, but remained rather dead, in order not to be obliged to see them." And having spoken thus he ran from the tomb.

84. And when John perceived the unchangeable soul of Fortunatus, he said, "O nature, which did not turn to the loftier! O source of the soul, remaining in the filth! O property of corruption, full of darkness! O death, dancing among those belonging to thee! O forest, with trees full of unhealthy shoots, neighbor of unbelief! O fruitless tree, full of fire! O wood, producing the coal as fruit! Thou didst show what thou art, and thou wilt be convinced with thy children. And the fac-

ulty of praise the higher things, thou knowest not; for thou hast it not. Wherefore as thy issue, so thy root and nature. Vanish away from those who hope in the Lord — from their thoughts, from their mind, from their souls, from their bodies, from their doing, from their life, from their conversation, from their activity, from their pursuit, from their counsel, from their resurrection to God, from their sweet savor of which thou wilt have a part, from their fasting, from their prayers, from their holy baptism, from their eucharist, from their food of flesh, from their drink, from their dress, from their love, from their recreation, from their continence, and from their righteousness. From all these, thou most unholy and abominable Satan, Jesus Christ, our God and <Lord?> of those who are like thee and have thy nature, will keep away."

85. After these words John prayed, fetched a loaf of bread to the tomb to break it, and said, " We praise thy name, who hast converted us from error and unmerciful lusts. We praise thee who hast brought before our eyes that which we saw. We bear witness to thy goodness manifested to us in various ways. We hallow thy good name, Lord <and thank thee>, that thou didst show those convicted by thee. We thank thee, Lord Jesus Christ, that we believe in thy unchangeable <mercy>. We thank thee that thou art in need of a saved human nature. We thank thee, that thou didst give us this sure <faith>, that thou alone art God, and, for ever. We, thy servants, thank thee, O Holy One,

who met with (good) reason, and they who raise (from the dead).

86. Having thus prayed and praised God, he left the tomb and made all brethren partake of the eucharist of the Lord. And when he had come into the house of Andronicus, he said to the brethren: "Dear brethren, a spirit within me has prophesied that, in consequence of the bite of the serpent Fortunatus died of blood-poisoning. Let one make haste and inquire whether it is so! And one of the young men ran and found him dead already, the poison having spread and reached the heart. And he returned to John, reporting that he had been dead three hours already. And John said, "Thou hast thy child, devil!"

Thus John rejoiced with the brethren in the Lord.[6]

Pertaining to the Life of Jesus and His Death.

(*Aa. pp.* 193-203).[1]

87. Those then, who were present inquired the cause,[2] and were especially perplexed, for that Dru-

---

[6] The last sentence is found in Codex R (codice Patmensi, 14th cent.), and by Abdias, who translates "and on that day he rejoiced with the brethren." Upon this follows in Abdias a story concerning the philosopher Craton, which is given in German in Zahn's *Acta Joannis*, p. 235-238; see also Lipsius, *Apokryphe Apostelgeschichten*, l. p. 422 f. There is no doubt a gap in the Greek and this marked also by . . . in Bonnet's edition, p. 193.

[1] The text is that of Codex C, a Vienna MS. written in 1324, and discovered by M. R. James.

[2] The beginning shows that the narrative followed imme-

siana had said, " The Lord appeared unto me in the tomb in the form of John and in that of a youth." For as much, therefore, as they were perplexed and were in a manner not yet confirmed in the faith so as to endure it steadfastly, John said:

88. " Men and brethren, ye have suffered nothing that is strange or incredible as concerning your conception of the <Lord>, inasmuch as we also, whom he chose for himself as apostles, were tried in many points, I, indeed, am neither able to set forth to you nor to write the things which I both saw and heard: and now it is needful that I should fit them to your hearing; and according as every one of you is capable I will communicate unto you those things whereof ye are able to become hearers, that ye may see the glory that is about him, which was and is both now and for ever.

"For when he had chosen Peter and Andrew, who were brethren, he cometh to me and to my brother James, saying, I have need of you, come unto me. And my brother said as follows: John, that child that called to us upon the shore, what does it want? And I said, What child? He replied, the one that is beckoning to us. And I answered, Because of our long watch which we kept at sea thou seest not aright, my brother James: but seest thou not the man that standeth there, fair and comely and of a cheerful countenance? But he

---

diately the Drusiana-story, but it shows also that the preceding narrative is not complete.

ACTS OF JOHN

said to me, Him I see not, brother; but let us go forth, and we shall see what it meaneth.

89. "And so when he had brought the ship <to land>, we saw Him also helping along with me to settle the ship. And when we departed from the place, wishing to follow him again, he was seen of me as having a head rather bald but a thick and flowing beard; but to James he appeared as a youth whose beard was newly come. We were therefore perplexed, both of us, as to what should mean which we had seen. But when we followed him, both of us little by little became more perplexed as we thought upon the matter. Yet unto me there appeared this, which was still more wonderful: for I would try to see him in private, and I never at any time saw his eyes closing, but only open. And oftentimes he appeared to me as a small man and uncomely, and then again as one reaching to heaven. Also there was in him another marvel; when I sat at meat he would take me upon his breast, and I would consider with myself; and sometimes his breast was felt of me to be smooth and tender, and sometimes hard, like stones, so that I was perplexed in myself and said, What does this mean? And when I was thinking of these things

. . .

90. "At another time he taketh me, James, and Peter into the mountain, where his custom was to pray, and we beheld in him such a light as it is not possible for a man that useth corruptible speech to

tell what it was like. Again in like manner he leadeth us three up into the mountain, saying, Come ye with me. And we again went, and we saw him at a distance praying. Now therefore I, because he loved me, drew nigh unto him softly as though he should not see, and stood looking upon his hinder parts. And I beheld him that he was not in any wise clad with garments, but was seen of us naked thereof, and not in any wise as a man; and his feet whiter than snow, so that the ground there was lighted up by his feet, and his head reaching unto the heaven; so that I was afraid and cried out, and he turned and appeared as a man of small stature, and took hold upon my beard and pulled it and said unto me, John, be not unbelieving, but believing, and be not a busybody. And I said unto him, What have I done, Lord? And I tell you, brethren, I suffered such pain at that place where he took hold upon my beard, for thirty days, that I said unto him, Lord, if thy twitch when thou wast in sport hath given me so much pain, what were it if thou hadst given me a buffet? And he said unto me, Let it be thine from henceforth not to tempt him who is not to be tempted.

91. "But Peter and James were wroth because I spake with the Lord, and beckoned unto me that I should come unto them, and leave the Lord alone. And I went, and they both said unto me, He that was speaking with the Lord when he was upon the top of the mountain, who was he? for we heard both of them speaking. And I, when I considered

ACTS OF JOHN

his great grace and his unity which hath many faces, and his wisdom which without ceasing looked upon us, said, That ye shall learn if ye inquire of him.

92. "Again, once, when all of us his disciples were sleeping in a house at Gennesaret, I alone, having wrapped myself up, watched what he did, and first I heard him say, John, go thou to sleep. And thereupon I feigned to be asleep; and I saw another like unto him, whom I also heard saying unto my Lord, Jesus, those whom thou hast chosen believe not on thee. And my Lord said unto him, Thou sayest well, for they are men.

93. "Another glory will I tell you brethren.[3] Sometimes when I would lay hold of him, I met with a material and solid body; and at other times again when I felt him, the substance was immaterial and bodiless and as it were not existing in any wise.[4] Now, if at any time, he were bidden by one of the Pharisees and went to the bidding, we went with him. And there was set before each one of us a loaf of bread by him that had bidden us, and he also with us received a loaf. And he would bless his own and divide it amongst us; and from that

---

[3] In the following Codex C can be supplemented by the Acts of the second Nicene Synod; see also Zahn, *loc. cit.*, p. 219 f.

[4] It is probably this passage to which Clement of Alexandria (*adumbrat. in ep. I, Joan.* ed. Potter, tom. II p. 1009) refers: "Fertur ergo in traditionibus Joannes, ipsum corpus quod erat extrinsecus tangens, manum suam in profunda misisse et ei duritiam carnis nullo modo reluctatam esse, sed locum manui præbuisse discipuli."

little each of us was filled, and our own loaves were saved whole, so that they who bade him were amazed. And often when I was walking with him I wished to see whether the print of his foot appeared upon the earth — for I saw him raising himself from the earth — but I never saw it. Now, these things, dear brethren, I speak to you to encourage you in your faith toward him, for we must at the present keep silence concerning his mighty and wonderful works, inasmuch as they are mysteries and peradventure cannot at all be either uttered or heard.

94. "Now, before he was taken by the lawless Jews, which received (their) law from a lawless serpent, he gathered us all together and said, Before I am delivered up unto them, let us sing a hymn[5] to the Father, and go forth to what lieth before us. So he commanded us to make as it were[6] a ring, holding one another's hands, and himself standing in the middle. He said, Respond Amen to me. He began, then, to sing a hymn, and to say:

Glory to thee, Father!
And we going about in a ring said, Amen.
  Glory to thee, Word! Glory to thee, Grace!
    Amen.

---

[5] On this hymn which the Priscillianists used, see Zahn, *loc. cit.*, p. 220 f.; Lipsius, *Apokryphe Apostelgeschichten*, I, 525 f.; Pfleiderer, *Urchristentum*, 2d. ed., II, 123 f.; Hilgenfeld, *Zeitschrift fuer wissenschaftliche Theologie*, 1900, p 30 ff.

[6] "As it were" not found in the Nicene Acts.

Glory to thee, Spirit! Glory to thee, Holy One!
Glory to the glory! Amen.
We praise thee, O Father. We give thanks to
thee,
O Light wherein dwelleth not darkness. Amen.
95. Now whereas we give thanks, I say:
I would be saved, and I would save. Amen.
I would be loosed, and I would loose. Amen.
I would be pierced, and I would pierce. Amen.
I would be born, and I would bear. Amen.
I would eat, and I would be eaten. Amen.
I would hear, and I would be heard. Amen.
I would be understood, being wholly understand-
ing. Amen.
I would wash myself, and I would wash. Amen.

Grace is dancing.

I would pipe, dance all of you! Amen.
I would mourn, lament all of you! Amen.[7]
An Ogdoad is singing with us. Amen.
The Twelfth number is dancing above. Amen
And the Whole that can dance. Amen
He that danceth not, knoweth not what is being
done. Amen.
I would flee and I would stay. Amen.
I would deck, and I would be decked. Amen.
I would be united, and I would unite. Amen.
I have no house, and I have houses. Amen.

---

[7] Thus far the text in the Nicene Acts.

I have no place, and I have places. Amen.
I have no temple, and I have temples. Amen.
I am a lamp to thee, who beholdest me. Amen.
I am a mirror [8] to thee who perceivest me. Amen.

I am a door to thee who knockest at me. Amen.
I am a way to thee, wayfarer. Amen.

96. "Now if you respond to my dancing, see thyself in me who speaks; and when thou hast seen what I do, keep silence about my mysteries! Thou that dancest, perceive what I do; for thine is this passion of the manhood which I am to suffer! For thou couldst not at all have apprehended what thou sufferest if I had not been sent unto thee as the Word by the Father. When you saw what I suffer, thou hast seen me as suffering; and seeing that, thou hast not stood firm, but wast moved wholly. Moved to become wise, thou hast me for a support. Rest upon me! Who am I? Thou shalt not know when I go away. What I am now seen to be, that I am not. Thou shalt see, when thou comest. If thou hadst known how to suffer, thou wouldst have had (the power) not to suffer. Know thou suffering, and thou shalt have (the power) not to suffer. That which thou knowest not, I will teach thee. Thy God am I, not that of the betrayer. I would

---

[8] In Pseudo-Cyprian, *De duobus montibus*, XIII, we read: "The Lord himself instructs and admonishes us in the epistle of his disciple John to the people, 'You see me thus in yourselves as one of you sees himself in the water or a mirror.'" Comp. also Pick, *Paralipomena*, p. 109.

keep time with holy souls. In me know thou the word of wisdom! Say thou again (with) me:

Glory to thee, Father; glory to thee, Word;
Glory to thee, Holy Ghost!

"Now concerning me, if thou wouldst know what I was (know): with a word did I once deceive all things, and was not put to shame in any wise. I have leaped; but do thou understand the whole, and having understood it say, Glory to thee, Father! Amen.[9]

97.[10] "After this dance, beloved, the Lord went out with us; and we as men gone astray or awakened out of sleep fled all ways. Nay even I that had seen him did not abide at his passion when he was suffering,[11] but fled unto the Mount of Ol-

---

[9] This hymn Augustine found in use among the Priscillianists, and treats of it in *epist.* 237 *ad Ceretium* (Opp. tom. II, col. 644 ff. Ed. Maur. II, 850 ff., Paris 1688). He quotes the following sentences:

> Salvare volo et salvari volo.
> Solvere volo et solvi volo.
> Generari volo . . .
> Cantare volo, saltate cuncti:
> Plangere volo, tundite vos omnes.
> Ornare volo et ornari volo.
> Lucerna sum tibi, ille qui me vides.
> Janua sum tibi, quicumque me pulsas.
> Qui vides, quod ago, tace opera mea.
> Verbo illusi cuncta, et non sum illusus in totum.

Thilo once promised to write a commentary on this hymn, but never fulfilled his promise. The Gnostic character of the hymn is obvious.

[10] Cod. C. can here again be supplemented by the Nicene Acts, see Zahn, loc. cit., p. 222 f.

[11] But see John XIX, 26 f.

ives, weeping over that which had taken place. And when he was hung upon the cross, at the sixth hour of the day, there came darkness over all the earth. And my Lord stood in the midst of the cave and lighted it up, and said, John, unto the multitude down below in Jerusalem I am being crucified, and pierced with lances and reeds, and gall and vinegar is given me to drink.[12] But unto thee I am speaking, and hearken thou to what I say. I put it into thy heart to come up into this mountain, that thou mightest hear matters needful for a disciple to learn from his teacher, and for a man to learn from his God.

98. "And having thus spoken, he showed me a cross of light set up, and about the cross a great multitude, not having one form; and in the cross was one form and one likeness. And the Lord himself I beheld above the cross, not having any shape, but only a voice, and a voice not such as was familiar to us, but a sweet and kind voice and one truly divine, saying unto me: "It is needful that one should hear these things from me, O John, for I have need of one that will hear. This cross of light is sometimes called the Word by me for your sakes, sometimes Mind, sometimes Jesus, sometimes Christ, sometimes Door, sometimes Way, someties Bread, sometimes Seed, sometimes Resurrection, sometimes Son, sometimes Father, sometimes Spirit, sometimes Life, sometimes Truth, some-

---

[12] i.e. the true Christ does not suffer, cannot suffer.

times Faith, sometimes Grace.[13] Now, so it is called as toward men. But in truth, as concerned in itself and in our mode of expression, it is the marking off of all things and the uplifting and foundation of those things that are fixed and were unsettled, and the harmony of the wisdom — and indeed the wisdom of the harmony. But there are on the right and on the left of its powers, principalities, dominions and demons, operations, threats, wrath, devils, Satan and the Lower Root, from which the nature of the things that come into being proceeded.

99. "This, then, is the cross which fixed all things apart by the Word, and marked off the things from birth and below it, and then compacted all into one. But this is not the cross of wood which thou wilt see when thou goest down hence; neither am I he that is upon the cross, whom now thou seest not, but only hearest a voice. I was reckoned to be what I am not, not being what I was unto many others; but they will call me something else, which is vile and not worthy of me. As, therefore, the place of rest is neither seen nor spoken of, much less shall I, the Lord of that place, be seen (or spoken of).

100. "Now the multitude about the cross which is the lower nature is <not> of one aspect; and those whom thou seest in the cross, even if they have not one form, it is because every member of him that came down has not yet been comprehended.

---

[13] Thus far the Acts of the Nicene Synod.

But when the nature of man shall be taken up, and the race which is repairing to me, in obedience to my voice, then that which now hears me shall be united with it and shall no longer be what it now is, but above them, as I am now. For as long as thou callest not thyself mine, I am not that which I was. But if hearing thou hearkenest unto me, then thou shalt be as I am, and I shall be what I was, when I have thee with myself. For from this thou art. Care not, therefore, for the many, and them that are outside the mystery despise! Know that I am wholly with the Father, and the Father with me.

101. "Nothing therefore of the things which they will say of me have I suffered: nay, that suffering also which I showed unto thee and unto the rest in the dance, I will that it be called a mystery. For what thou art, thou seest, that did I show thee; but what I am, that I alone know, and none else. Let me, therefore, keep that which is my own, and that which is thine behold thou through me, and behold me in truth not <what> I am, as I said, but what thou art able to know, because being akin. Thou hearest that I suffered, yet I suffered not; that I suffered not, yet did I suffer; that I was pierced, yet was I not smitten; hanged, and I was not hanged; that blood flowed from me, yet it flowed not; and, in a word, those things that they say of me I had not, and the things that they say not those I suffered. Now what they are I will signify unto thee, for I know thou wilt understand. Perceive thou, therefore, in me the rest of the Logos,

the piercing of the Logos, the blood of the Logos, the wound of the Logos, the nailing of the Logos, the passion of the Logos, the nailing of the Logos, the death of the Logos. And thus speak I, separating off the manhood. Think thou, therefore, in the first place of the Logos, then shalt thou perceive the Lord, and in the third place the man, and what he hath suffered.

102. "When he had spoken unto me these things, and others which I know not how to say as he would have me, he was taken up, no one of the multitude having beheld him. And when I went down, I laughed them all to scorn, inasmuch as he had told me the things which they said concerning him; and I held firmly this one thing in myself, that the Lord contrived all things symbolically and by a dispensation toward men, for their conversion and salvation.

103. "Having therefore beheld, brethren, the grace of the Lord and his kindly affection toward us, let us worship him as those unto whom he hath shown mercy. Not with our fingers, neither with our mouths, nor with the tongue, neither with any part of our body, whatsoever, but with the disposition of our soul, even him, who became man apart from this body. And let us watch because now also he keepeth ward over prisons for our sakes, in tombs also, in bonds and dungeons, in shame and reproaches, by sea and land, at scourgings, condemnations, conspiracies, frauds, punishments, and, in a word, he is with all of us, and suffereth with us

when we suffer, brethren. When he is called by any one of us he endureth not to shut his ears to us, but as being everywhere he hearkeneth to all of us, and just now (has hearkened) to both me and Drusiana — forasmuch as he is the God of them that are shut up — bringing help to us by his own compassion.

104. "Be ye also persuaded, therefore, beloved, that it is no man whom I preach unto you to worship, but God unchangeable, God invincible, God higher than all authority, and all power, and older and mightier than all the angels and creatures that are spoken of, and all ages (æons). If ye then abide in him, and in him are builded up, ye shall possess your soul indestructible."

105. And when he had delivered these things unto the brethren, John departed with Andronicus to walk; and Drusiana also followed afar off together with all, that they might behold the acts that were done and hear his word always in the Lord.[14]

THE END OF JOHN

(*Aa. pp.* 203-215).[1]

106. On the following day, which was the Lord's day, and in the presence of the brethren, he

---

[14] Codex C. adds after "Lord": now and always and for ever and ever. Amen.

[1] For the text see also Tischendorf, *Acta*, pp. 272-276; Zahn, *loc. cit.*, pp. 239 ff.; comp. also Lipsius, I, p. 490 ff. The whole consists of two parts: the first describes a Sunday-service — the last of John (c. 106-110), the second the burial of the apostle (c. 111-115).

began to say to them: "Brethren, fellow-servants, coheirs, and copartners of the Kingdom of the Lord, ye know the Lord, how many powers he hath given you through me, how many miracles, what cures, signs, what gifts, teachings, rulings, rests, services, knowledge, glories, graces, gifts, faiths, communions, all gifts that you have seen with your eyes, were given you by him, as they cannot be seen with these eyes and cannot be heard with these ears. Be strong, therefore, in him, remembering him in all your doings, knowing the mystery of the dispensation that has come to men, for the sake of which the Lord hath worked. He, then, through me, exhorts you, since he wishes to remain without grief, without insult, without treachery, without punishment. For he also knows insult from you, he knows also dishonor, treachery and punisment, if you disobey his commandments.

107. "Let not, therefore, our good God be grieved, the compassionate, the merciful, the holy, the undefiled, the incorporeal, the only, the one, the immutable, the sincere, the guileless, the slow to anger, he that is higher and more exalted than every name that we speak or think of, our God Jesus Christ! Let him rejoice along with us, because we live in purity; let him rest because we behave reverently. Let him be unconcerned, because we are temperate; let him be pleased because we live in fellowship; let him smile because we are sober-minded, and let him be delighted because we love him! These things, brethren, I communicate to you, press-

ing on to the work set before me, already perfected for me by the Lord. For what else have I to say to you? You have the sureties of our God. You have the pledges of his goodness, you have his sure presence. And if ye, then, sin no more, he will forgive you what you have done in ignorance. But if, after ye have known him, and he has had compassion upon you, you return to the like courses, even your former offenses will be laid to your charge, and ye shall have no portion in him, or compassion before his face."

108. And when he had said this to them, he thus prayed: "Jesus, who didst wreathe this crown by thy twining, who hast inserted these many flowers into the everlasting flower of thy countenance, who hast sown these words into my soul, who art the only fosterer and physician of thy servants, who healest freely, who art benignant and not haughty, alone merciful and kind, alone a Saviour and just; thou who always seest what concerns all, and art all, and everywhere present, comprising all and replenishing all, Christ Jesus God Lord, who with thy gifts and thy compassion protects those that hope in thee; who knowest intimately all the cunnings and threats by which our adversary follows us everywhere, do thou alone, O Lord, help thy servants with thy watchful care. So be it, Lord."

109. And having asked bread, he gave thanks thus, saying: "What praise or what sort of offering or what thanksgiving, shall we, breaking the bread, invoke, but thee only, Lord Jesus? We

glorify the name of the Father called by thee. We glorify the name of the Son called through thee. We glorify thy resurrection manifested to us through thee. We glorify thy way; we glorify thy seed, the word, the grace, the faith, the salt the unspeakable pearl, the treasure, the plow, the net, the greatness, the diadem, him called Son of man for our sakes, who has given us the truth, the rest, the knowledge, the power, the commandment, the trust, the hope, the love, the freedom, and the place of refuge in thee. For thou alone, O Lord, art the root of immortality and the fountain of incorruption, and the seat of the ages; thou who hast been called all these names for our sakes, that now we, calling upon thee through these, may recognize thy greatness, which we cannot really see in the present, but only, when we are pure, and solely in the image of the man belonging to thee!"

110. And having broken the bread, he gave it to us, praying for each of the brethren, that he might become worthy of the grace of the Lord and his most holy eucharist. He also, therefore, having likewise tasted it, said: "To me also let there be a portion with you, and grace be with you, O be-

111. And he said to Berus:[2] "Take two

---

[2] Tischendorf reads here thus: "And having thus spoken and confirmed the brethren, he said to Eutyches, also named Verus: Behold, I appoint thee a minister of the Church of Christ, and I entrust to thee the flock of Christ. Be mindful, therefore, of the commandments of the Lord; and if thou shouldst fall into trials or dangers, be not afraid, for thou shalt fall under many troubles, and thou shalt be shown to be an eminent witness of the Lord. Thus, then, Verus

brethren with baskets and vessels with thee and follow me!" And Berus did immediately what John, the servant of God, had bidden him. And the blessed John, having gone forth from the house, went outside of the gates, having told the multitude to stand off from him. And having come to the tomb of one of our brethren, he told to the young men: "Dig, children!" And they dug, and he said to them: "Let the trench be deeper." And as they dug, he preached to them the word of God, and exhorted those who had come out of the house with him, building them up, and furnishing them thoroughly into the majesty of God, and praying for each one of us. And when the young men had finished the trench, as he had wished, while we knew nothing, he takes off the clothes he had on, and throws them, as if they were some bedding, into the depths of the trench; and standing in only his drawers, stretched forth his hands, and prayed thus:

112. "O God, who hast chosen us for the apostleship among the Gentiles, who hast sent us into this world, who hast declared thyself through the Law and the prophets; who hast never rested, but always savest from the foundation of the world those who can be saved; who hast made thyself known through all nature, even among the animals,

---

attend to the flock as a servant of God, until the time appointed for thy testimony. And when John had spoken this, and more than this, having entrusted to him the flock of Christ, he says to him," etc., etc.— Zahn and Bonnet considered this whole clause as an interpolation and omitted it from their texts.

who hast made the lonely and wild soul quiet and peaceable; who hast given thyself to it when thirsting after thy words; who didst quickly show thyself to it when about to die, and didst appear as law when sinking into lawlessness; who didst manifest thyself to it when overcome by Satan; who didst overcome its adversary when it took refuge in thee; who hast given it thy hand, and raised it from the Kingdom of Hades; who didst not leave it in the body; who hast shown it its own enemy; who hast given it a pure knowledge concerning thee, God Jesus, Father of the supernatural, ruler of the heavenly law of things ethereal, the course of things aerial, guardian of those on earth and fear of those under the earth, and grace of thine own people; receive also the soul of thy John, which is certainly deemed worthy of thee!

113. "Thou who hast preserved me also till the present hour pure to thyself, and free from intercourse with a woman; who, when I inclined in my youth to marry, didst appear to me and say, I am in need of thee, John; who didst prepare for me beforehand my bodily weakness; who, in the third place,[8] when I wished to marry, didst prevent me at once, but didst say to me at the third hour, in the sea, John, if thou wert not mine, I would let thee

---

[8] Thus we render the Greek word *triton*, which may also be translated "a third time." The idea seems to be that John speaks of three impediments; one was the appearing of the Lord and call of John; the second his bodily weakness; the third the express prohibition of the Lord to John. with the declaration: "If thou wert not mine, I would let thee marry."

marry; who for two years madest my eyesight weak, didst make men mourn and dependent on thee; who in the third year hast opened up the spiritual eyes, and favored my visible eyes; who by thy representations didst make the steady gaze upon a woman hateful to me; who didst deliver me from temporary show, and didst become my leader to eternal life; who didst separate me from the filthy madness of the flesh; who didst wrest me from bitter death, and alone didst bring me to thee; who didst stop up the secret disease of the soul, and cut out its open sections; who didst afflict and banish him who rebelled in me; who didst establish a spotless friendship to thee; who didst prepare a safe way to thee, who didst give me undoubting faith in thee; who hast drawn out for me pure thoughts toward thee; who hast given the due reward to every deed; who hast set it in my soul to have no other possession than thee alone — for what can be more precious than thou? — now, since I have accomplished thy stewardship with which I was intrusted, make me worthy, O Lord, of thy repose, and give me the end in thee, which is the unspeakable and ineffable salvation.

114. "And as I go to thee, let the fire withdraw; let darkness be overcome; let the gulf be powerless; let the furnace be slackened; let hell be extinguished, let the (evil) angels get behind me; let the demons be afraid; let the princes be broken in pieces; let the powers (of darkness) fall. Let the devil be brought to silence; let Satan be laughed to scorn; let

his madness be tamed; let his wrath be broken; let his vengeance behave itself unseemly; let his attack suffer sorrow. Let his children be trodden under foot, and let all his root be uprooted. And grant to me to accomplish my journey to thee, without suffering insults and abuses; and let me receive what thou hast promised to those, that live in purity, and love thee only!"

115. And having sealed (crossed) himself altogether, he stood and said, "Be thou with me, Lord Jesus Christ"; he laid down in the grave in which he had spread out his garments. He then said to us, "Peace be with you, brethren!" and peacefully yielded up the ghost.[4]

---

[4] In Tischendorf's text the last section reads as follows: And gazing towards heaven, he glorified God; and having sealed himself altogether, he stood and said to us, Peace and grace be with you, brethren! and sent the brethren away. And when they went on the morrow they did not find him, but his sandals, and a fountain welling up. And after that they remembered what had been said to Peter by the Lord about him: "For what does it concern thee if I should wish to remain until I come?" And they glorified God for the miracle that had happened. And having thus believed, they retired praising and blessing the benignant God; because to him is due glory, now and ever, and to ages of ages. Amen.

The story of John going down alive into his grave is related at length by Augustine (*Tractat. 124 in Joannen*, opp. T., III, 2 col., 597 ff.). See Zahn, *loc. cit.*, p. XCVIII f.; Lipsius, *loc. cit.*, I, 494 ff. A modern German poet, R. Binder speaks thus of John's grave:

"Nicht tot ist er, nein, er schlummert bloss,
Und harrt auf den Meister, der Erd im Schoss.
Sich selbst grub er lebensmüde sein Grab
Und legte zum Schlummer sich dann hinab.
Das Atmen der Brust hört das lauschende Ohr,
Aus dem Boden quillt heilendes Manna hervor."

APPENDIX

John and the Robber.

In his *Quis div. salv.*, c. 42, Clement of Alexandria mentions the story of John and the robber, which forms the theme of "Der gerettete Jüngling" by the poet Herder. In the Acts of John the story is not mentioned though it is found by Abdias immediately before the Drusiana-story (c. 62). Whether the story preserved by Clement ever formed a part of the Acts, is difficult to tell. But be this as it may, we add it for the reader's benefit in Wilson's translation (Clement's works in the Ante-Nicene Library):—

(John) Having come to one of the cities not far off (the name of which some give),[1] and having put the brethren to rest in other matters at least, looking to the bishop appointed, and seeing a youth, powerful in body, comely in appearance, and ardent, said, "This (youth) I commit to you in all earnestness, in the presence of the Church, and with Christ as witness." And on his accepting and promising all he gave the same injunction and testimony. And he set out for Ephesus. And the presbyter taking home the youth committed to him, reared, kept, cherished, and finally baptized him. After this he relaxed his stricter care and guardianship, under the idea that the seal of the Lord he had set on him was a complete protection to him. But on his obtaining premature freedom, some youths of his age, idle, dissolute, and adepts in evil courses, corrupt him. First they entice him by many costly

---

[1] Said to be Smyrna.

entertainments; then afterwards by night issuing forth for highway robbery, they take him along with them. Then they dared to execute together something greater. And he by degrees got accustomed; and from greatness of nature, when he had gone aside from the right path, and like a hard-mouthed and powerful horse, had taken the bit between his teeth, rushed with all the more force down into the depths. And having entirely despaired of salvation in God, he no longer meditated what was insignificant, but having perpetrated some great exploit, now that he was once lost, he made up his mind to a like fate with the rest. Taking them and forming a band of robbers, he was the prompt captain of the bandits, the fiercest, the bloodiest, the cruelest.

Time passed, and some necessity having emerged, they sent again for John. He, when he had settled the other matters on account of which he came, said, "Come now, O bishop, restore to us the deposit which I and the Saviour committed to thee in the face of the Church over which you preside, as witness." The other was at first confounded, thinking that it was a false charge about money which he did not get; and he could neither believe the allegation regarding what he had not, nor disbelieve John. But when he said, "I demand the young man, and the soul of the brother," the old man groaned deeply, and bursting into tears, said, "He is dead." "How and what kind of death?" "He is dead," he said, "to God. For he turned wicked and abandoned, and at last a robber; and now he has taken possession of the mountain in front of the church, along with a band like him." Rending therefore, his clothes, and striking his head with great lamentation, the apostle said, "It was a fine guard of a brother's soul I left! But let a horse be brought me, and let some one be my guide on the way." He rode away, just as he was, straight from the church. On coming to the place, he was arrested by the robbers' outpost; neither fleeing nor entreating, but crying, "It was for this I came. Lead me to your captain;" who meanwhile was waiting, all armed as he was. But when he recognized John as he advanced, he turned, ashamed, to flight. The other followed with all his might, forgetting his age, crying, "Why, my son, dost thou flee from me, thy father, unarmed, old? Son, pity me. Fear not; thou hast still hope of life. I will give account to Christ for thee. If need be, I will willingly endure death, as the Lord did die for us. For thee I will surrender my life. Stand, believe; Christ hath sent me."

And he, when he heard, first stood, looking down; then threw down his arms, then trembled and wept bitterly. And on the old man approaching, he embraced him, speaking for himself with lamentations as he could, and baptized a second time with tears, concealing only his right hand. The other pledging, and assuring him on oath that he would find forgiveness for himself from the Saviour, beseeching and falling on his knees, and kissing his right hand itself, as now purified by repentance, led him back to the church. Then by supplicating with copious prayers, and striving along with him in continual fastings, and subduing his mind by various utterances of words, did not depart, as they say until he restored him to the Church, presenting in him a great example of true repentance and a great token of regeneration, a trophy of the resurrection for which we hope; when at the end of the world, the angels, radiant with joy, hymning and opening the heavens, shall receive into the celestial abodes those who truly repent, before all, the Saviour Himself goes to meet them, welcoming them; holding forth the shadowless, ceaseless light; conducting them to the Father's bosom, to eternal life, to the kingdom of heaven.

IV

THE ACTS OF ANDREW

LITERATURE.

Lipsius, *Die apokryphen Apostelgeschichten,* I (1883), 543–622; Ergänzungsheft, 1890, 28–31.

Harnack, *Geschichte der altchristlichen Literatur,* I (1893), 127 ff.; II, 1 (1897), 543–545.

Speranskij, *Die apokryphen Akten des Apostels Andreas in den altrussischen Texten,* Moskau, 1894.

Bonnett, "La passion de l'apôtre André, dans quelle langue a-t-elle été écrite?" (*Byzantinische Zeitschrift,* 3 (1894), 458–469. Supplementum Codicis apocryphi, II: Acta Andreæ cum Laudatione contexta, et Martyrium Andreæ græce, Passio Andreæ latine a se primum edita ex Analectis Bollandianis (XIII, 1894, p. 309–378), repetiit præfatus est indices adjecit, Paris, 1895.

Acta Apostolorum Apocrypha, II, 1 (1898), pp. XI–XXIV; 1–127.

Ehrhard, *Die altchristliche Literatur,* I (1900), 161–163.

Bardenhewer, *Geschichte der altchristlichen Literatur,* I (1902), 432 ff.

Schimmelpfeng-Hennecke in Hennecke, *Neutestamentliche Apokryphen,* 1904, 459 ff.; Handbuch, 1904, 544 ff.

Bardenhewer, *Patrology,* p. 103 f.

Of Andrew, the brother of Peter (Matt. IV, 18; Mark I, 16; XIII, 3; John I, 40, 44; VI, 9; XII, 22) we know very little. According to Eusebius, Andrew labored in the countries north of the Black Sea (*Hist. Eccl.,* III, 1, 1). Some make Greece the sphere of his activity (Lipsius, *loc. cit.,* 63); only the Muratorian Fragment (line 13) records that, in consequence of a revelation given to Andrew, John wrote his gospel, which would point to Ephesus.

Leucian Acts of Andrew, like those of other apostles, are mentioned first by Eusebius (*loc. cit.*, III, 25). Ephiphanius (d. 403) states that the Acts of Andrew were in favor with the Encratites (i.e., those sects which rejected as absolutely unlawful the use of marriage, of flesh meat, and of wine, *hæres,* 47, where the Acts of John, Thomas and other Acts are also mentioned); the Apostolics (also called Apotactici, i. e., "Renunciants," who condemned marriage and rejected private property. They appealed chiefly to the Acts of Andrew and of Thomas, *hæres,* 61); the Origenians, or eunuchs (*hæres,* 63). These sects point to Asia Minor, where the Leucian Acts, as we stated above, were composed. Augustine (d. 430) mentions that the Acts of the Apostles, written by Leucius Charinus — "discipulus diaboli" (i. e., a disciple of the devil), as Pope Gelasius (d. 496) calls him — were held in estimation by the Manichæans (*contra adversar. legis et prophet.,* I, 20). Philastrius of Brescia (*hæres,* 88) speaks of two kinds of Acts of Andrew. The authorship generally is attributed to Leucius by early writers; Innocentius, I. (d. 417), however, says that the Acts of Andrew were composed by the philosophers Nexocharis and Leonidas, which may perhaps be a mistake for Leucius Charinus.

Of the material of the Acts of Andrew, which still recently has come to us, two passages preserved by Euodius of Uzala, a cotemporary of Augustine, in his *De fide contra Manichæos,* c. p. XXXVIII, have been designated as original. Later revisions of the original Acts made it impossible to obtain a true state of the original Acts, and it is due to the labors of Prof. Bonnet, that we now have what may be considered a part of the ancient Acts. Following Hennecke, who also gives a critique of the sources, we give:

I.

THE DOUBLE FRAGMENT BY EUODIUS [1]

a. [Listen what you hear in the Acts of Leucius, which he wrote under the name of the apos-

---

[1] The Latin text of the fragment is given by Lipsius, *loc. cit.,* 590 f., and Schmidt, *Die alten Petrusakten,* p. 53.

tles concerning Maximilla, the wife of Egetes:[2]] As she would not give to her husband what she owed to him, though the apostle said, Let the husband render unto the wife due benevolence: and likewise also the wife unto the husband, she subsituted her maid Euclia, supplying her with repugnant adornment and attire and in the night made her her substitute, so that her husband, without knowing it, went in to her as to his wife.

b. We also read there that when Maximilla and Iphidamia [3] went to hear Andrew the apostle, a beautiful boy, whom Leucius regarded as a god or at least as an angel, delivered them to Andrew and then went to the pretorium of Egetes. He there entered her bedchamber and imitated the voices of women, as if Maximilla were complaining of the sufferings of the female sex and Iphidamia were answering. Upon hearing this, Egetes, thinking that the women were there, went away.[4]

---

[2] Euodius writes: Egetes; the Greek versions: Ægeates; the Latin: Ægeas.

[3] This name is also differently written, as Iphidama, Ephidonna, Ephidamia.

[4] In the present texts of the Acts of Andrew, we find nothing of what Euodius narrates, and it is possible that the words were eliminated as offensive.

2.

Andrew in Prison [1]

(Aa. II, 1, pp. 38-45.) [2]

1. ". . . . . . . Are ye all so slack? Are ye not yet convinced of yourselves, that ye are not yet carrying his goodness? Let us reverently rejoice with one another over the rich communion which we have with him. Let us say among ourselves, Happy is our generation, by whom is it loved? Blessed our existence, of whom did it receive compassion? We are not prostrated, since we are known from such a height. We belong not to time, to be afterward destroyed by it. We are not the product of moving, to be again annihilated by it, nor of earthly generation, to return again (to earth). We belong to that greatness after which we follow, and to him who pities us. We belong to the better. Therefore, we run away from the baser. We belong to the noble, by whom we reject the ignoble; to the righteous, by whom we thrust away the unrighteous; to the merciful by whom we repel the unmerciful; to the Saviour, by whom we have known the destroyer; to the light, by which we banished the darkness; to the One, by whom we removed the many; to the heavenly, by whom we perceived the earthy; to the permanent, by whom

---

[1] The heading is for the sake of convenience.
[2] The text is according to cod. Vatic. gr., 808 saec: X aut XI (Aa., p. XIV), and it seems to present the close of an address delivered by the apostle in prison.

we understood the transient. If we, as he deserves it, resolve to pay to the God, who had mercy upon us, with thanksgiving or trust, with praises or glorifications, let us glory before him of nothing more than that we are known of Him!"

2. Having said these things to the brethren, he dismissed every one to his house, and said to them, "As servants of Christ you shall neither be forsaken by me for the sake of the love which is in him, nor shall I also be forsaken by you because of his mediatorship." And each returned to his house. And there was joy among them for many days, during which Aegeates did not think of instituting proceedings against the apostle. Thus every one was confirmed in the faith in the Lord. And though they all met fearlessly in the prison together with Maximilla and Iphidamia and the others, they unceasingly considered the love and mercy of the Lord.

3. One day, when Aegeates sat in judgment, he remembered the case against Andrew. And like a mad man, he abandons the case before him, leaves the seat and runs to the pretorium (the official residence). He passionately addresses Maximilla with flatteries, which had reached the house before him coming from prison.

4. And coming to her he said, "Thy parents, Maximilla, deemed me worthy to become thy husband and gave thee to me in marriage, without regard to riches, descent, or glory, but on account of the nobility of my heart. Not to mention many

things, what I meant to tell to thy shame, not to mention the good which I received from thy parents and which thou didst receive from me all our life, I came here, leaving the court, to hear one thing from thee. Answer, therefore, intelligently. If thou wert as formerly, lived with me in an intimate manner, slept with me, and would unite with me to procreate children, I should then please thee in every respect. Yea, I will do still more and set free the stranger whom I have in prison. But if thou refusest, I shall do no harm to thee — for this is not in my power; but him whom thou lovest the most, more than thou lovest me, I shall torment the more. Consider, therefore, both, and give me thy decision to-morrow! For I am fully prepared for it."

5. Having thus spoken, he went away. At the usual hour Maximilla and Iphidamia went to Andrew. And putting his hands before her face, she kissed them, and she told him what Aegeates had said. And Andrew answered: "I understand, Maximilla, my dear child, that thou art so excited and that the demand of conjugal intercourse is repugnant to thee, who wishest to keep away from an impure and filthy conduct. And this separation was enjoined upon thee long ago by thy view. Now thou wishest to have my opinion also for a testimony. I adjure three, Maximilla, do it not! Submit not to the threat of Aegeates! Be not persuaded by him! Fear not his infamous designs! Be not decided by his flattering or winning ways.

Yield not to his unclean delusions! But suffer every trial, which he puts on thee, and look a little at us, and thou shalt see how he wholly flags and wastes away, far from thee and those which are inwardly related to thee. What I indeed should have told thee — for I rest not to accomplish the task seen and imposed by thee — has escaped me. Yea, justly I see in thee repenting Eve and in me converting Adam. For what she suffered unknowingly, thou, to whose soul I address my words, being converted, bringest to a happy end. And what the spirit suffered, being dragged down by her, became unfaithful to itself, I now settle with thee, which perceivest that thou art drawn upwards. Of what she was ill thou hast cured, without suffering the same. And wherein she was disobedient, in that thou didst obey. And what he yielded, I flee. And wherein they were deceived, we have known. For it is appointed that each should make amends for his case.

6. "I said as I meant, but could say yet the following: Well for thee, nature of man, that thou art saved in spite of thy weakness, without being hidden! Well for thee, soul, which didst cry what thou hast suffered, and hast found the way again to thyself! Well for thee, man, who knowest that which is not thine and longest after thine own! Well for thee, that thou hearest the things which were spoken! For I conceive that thou art greater than can be thought of or expressed. For I know that thou art mightier than those which seem to

have power over thee; that thou art more glorious than those which brought thee into disgrace; than those which imprisoned thee. Having carefully considered all this in thyself, O man, that thou art immaterial, holy, light, related to the uncreated, rational, heavenly, transparent, pure, exalted over flesh, world, dominions, and powers, above whom thou art, having conceived thyself in the condition, take also along the knowledge, in which thou art prevalent. And when thou hast seen thy face in thy essence, break all bonds. I mean not those which belong to thine own origin, but those which lie beyond thy origin, for which we laid down for thee enormous denominations, and long to see him who has revealed himself unto thee, the uncreated, whom thou shalt soon see alone!

7. "This Maximilla, I say, with respect to thee. For according to their meaning my words refer to thee. As Adam lived in Eve, because he completely yielded to her, thus I also live now in thee, since thou obeyest the commandment of the Lord, and livest a life worthy of thy essence. But the threats of Aegeates despise in the consciousness that we have a God who has mercy upon us. Let the verbosity of that man also not influence thee, but remain chaste! And let him revenge himself on me not only through the torture in prison, but let him also cast me to the wild beasts, burn me at the stake, throw me down the precipice! What more can be done to me? Since it concerns this body, let him do with it as he pleases, since it is related to him!

8. "My word, Maximilla, concerns thee again. I say to thee, Yield not to Aegeates! Resist his designs, especially as I have seen the Lord, Maximilla, whose voice was to me: the father of Aegeates, the devil, shall deliver thee from this prison! Therefore, let it be thy care to keep thyself in future chaste and pure, holy, undefiled, sincere, discreet, not consenting to the persuasive attempts of our enemy, inviolated, infrangible, unbroken, unwounded, undivided, not giving offense, without part in Cain's works! For if thou, Maximilla, resignest not thyself to the opposite conduct, I shall also rest, since I am obliged to leave this life for thee, i. e., for me. But should I be driven hence, whereas I could help other souls related to me through thee, and thou yieldest to the persuasive arts of Aegeates and the alluring arts of his father, the serpent, and turnest again to thy former way, know that I shall suffer on thy account, till thou hast seen thyself, that I refused to live longer for any unworthy soul!

9. "I beseech thee, therefore, to endure in the sense which becomes the wise. I pray thy invisible mind, to keep with thee. I beseech thee, love the Lord Jesus, yield not to the baser! Assist me also, when as man I call for help, that I become perfect! Help me also, that thou mayest know thy true nature! Suffer with my affliction, that thou mayest know what I suffer, and thou shalt escape affliction. See what I see, and what thou seest, will blind thee. See that which is needful,

ACTS OF ANDREW

and what is not needful thou shalt not see. Listen to that which I say, and what thou hast heard, reject!

10. "These things I spoke to thee and to every hearer who listened to me. And thou, Stratocles"[3] —with these words he looked at him—"why dost thou shed so many tears and weepest thou? What sadness has overtaken thee? What meaneth thy great affliction or thy great grief? Dost thou understand my words and why I ask of thee, child, to come to thy senses? Knowest thou whom my words concern? Has each taken hold of thy mind? Has it penetrated into the heart of thy thoughts? Have I only thee, who didst listen to me? Do I find me in thee? Does some one speak in thy heart, whom I regard as mine own? Does he love the one speaking in me and will join him? Will he be united with him? Does he hasten to make friends with him? Does he long to be connected with him? Does he find a certain repose in him? Has he a place where to lay his head? Is anything there to oppose him? Does he get incensed — pursued — hated? Does he go away — does he get provoked — does he turn away — does he renounce — does he move out — is he troubled with anxiety? Has he any quarrel? Does he speak with others? Do others flatter him? Does he agree with others? Does something else disturb him? Dost thou enter-

---

[3] As the manuscript is imperfect, both at the beginning and at the end, we must suppose that before the beginning of the present text mention must have already been made of Stratocles, the brother of Ægeates.

tain an opponent of mine? An adversary? a disturber of the peace? an enemy? a juggler? a sorcerer? a word twister? an obdurate? a treacherous? a plotter? a misanthrope? an enemy of the word? a tyrant? a boaster? an insolent? a mad? a relative of the serpent? an instrument of Satan? an advocate of the hellish fire? a servant of darkness? Does anyone dwell in thee, who, when I thus speak, Stratocles, could not bear it? For who should it be? Answer! Do I speak in vain? Have I spoken in vain? No, saith the man who in thee, Stratocles, sheds tears again."

11. And Andrew took the hand of Stratocles and said, "I have him whom I loved. I shall rest on him for whom I have waited. For thine ever intenser sighing and unceasing weeping has given me a sign for my already approaching end, that I have not spoken my words in vain to thee."

12. And Stratocles answered him, "Think not, most blessed Andrew, that I suffer under any other affliction, but for thee! For the words which come out of thy mouth are like a stream of fire, emptying itself in me, and each seizes me and truly influences me. My soul is in that which is heard, and in anticipation of an approaching affliction it is chastised. Thou findest thy death, and I well know, a beautiful one. But when I afterward seek thy thoughtful care, where shall I find it and by whom? The seed-corns of the word of salvation I have received, when thou wast the sower. That they grow and spring up, they need none else but thee, most blessed

Andrew. What else could I have said to thee than this? I need great compassion and thy help, to show myself worthy of the seed received from thee. But it will only grow unceasingly and visibly spring, if thou willst, and by praying for it and my whole self."

13. And Andrew answered him, "It is this, child, that I myself saw in thee. And I praise my Lord that my spiritual efforts for thee have not fallen upon an empty soil; that I know, however, what he preached. But that thou may know it, tomorrow Aegeates will have me crucified. For Maximilla, the Lord's maid, will excite the evil enemy that dwells in him and whom he serves, because she denies to him what is hateful to her. And he will imagine to comfort himself by killing me."

14. And Maximilla was not present when the apostle said this. Having heard the words of his reply, and having in manner collected herself and decided as the words demanded, she gave up every worldly enjoyment of life, and fully decided she went straightway to the pretorium. Ageates made the same request, which she was to consider, whether she would not share with him in his couch. And as she refused, he plotted to kill Andrew, and reflected which capital punishment he was to inflict. And having made up his mind to the death upon the cross, he went away and had a banquet with his equals. But Maximilla, the Lord going before her in the form of Andrew, went with Iphidamia to the prison. And when a greater number of brethren

had met, Andrew felt compelled to speak thus:

15. "I was sent, dear brethren, by the Lord as an apostle into these regions, of which the Lord deemed me worthy, not to teach but to exhort all men inwardly related to the words, that they live in transitory sufferings, if they rejoice in the noxious notions of their imagination. To give them up I always asked you, and I have admonished you to hasten toward the permanent and to flee everything changeable. For, as you see, none of you is firm, but all things are easily changeable, even to the human character. And this is the case on account of the uneducated soul which had gone astray to the nature of man and retains pledges from its vagary. I therefore regard those blessed who have become hearers of the words and through them as in a mirror behold the mysteries of their own nature, on whose account all things are created.

16. "I charge you, therefore, beloved children, to firmly build upon the foundation which is laid for you, which is immovable and is unassailable for all evil ones. In this foundation take root. Become firm in the recollection of that which you have experienced, of that which took place, when I walked with you all! You saw works performed by me which you must believe, such signs at which the dumb nature even would cry out. I communicated words to you which I should like to have you receive, as the words themselves wish it. Therefore, dearly beloved, be firm in everything which you saw, which you heard, of which you had part! And the

God on whom ye believed has had mercy upon you and will have his pleasure in you and give you rest in all eterntiy.

17. "But what will happen to me should not frighten you as some strange thing, that the servant of God, to whom God has shown so many things by words and deeds, should be forcibly driven from this earthly life by a bad man! For such will not only happen unto me, but also unto all who love him, believe on him, and confess him. The devil, shameless in every respect, will arm his own children against them, that they adhere to him. And yet he shall not accomplish what he wishes. And why he undertakes it, I will tell: from the beginning of all things, and, if it may be said, since he who is without beginning came down into his dominion, the evil enemy who is averse to peace, estranges him who is not his (from God), but only one of the weaker ones, which has not yet come to full clearness and could not yet be known. And since he also does not know him, he should have been opposed by him. And because that one thought to own him and to be his master for ever, he behaves toward him so that their enmity became a kind of friendship. For he often sketched pictures of that which is his own, to father it upon him, namely, of deceitful sensual pleasures, by which he thought to rule over him fully. He did not come out openly as enemy, because he pretended a friendship worthy of him.

18. "And this work he carried on for a long

time, that man did not understand it; only he knew it; that is, because of his gifts he was not regarded as an enemy. But when the mystery of grace shone forth and the counsel of the everlasting rest was manifest and the light of the word appeared and it was seen how the saved human race had to fight with many hosts, the enemy himself, however, being despised and on account of the goodness of mercy was ridiculed for his gifts by which he proudly appeared to triumph over him, he began to rise up in hatred and enmity and to turn the tables upon us. And he has undertaken not to desist from us, till he thinks to have separated us (from God). In former times our adversary was careless and associated with us, pretending a friendship worthy of him. He was not even afraid that we, deceived by him, might leave him. But the light that rose unto us of the possession of the order of salvation has, I will not say <intensified his enmity, but manifested>. For it brought to light the mercy of his essence and what seemed to be hidden of him, and brought out his true nature. Therefore, dear brethren, since we know what is to come, let us wake up without being discontented, without assuming an air, without walking with our souls in his tracks, which are not ours; but being completely bound up in the whole word, let us arise spiritually, and let us all joyfully wait for the end and flee from him, that in future he may also be manifested as that, who our nature against our . . .

The Death of Andrew.[1]

(*Aa. II, 1, pp. 23, lines 28-29; 24 l. 19; 25, l. 23-26; 54, l. 18-55 l. 19; 25 l. 26-36 l. 11.*)

19. And he left them, went to the cross, and exclaimed: "Hail, cross!"

(p. 25) For thou also canst rejoice indeed. I well know that thou shalt rest henceforth, since thou art tired long since, and standest awaiting me. <I have come to thee whom I claim as mine own; I have come to thee who longest for me. I know thy mystery, that, for whose sake thou hast been stablished. For thou art placed in the world to strengthen the wavering. And thou reachest up to heaven, to proclaim the upper Logos. Thou art spread out to the right and to the left to put to flight the fearful, hostile power and to bring together the dispersed. Thou art fastened in the earth to connect that which is in the earth and under the earth with that which is in heaven. O cross, salvation-instrument of the Most High! O cross, sign of Christ's victory over his enemies! O cross, planted on earth, and bearing fruit in heaven! O name of the cross, which beareth the universe!

---

[1] Whether this part belonged to the ancient Acts of Andrew is not so evident as far as the present form is concerned. Since there are so many recensions and versions, this part is composed of different portions supplemented by portions from parallel narratives. In the original the constituent parts are distinguished by a different print. For the convenience of the student the lines in the original are also marked. The chapter-number is also retained for the sake of convenience.

Well for thee, O cross, which bindeth the world in its extent! Well for thee, O cross, which hast formed thy deformed outward appearance to a form full of intelligence! Well for thee the invisible chastisement, with which thou chastisest the nature of the doctrine of polytheism and drivest its inventor out of this humanity! Well for thee, O cross, which hast put on the Lord, hast gathered in the robber, hast called the apostle to repentance, and hast not deemed us unworthy to be received by thee! But why do I speak yet so long and allow not the cross to embrace me, in order to be raised to life in the cross, when I, through the cross, have gone from life to death, which is the lot of all? Come then, servants of my joy and beadles of Aegeates, and fulfill the wish of both of us and bind the lamb to the cross of suffering, the man to the demiurge, the soul to the Saviour!">[2]

20. (p. 25) And when most happy Andrew, standing on the ground and incessantly looking at the cross, had spoken these words, <he approached it> after having called to the brethren that the hangman should come and execute their order; for they stood afar off. <So they came and> (p. 26) only bound his feet <without piercing his hands and feet>, without cutting the hollows of the knee, having received this order from the proconsul, for he wished him to be in distress while on the cross, and in the night time to be eaten up alive by the

---

[2] This paragraph is inserted from the *Martyrium Andreæ prius*, p. 54, line 18 to p. 55, line 19.

dogs. <And they left him suspended and went away from him.>

21. <And a great multitude of the brethren stood by.> And having beheld the executioners standing afar off, and that they had done to the blessed one nothing of that which those who were hanged generally experience, they thought that they would again hear something from him; for assuredly, as he was hanging, he moved his head smiling. And Stratocles inquired of him, "Why art thou smiling, Andrew, servant of God? Thy laughter makes us mourn and weep, because we are deprived of thee." And the blessed Andrew answered him, "Shall I not laugh at all, my son Stratocles, at the empty stratagem of Aegeates, through which he thinks to take vengeance upon us? We have nothing to do (p. 27) with him and his plans. He cannot hear; for if he could, he would be aware, that a man who belongs to Jesus, because he is known of him, is henceforth armed against every vengeance."

And having thus spoken, he discoursed to them all in common — for even heathen ran together enraged at the unjust judgment of Aegeates — "Ye men, standing by me, and women, and children, and elders, born and free, and as many as will hear; I beseech you, give up this life, ye who have for my sake assembled here; and hasten to take a hold of my soul, which leads to heavenly things, and once for all despise all temporary things, confirming the hearts of those who believe in Christ!"

22. (p. 28) And the multitude, hearing what was said by him, did not stand off from the place, and the blessed Andrew continued the rather to say to them more than he had spoken. And so much was said by him, that a confirmation of the hearers in the faith could be inferred. A space of three days and nights was taken up, and no one was tired and went away from him. And when also on the fourth day they beheld his nobleness, and the unweariedness of his intellect, his eloquence, his kind exhortations, his serene calmness, his intelligent spirit, his firm mind, and his pure word; they were enraged against Ageates, and all with one accord hastened to the tribunal and cried out against him who was sitting there, saying, "What is thy judgment, O proconsul? Thou hast judged wickedly; thy awards are impious. In what has the man done wrong; what evil has he done? The city has been put in an uproar. Thou grievest us all; do not betray Cæsar's city. Grant willingly to the Achaians the just man; do not put to death the God-fearing man; destroy not the godly! Four days he has been hanging and is alive. Having eaten nothing he has filled us all. Take down the man from the cross, (p. 29) and we shall all seek after wisdom. Release the man, and to all Achaia will mercy be shown."

23. And when Aegeates refused to listen to them, at first indeed signing with his hand to the crowd to take themselves off, they began to be emboldened against him, being in number about twenty

thousand. And the proconsul having beheld that they had somehow become maddened, afraid that something frightful would befall him, rose up from the tribunal and went away with them, having promised to set free the blessed Andrew. And some went on before to tell the apostle the cause for which he came to the place of execution. While the crowd, therefore, was exulting that the blessed Andrew was going to be set free, the proconsul having come up, and all the brethren rejoicing along with Maximilla, Andrew, having heard this, said to the brethren standing by, "What it is necessary for me to say to him, when I am departing that will I also say. For what reason hast thou again come to us, Aegeates? On what account (p. 30) dost thou, being an adversary, come to us? What wilt thou again dare to do, what to contrive? Tell us. Hast thou come to release us, as having changed thy mind? I would not consent to thee even if thou hadst really changed thy mind, Aegeates. <I would not become faithless to me, though thou didst promise me everything thou ownest.> Nor would I believe thee, though thou didst claim to be my friend. Wilt thou, O proconsul, release him that has been bound? release him, who is redeemed? release the free? <Release him who was known by him related to him; him, who obtained mercy? him, beloved of him? thy opponent? the stranger? him who appeared to thee as law?> But I have him with whom I shall be for ever; I have him in whose Kingdom I shall live to countless ages. To him I go; to him I hasten, who also having made thee known to me, when he said to me: <Know, Aegeates and his gifts!> Let not that fearful man terrify thee! Let him not think to have power over thee, who art mine! For he is thine enemy. <He is a disturber of the peace, a deceiver, a seducer, a madman, a sorcerer, a juggler, a murderer, a choleric; without sympathy.> Therefore I knew thee fully through him, who has turned toward me. I leave thee. For I and my kinsmen depart to our own, allowing thee to be what thou art, and what thou dost not know about thyself."

24. (p. 31). When, therefore, he attempted to come near to the tree of the cross, so as to release the blessed Andrew, with all the city applauding him, the holy Andrew said with a loud voice, "Do not suffer, Andrew, bound upon thy cross, to be released, O Lord! Do not give me who am in thy mystery to the shameless devil! O Jesus Christ, let not thine adversary release me, who has been hanged by thy favor! O Father, him who has known thy (p. 32) greatness, let this insignificant man no longer humble! Thou, whom I know, whom I have, whom I love, to whom I belong, receive me, O Lord, that through my departure to thee there may be access to thee of many kindred, (p. 33) when they rest in thy glory!" <And when he had thus spoken and glorified the Lord still more, he gave up the ghost> (p. 34) with thanksgiving.

25. After the decease of the most blessed An-

drew <Maximilla came> together with Stratocles, taking no heed at all of those standing by, <and took down the body> of the most blessed Andrew. And when it was evening, bestowing upon him the necessary care, she buried him. And she separated from Aegeates on account of his brutal disposition and lawless conduct, having chosen for herself a holy and quiet life, and having been united to the love of Christ, she spent her life blessedly along with the brethren. And though Aegeates had been very importunate with her and promised her that he would make her mistress of his wealth, yet he could not persuade her. <And his heart being smitten and troubled in his conscience> (p. 36) he rose up at the dead of the night, and, unseen by all his people, he fell down from a great height, <and falling headlong he burst asunder in the midst and died. And Stratocles, the brother of Aegeates, sought nothing of his substance — the unhappy one having died childless — but said, "Let that which is thine, Aegeates, go with thee! Christ shall be my friend and I his servant!">[8]

---

[8] For the material within <> I have availed myself of the researches of Schimmelpfeng. A carefully prepared list of parallel passages is given by Bonnet, p. XVII-XIX.

V

THE ACTS OF THOMAS.

LITERATURE.

Thilo, *Acta S. Thomæ apostoli*, Lipsiæ, 1823.
Tischendorf, *Acta Apost. apocrypha*, 1851.
Lipsius, *Apokryphe Apostelgeschichten*, I, 225-347; II, 2, 422 f.
Macke, *Theologische Quartalschrift*, 1874, p. 1 f.
Harnack, *Geschichte der altchristlichen Litteratur*, II, 1, p. 545-549.
Bevan, The hymn of the Soul contained in the *Syriac Acts of Thomas* in Texts and Studies, 5, 3 (1897).
Ehrhard, *Die altchristliche Literatur*, 1900, p. 163-165.
Burkitt in *Journal of theological studies*, I (1900), p. 280 ff.; II (1901), p. 429; IV (1903), p. 125 ff.
Philipps, "The connection of St. Thomas the Apostle with India" (*Ind. Antiq.*, 1903, 1, p. 1-15).
Bonnet, *Acta Apostolorum Apocrypha*, II, 2 (1903), p. 99-291.
Hoffman in *Zeitschrift fuer neutestamentliche Wissenschaft*, 1903, p. 273-309.
Preuschen, *Zwei gnostiche Hymnen*, Gieszen, 1904.
Hilgenfeld, "Der Königssohn und die Perle" (*Zeitschrift fuer wissenschaftliche Theologie*, 1904, 229-241).
Raabe-Preuschen in Hennecke, *Neutest. Apokryphen*, 1904, 473 ff., and in Handbuch (1904) 563 ff.
Bardenhewer, *Patrology*, p. 106 ff.

According to a tradition, known already to Origen, Thomas is said to have preached in Parthia. According to a Syriac tradition he died at Edessa, where a beautiful church was erected in his honor, in the fourth century. According to the Acts of Thomas, he is said to have labored in India. This tradition has been accepted by most writers since the fourth century (see Lipsius, I, 227 ff.). To harmonize it with the already existing tradition which speaks of his labors or death in Syria, it has been assumed that his remains were transferred from India to Edessa. Barhebræus (d. 1286) even records that the coffin was brought to Edessa under Bishop Eulogius (end of the fourth century). According to the Latin Passio (i.e. Consummation) of Thomas (see Lipsius, I, 144) the transference took place under Alexander Severus after his victory over Ardasir (233 A. D.).

Of his early life we learn from the Acts just as little as from the New Testament. Here he is sometimes connected with Matthew (Matt. X, 3), sometimes with Philip (Acts I, 13). Only from the gospel of John we learn that his name signifies "twin" (XI, 16; XX, 24; XXI, 2). In the Acts he is called Judas (thus already an ancient Syriac version in John XIV, 22) with the surname of Thomas (comp. Euseb., I, 13, 11), and the surname is explained by this that he was a twin of Jesus whom he resembled very much (c. 11 f., 31, 39).

Among the books read by Photius (B.bl., 114) was a volume purporting to be written by Leucius Charinus and containing the travels of Peter, John, Andrew, Thomas and Paul. The stichometry of Nicephorus contains a record of the number of stichoi in the travels of Peter, John, and Thomas, respectively, viz.: 2,750, 2,600, 1,600. The Acts of Thomas were held in great estimation especially in Gnostic circles, among the Encratites (Epiphan, 47, 1), the Apostolici (Epiphan, 61, 1), the Manichæans (August *against Faustus*, XXII, 79; *against Adinatus*, 17, and others), the Priscillians (Turribius of Astorga in a letter to Idacius and Ceponius 5; see Zahn, *Acta Joannis*, p. 200).

In preparing his text Bonnet collated twenty-one Greek manuscripts, the most important of which are a Paris Codex (1510 from the XI or XII cent. cod. P.) and a Latin Codex (Vallicellanus B. 35 from the XI cent. cod. U.). Both these codices alone contain the Acts in a complete form; the hymn to the soul, hitherto extant only in the Syriac, is found only in cod. U

Besides the Greek witnesses the Syriac Acts edited from a London codex (Mus. Brit. Syr. Add., 14645, from the year

936) and translated by W. Wright (*Apocryphal Acts of the Apostles*, London, 1871, I, p. 172–333; II, p. 146 f., the text reprinted, 1892, by Bedjan, *Acta martyrum et sanctorum*, III (1892), p. 3 ff.) are of importance, although they have been revised already in a Catholic manner. A free Ethiopic rendering of our Acts has been made into English by J. C. Malan, in *The Conflicts of the Holy Apostles*, London, 1871, p. 187 ff.; E. W. Budge, *The Contendings of the Apostles*, I (Ethiopic text, London, 1899); II (Engl. transl., 1901), p. 319 ff., 404 ff. A short Greek version closely following the Ethiopic was published by James in Text and Studies, V. I (1897), p. 27 ff.

In Latin are extent a *Passio* and the *Miracula beati Thomæ* ("the Miracles of Blessed Thomas") but in a revised form. There is also extant an Armenian translation of our Acts; but the hymn to the soul is wanting.

In the Greek MSS. the matter is divided into thirteen "deeds," to which may be added as fourteenth the martyrdom of Thomas. The Acts of Thomas, whose Gnostic character is beyond mistake, include some hymns, copied in all simplicity by orthodox transcribers, who, being ignorant of Gnostic mythology, did not understand what was meant, but which betray their heretical origin at once to those who are acquainted with Gnostic speculations.

It is mainly for the light they throw on Gnostic ideas that the Acts of Thomas deserve to be studied; for they are a mere romance without any historic value. The object of the Acts seems to have been to delineate a Christian ideal as presented in Thomas, whose "acts of compassion, and the cures done by him as a free gift, and still more, his single-mindedness, and gentleness, and fidelity, show that he is a just man, or an apostle of the new God whom he preaches; for he continually fasts and prays, and eats only bread with salt, and his drink is water, and he wears one coat, whether in warm weather or in cold, and he takes nothing from anyone, but gives to others even what he has" (c. 20).

From the Acts we learn some interesting details about the Gnostic rites, and the agreement of the ritual with that described by Cyril of Jerusalem shows that, though most of the words of the prayers put into the apostle's mouth may be regarded as the invention of the heretical composer of the Acts, much of the ritual, and possibly even some of the words, simply represent the usage of the church before these Encratites branched off, and which they retained after their separation.

We also find in these Acts some interesting notices on "Baptism" and the "Eucharist," besides the copious use made in these Acts of the New Testament.

Whether the Syriac or the Greek was the original language of the Acts is difficult to decide, although the opinion is in favor of the latter. Where we followed another text, especially the Syriac, the matter is put within < >. A small portion of the Acts has been translated into English by A. Walker for the Ante-Nicene Christian Library (Edinburgh, 1867 seq.); chaps. 39, 40, 41, 62–158 are omitted, because the matter was not in Tischendorf's text. We refer to this fact to show the importance of the recension of the text now extant in Bonnet's edition, which we followed throughout.

THE DEEDS OF THE HOLY APOSTLE THOMAS.

(Aa. II, 2, p. 99-288.)

<FIRST DEED OF THE APOSTLE JUDAS THOMAS, HOW THE LORD SOLD HIM TO THE MERCHANT ABBAN, THAT HE SHOULD GO DOWN AND CONVERT INDIA.>

1. At that time we the apostles were all in Jerusalem — Simon called Peter, and Andrew his brother; James the son of Zebedee, and John his brother; Philip and Bartholomew; Thomas and Matthew, the taxgatherer; James son of Alphaeus and Simon the Cananaean, and Judas the son of James — and we portioned out the regions of the world, in order that each one of us might go into

the region that fell to him, and to the nation to which the Lord had sent him.[1] By lot, then, India fell to Judas Thomas, also called Didymus. And he did not wish to go, saying that he was not able to go on account of the weakness of his body, and said, " How can I, being a Hebrew, go among the Indians to proclaim the truth? " And while he was thus reasoning and speaking, the Saviour appeared to him during the night and said to him, " Fear not, Thomas, go away to India and preach the word there, for my grace is with thee." But he obeyed not, saying, " Wherever thou wishest to send me, send me, (but) elsewhere. For to India I am not going."

2. And as he was thus speaking and considering, it happened that a merchant who had come from India, named Abban, was there, sent from the King of Gundafor, and having received an order from him to buy a carpenter and bring him to him. And the Lord, having seen him walking about in the market at noon, said to him, " Dost thou wish to buy a carpenter? " He replied, " Yes." And the Lord said to him, " I have a slave a carpenter, and I wish to sell him." And having said this, he showed him Thomas at a distance, agreed with him for three pounds of uncoined (silver), and wrote a bill of sale, saying, " I, Jesus,

---

[1] The legend concerning the labors of the apostles in various countries are all originally connected with that of their separation at Jerusalem, which is as old as the second century. See " Die Legende von der Aposteltheilung " in Lipsius, *loc cit.*, p. 11–34.

son of the carpenter Joseph, declare that I have sold my slave, Judas by name, to thee, Abban, a merchant of Gundafor, King of the Indians." And the purchase being completed, the Saviour took Judas, also called Thomas, and led him to Abban, the Merchant. When Abban saw him, he said to him, "Is this thy master?" The apostle answered and said, "Yes, he is my Lord." And he said, "I have bought thee from him." And the apostle held his peace.

3. On the following morning the apostle prayed and entreated the Lord, saying, "I go wherever thou wishest, O Lord Jesus; thy will be done." And he went to the merchant Abban, carrying nothing at all with him, but only his price. For the Lord had given it to him, saying, "Let thy worth also be with thee along with my grace, wherever thou mayest go." And the apostle came up with Abban, who was carrying his effects into the boat. He began, therefore, also to carry them along with him. And when they had gone on board and sat down, Abban questioned the apostle, saying, "What kind of work dost thou know?" And he said, "In wood, plows, and yokes, and balances, and boats, and boats' oars, and masts and small blocks; in stone, slabs, and temples and royal palaces." And Abban the merchant said to him, " (it is well,) for such a workman we also need." They began therefore, to sail way. And they had a fair wind; and they sailed cheerfully till they came to Andrapolis, a royal city.

4. And having left the boat, they went into the city. And, behold, the voices of flute-players and of water-organs, and trumpets sounding round them. And the apostle inquired, saying, "What festival is this in this city?" And the inhabitants there answered, "the gods have brought thee also, that thou mayest be feasted in this city. For the King has an only daughter and now he is going to give her to a husband in marriage. This festival, then, which thou seest to-day, is the rejoicing and public assembly for the marriage. And the King has sent forth heralds to proclaim everywhere that all are to come to the marriage, rich and poor, bond and free, strangers and citizens. But if anyone should refuse and not come to the marriage, he is answerable to the King. And Abban, having heard, said to the apostle, "Let us also go, that we give no offense to the King, and especially as we are strangers." And he said, "Let us go." And having turned into the inn, and rested a little, they went to the marriage. And the apostle, seeing them all reclining, reclined also in their midst. And they all looked at him as a stranger, and coming from a foreign land. And Abban the merchant, as being a lord, reclined in another place.

5. And whilst they were eating and drinking, the apostle tasted nothing. Those about him said to him, "Why hast thou come hither, neither eating nor drinking?" And he answered and said to them, "For something greater than food or

even drink have I come hither, that I might accomplish the will of the King. For the heralds proclaim the wishes of the King, and whoever will not hear the heralds will be liable to the judgment of the King." When, therefore, they had dined and drunk, and crowns and perfumes had been brought, each took perfume, and one anointed his face, another his chin, and one one part of his body, and another another. And the apostle anointed the crown of his head, and put a little of the ointment in his nostrils, and dropped it also in his ears, and applied it also to his teeth, and carefully anointed the parts round about his heart; but the crown that was brought to him, wreathed of myrtle and other flowers, he put on his head, and took a branch of reed in his hand, and held it. And the flute-girl, holding the flutes in her hand, went round them all; and when she came to the place where the apostle was, she stood over him, playing the flute over his head a long time. And that flute-girl was Hebrew by race.

6. And as the apostle looked to the ground, one of the cupbearers stretched forth his hand and struck him. And the apostle, having raised his eyes, looked at him who had struck him, saying, "My God will forgive thee for this wrong in the world to come, but in this world he will show his wonders, and I shall soon see that hand that struck me dragged along by dogs. And having thus spoken, he began to sing and to repeat this song:

"The maiden is the daughter of the light,
On whom rests the majestic splendor of Kings;
Delightsome is her sight,
Resplendant with brilliant beauty.
Her garments are like spring flowers
Sending forth sweet fragrance.
On the crown of her head the King is seated
Feeding with his ambrosia those who live under him
Truth rests upon her head,
Joy she shows forth with her feet.
Her mouth is opened, and becomingly
<She sings all hymns with it.>
Thirty-and-two are they who praise her.
Her tongue is like a door-curtain,
Drawn back for them who go in.[2]
Her neck ascends like steps
Made by the first creator.
Her two hands point predicting at the chorus of the blessed ages,
Her fingers at the gates of the city.
Her chamber is bright,
Breathing forth scent from balsam and every perfume,
Sending forth sweet odor of myrrh and savory herbs.
Within are strewn myrtle-branches and all manner of sweet smelling flowers,
The ingress is adorned with calamus.

---

[2] The Syriac reads here: drawn back by the priest who goes in.

7. She is surrounded by her groomsmen, seven in number,
Chosen by herself;
Her bridesmaids are seven,
Who dance before her.
Twelve are they in number who minister before her
And are at her bidding.
Their gaze is attentively directed at the bridegroom,
That they be enlightened by his sight,
And be for ever with him for that everlasting joy
And sit down in that wedding to which the great ones assemble,
And abide in the supper, of which the eternals are deemed worthy,
And put on royal garments, and be dressed in shining robes
That both may rejoice and exult
And praise the Father of the universe,
Whose majestic light they have received
And have been enlightened by the sight of their Lord,
Whose ambrosial food they received
Of which there is no failing,
And drink also of his wine,
Which brings to them no thirst nor desire,
Praised and glorified with the living spirit
The Father of truth and the mother of wisdom." [3]

---

[3] On this ode which Thomas is said to have recited in Hebrew, see Lipsius, *loc. cit.*, p. 301 f.; Preuschen, *loc. cit.*, p. 28 f.

8. And when he had sung and finished this song, all who were present looked at him. He kept silence. They also saw his form changed, but they understood not his words, as he was a Hebrew and his words were spoken in Hebrew. Only the flute-girl understood it, being of the Hebrew race; and hearing him, she played the flute to the others, but repeatedly looking at him. For she loved him as one belonging to her nation, and he was also beautiful in appearance above all who were there. And when the flute-girl had finished her flute-playing, she sat down opposite him, and looked and gazed at him. But he looked at no one at all, neither did he regard any one, but only kept his eyes on the ground, waiting until he could depart thence. And the cup-bearer that struck him came down to the fountain to draw water. And there happened to be a lion there which killed him and left him lying in the place, after tearing up his limbs. And dogs immediately seized his limbs, among which also one black dog, laying hold of his right hand in his mouth, brought it to the place of the banquet.

9. When they saw it, they were frightened and all inquired who it were which had left them. And when it became known that it was the hand of the cup-bearer that struck the apostle, the flute-girl broke her flutes and threw them away, and went and sat at the feet of the apostle, saying, " This man is either God or God's apostle. For I heard him say in Hebrew to the cup-bearer, I shall soon see the hand that struck me dragged about by dogs —

ACTS OF THOMAS

which also you have now seen. For as he said, so also it has come to pass." Some believed her, and some not. And when the King heard of it, he came and said to the apostle, "Rise up and go with me, and pray for my daughter. For she is my only child and to-day I give her away." And the apostle would not go with him, for the Lord had not yet been revealed to him there. But the King took him away against his will to the bridal chamber, that he might pray for them.

10. And the apostle stood, and began to pray and speak thus: "My Lord and my God, who accompanies thy servants, guide and leader of those who believe on thee, refuge and repose of the afflicted, hope of the poor and deliverer of the captives, physician of the souls that are lying under disease, and Saviour of every creature, who gives life to the world and invigorates the souls, thou knowest the future, who also accomplishes it through us; thou, Lord, who revealest hidden mysteries and declarest secret words; thou, Lord, art the planter of the good tree and by thy hand all good works are produced; thou, Lord, art in all, and comest through all, and exists in all thy works and makest thyself manifest through the working of all; Jesus Christ, the Son of compassion and perfect Saviour; Christ, Son of the living God, the undaunted Power which has overthrown the enemy; the voice, heard by the rulers, which shook all their powers; messenger, sent from on high, who wentest down even to Hades; who also, having opened the

doors, didst bring out thence those that had been shut in for many ages in the treasuries of darkness, and didst show them the way up that leads up on high — I beseech thee, Lord Jesus, offering thee supplication for these young persons, that thou mayest do unto them what helps, benefits them, and is good for them." And having laid his hands on them and said, "The Lord be with you," he left them in the place, and went away.

11. And the King requested the groomsmen to leave the bridal chamber. When all had left, and the doors were shut, the bridegroom raised the curtain of the bridal chamber, that he might bring the bride to himself. And he saw the Lord Jesus talking with the bride, and having the appearance of Judas Thomas, the apostle, who shortly before had blessed them, and gone out from them; and he says to him, "Didst thou not go out before them all? And how is it that thou art here now? And the Lord said to him, "I am not Judas, sur-named Thomas; I am his brother." And the Lord sat down on the bed, and ordered them to sit down on couches, and he began to say to them:

12. "Remember, my children, what my brother said to you, and to whom he commended you; and know, that if you refrain from this filthy intercourse you become temples holy and pure, being released from afflictions and troubles, known and unknown, and you will not be involved in the cares of life, and of children, whose end is destruction. But if you get many children, for their sakes you become

ACTS OF THOMAS

grasping and avaricious, plundering orphans, deceiving widows, and by doing this you subject yourselves to most grievous punishments. For most children become unprofitable, being harassed by demons, some openly and others secretly. For they become either lunatics, or half-withered, or frail, or deaf, or dumb, or paralytics, or idiots. And though they be healthy, they will be again good-for-nothing, doing unprofitable and abominable works. For they will be detected either in adultery, or in murder, or in theft, or in unchastity, and by all these you will be afflicted. But if you obey and preserve your souls pure to God, there will be born to you living children, untouched by these hurtful things, and you will be without care, spending an untroubled life, free from grief and care, looking forward to receive that incorruptible and true marriage, and you will enter as groomsmen into that bridal chamber full of immortality and light."

13. And when the young people heard this, they believed the Lord and gave themselves over to him, and refrained from filthy lust, and remained thus spending the night in the place. And the Lord went away from them, after having said to them: " the grace of the Lord be with you!.' And the dawn having come on, the King arrived, and having supplied the table, brought it in before the bridegroom and the bride. And he found them sitting opposite each other, and he found the face of the bride uncovered, and the bridegroom was quite cheerful. And the mother came in and said

to the bride, "Wherefore dost thou sit thus, child, and art not ashamed, but actest as if thou hadst for a long time lived with thine own husband?" And her father said, "It is because of thy great love to thy husband that thou art uncovered?"

14. And the bride answered and said, "Truly, father, I am in great love, and I pray to my Lord to continue to me the love which I have experienced this night, and that I obtain that man whom I have experienced to-day. That I do not cover myself is, because the mirror of shame has been taken away from me; I am no longer ashamed or abashed, since the work of shame and bashfulness has been removed far from me. And that I am not frightened is, because fright did not abide in me. And that I am cheerful and glad is, because the day of joy has not been disturbed. And that I have lightly esteemed this husband, and these nuptials that have passed away, from before mine eyes, is, because I have been joined in a different marriage. And that I had no conjugal intercourse with a temporary husband, whose end is repentance and bitterness of soul, is, because I have been united to the true husband."

15. And when the bride was saying yet more, the bridegroom answered and said, "I thank thee, Lord, who hast been proclaimed by the stranger and found by us; who hast put corruption far from me, and hast sown life in me, who hast delivered me from this disease, hard to heal, and hard to treat, and abiding for ever, and established in me

sound health; who hast shown thyself to me, and hast revealed to me my condition, in which I am; who hast redeemed me from falling, and hast led me to something better and who hast released me from things temporary, but hast deemed me worthy of things immortal and ever existing; who hast brought thyself down even to me and my weakness, to place me beside thy greatness and to unite with thee; who hast not kept thy compassion from me, who was lost, but hast shown me how to search myself, and to know who I was and who and how I am now, that I may become again what I was; whom I did not know, but thou hast sought me out; of whom I did not know, but thou stoodst by me; whom I have experienced and am not able to forget; whose love is fervent in me and of whom I cannot speak as I ought. But what I have to say about him is short and very little, and is not in proportion to his glory; but he does not find fault with me if I dare to tell him that also, that I know not; for out of love to him I say even this."

16. And when the King heard these things from the bridegroom and the bride, he rent his garments, and said to those standing near him, "Go out quickly, and search the whole city, and seize and bring that man, the sorcerer, who has come for evil into this city. For I led him with my own hands into my house, and I told him to pray for my most unfortunate daughter. Whoever shall find him and bring him to me, I give him whatever he shall ask of me." They went away, therefore, and

went round seeking him, and found him not; for he had sailed. They also went into the inn where he had stayed, and found there the flute-girl weeping and in distress, because he had not taken her with him. And when they told her what had taken place with the young people, she rejoiced greatly upon hearing it, dismissed her grief, and said, "Now I also have found repose here!" And she arose and went to them, and was with them a long time, until they had instructed the King also. And many also of the brethren met there, until the rumor had spread that the apostle had gone to the cities of India, and was teaching there. And they went away and joined him.

Second Deed of the Apostle Thomas

HIS APPEARANCE BEFORE KING GUNDAFOR.

(Aa. II, 2, pp. 124-146.)

17. When the apostle came into the cities of India, with Abban the merchant, Abban went away to salute King Gundafor, and reported to him about the carpenter whom he had brought with him. And the King was glad, and ordered him to appear before him. Having come in, the King said to him, "What trade knowest thou?" The apostle said to him, "That of the carpenter and the housebuilder." Says the King to him, "What work in wood knowest thou, and what in stone." The apostle says, "In wood, plows, yokes, balances,

pulleys, and boats, and oars and masts; in stone monuments, temples, and royal palaces." And the King said, "Wilt thou build me a palace?" And he answered, "Yes, I shall build it, and finish it; for because of this I have come, to build and to do carpenter's work."

18. And the King having accepted him, took him out of the gates of the city, and began to talk with him on the way about the building of the palace, and how the foundations should be laid, till they came to the place where the building was to be carried out. And he said, "Here I wish the building to be!" And the apostle said, "Yes, for this place is appropriate for the building." For the place was like a wood, and much water was there. And the King says, "Begin at once!" And he answered, "Now I cannot commence." Says the King, "When wilt thou?" He said, "I shall begin in November and finish in April." And the King was surprised, and said, "Each building is built in the summer, but canst thou build and finish a palace in the winter?" And the apostle says, "Thus it must be done, and otherwise it is impossible." And the King said, "If thou hast resolved upon this, mark out for me how the work is to be done, since I shall come here after some time." And the Apostle took a reed, measured the place, and marked it out; the doors to be set towards the rising of the sun to look to the light, the windows toward the west, to the winds; the bakehouse he made toward the south, and the water-pipes neces-

sary for the service, toward the north. When the King saw this, he said to the apostle, "Thou art truly a craftsman, and it is fitting that thou shouldst serve Kings." And having left many things for him, he went away.

19. And at the appointed time he sent coined silver and the necessaries for his and the workmen's living. And he took everything and divided it, going about in the cities and surrounding villages, distributing to the poor and needy, and spending alms, and gave them recreation, saying, "The King knows how to obtain royal recompense, but the poor must be refreshed, as the condition requires it." After this the King sent a messenger to the apostle, having written the following: "Let me know what thou hast done, or what I should send to thee or what thou needest." The apostle sends to him word, saying, "The palace is built, and only the roof remains to be done." Upon hearing this, the King sent him again gold and uncoined silver and wrote, "Let the palace, if it be done, be roofed." And the apostle said to the Lord, "I thank thee, Lord, in every respect, that thou didst die for a short time, that I may live in thee for ever, and that thou hast sold me, to deliver many through me." And he did not cease to teach and refresh the afflicted, saying, "The Lord hath dispensed this to you, and he gives to each his food. For he is the support of the orphans and the provider of the widows, and rest and repose to all that are afflicted."

20. When the King came to the city, he inquired of his friends concerning the palace which Judas, surnamed Thomas, had built for him. And they said to him, "He has neither built a palace nor did he do anything of that which he promised to do but he goes about in the cities and villages, and if he has anything, he gives it to the poor, and teaches a new God, takes care of the sick, drives out demons, and performs many miracles. And we believe that he is a magician. But his acts of compassion and the cures done by him as a free gift, still more his single-mindedness, and gentleness, and fidelity, show that he is a just man, or an apostle of the new God, whom he preaches. For he continually fasts and prays, and eats only bread with salt, and his drink is water, and he wears one coat, whether in warm weather or in cold, and he takes nothing from anyone, but gives to others what he has." Upon hearing this, the King stroked his face with his hands, shaking his head for a long time.

21. And he sent for the merchant who had brought him, and for the apostle, and said to him, "Hast thou built the palace?" And he said, "Yes, I have built it." The King said, "When shall we go to inspect it?" And he repeated and said, "Now thou canst not see it, but thou shalt see it when thou hast departed this life." And the King was very wroth, and ordered both the merchant and Judas Thomas to be bound and cast into prison, until he should find out to whom the property of the King had been given, and thus destroy him and

the merchant. And the apostle went to prison rejoicing, and said to the merchant, "Fear nothing, believe only in the God which is preached by me, and thou shalt be freed from this world, and obtain life in the world to come."

And the King considered by what death he should kill them. Having decided to flog them and burn them with fire, on that very night Gad, the King's brother fell ill; and through the grief and imposition which the King suffered he was grievously depressed. And having sent for the King, he said to him, "Brother King, I commend to thee my house and my children. For I have been grieved on account of the insult that has befallen thee, and lo! I am dying, and if thou dost not proceed against the life of that magician, thou wilt give my soul no rest in Hades." And the King said to his brother, "I considered the whole night by what death I should kill him, and I have decided to flog him and burn him with fire together with the merchant who brought him hither."

22. While they were talking, the soul of Gad, his brother, departed, and the King mourned for Gad exceedingly, because he loved him, and ordered him to be prepared for burial in a royal and costly robe. While this was going on, angels received the soul of Gad, the King's brother, and took it up into heaven, showing him the places and mansions there, asking him, "In what place dost thou wish to dwell?" And when they came near the edifice of the apostle Thomas, which he had

erected for the King, Gad, upon beholding it, said to the angels, "I entreat you, my lords, let me dwell in one of these subterranean chambers." But they said to him, "In this building thou canst not dwell." And he said, "Why not?" They answered, "This palace is that which that Christian has built for thy brother." But he said, "I entreat you, my lords, allow me to go to my brother to buy this palace from him. For my brother knows not what it is like, and he will sell it to me."

23. And the angels let the soul of Gad go. And as they were putting on him the burial robe his soul came into him. And he said to those standing round him, "Call my brother to me, that I may beg of him a request." Straightway they sent the good news to their King, saying, "Thy brother has become alive again!" And the King started up, and with a great multitude went to his brother. And having come in he went to the bed as if stupefied, unable to speak to him. And his brother said, "I know and I am convinced, brother, that if anyone had asked of thee the half of thy kingdom, thou wouldst give it for my sake. Wherefore I entreat thee to grant one favor, which I beg of thee to do me, that thou sellest to me that which I ask of thee." And the King answered and said, "And what is it that thou wishest me to sell to thee?" And he said, "Assure me by an oath that thou wilt grant it to me." And the King swore to him, "Whatever of my possession thou shalt ask, I will

give thee." And he says to him, "Sell me the palace which thou hast in heaven." And the King said, "A palace in heaven — whence comes this to me?" And he said, "(it is) that which that Christian built for thee, who is now in prison, whom the merchant brought, having bought him from a certain Jesus. I mean that Hebrew slave whom thou didst wish to punish, as having suffered some imposition from him, on account of whom I also was grieved and died, and now have come alive again."

24. Then the King heard and understood (his words) about the eternal benefits that were conferred upon him and destined for him, and said, "the palace I cannot sell thee, but I pray to be permitted to enter into it and to dwell there, being deemed worthy to belong to its inhabitants. And if thou wilt really buy such a palace, behold, the man is alive, and will build thee a better one than that." And having sent immediately, he brought out of prison the apostle, and the merchant who had been shut up along with him, saying, "I entreat thee, as a man entreating the servant of God, pray for me, and to ask him whose servant thou art to pardon me and to overlook what I have done to thee or intended to do, and that I may become worthy to be an inhabitant of that house for which indeed I have done nothing, but which thou laboring alone hast built for me with the help of the grace of thy God, and that I may also become a servant and serve this God, whom thou preachest." His brother also fell down before the apostle, and said, "I entreat thee

and supplicate before thy God, that I may become worthy of his service and become partaker of that which was shown to me by his angels."

25. And the apostle seized with joy, said, "I give thanks to thee, Lord Jesus, that thou hast revealed thy truth in these men. For thou alone art the God of truth and not another; and thou art he who knowest all things that are unknown to many; thou, O Lord, art he who in all things showest mercy and compassion to men. For men, through the error that is in them, have overlooked thee, but thou hast not overlooked them. And now, because I entreat thee and supplicate thee, accept the King and his brother, and unite them into thy fold, cleanse them by thy baptism, and anoint them with thy oil from the error which encompasses them. Protect them also from the wolves and bring them into thy meadows. Give them to drink of thy ambrosial fountain, which is never muddy and never faileth. For they entreat and supplicate thee, and wish to become thy servants, and on this account they have also resolved to be persecuted by thine enemies, and to endure for thy sake hatred, insult, and death, as thou also hast suffered all this for our sakes, in order to gain us, who art Lord and a truly good shepherd. Do thou grant unto them that they put their trust alone in thee, and obtain the hope coming from thee and hope of their salvation, which they expect alone from thee, and that they may be confirmed in thy mysteries and receive the perfect benefits of thy graces and gifts, and flourish in thy

service and bear fruit to perfection in thy Father."

26. Very friendly disposed now toward the apostle, King Gundafor and his brother Gad followed him, never leaving him, providing for the poor, giving to all, and relieving all. And they entreated him that they might also receive the seal of the word, saying to him, "Since our souls are at ease, and as we are earnest about God, give us the seal. For we heard thee say, that the Lord whom thou preachest knoweth his sheep through his seal." And the apostle said to them, "I am glad and entreat you also to receive this seal, and to take part with me in this eucharist and blessed meal of the Lord, and to be made perfect by it. For he is the Lord and God of all, Jesus Christ, whom I preach, and he is the Father of truth, in whom I have taught you to believe." And he ordered them to bring oil, that through the oil they might receive the seal. And they brought oil and lighted many lamps. For it was night.

27. And the apostle arose, and sealed them. And the Lord was revealed to them, through a voice saying, "Peace to you, brethren!" And they heard his voice only, but his form they saw not. For they had not yet received the sealing up of the seal. And the apostle took the oil, poured it over their head, salved and anointed them, and began to say:[1]

---

[1] On this Gnostic dedication-prayer, see Lipsius, l. c., p. 311 ff.

"Come, holy name of Christ, which is above every name;[2]

Come, power of the Most High, and perfect compassion;

Come, gift most high;

Come, compassionate mother;[3]

Come, communion of the male;[4]

Come, revealer of secret mysteries;

Come, mother of the seven houses, that there may be rest for thee in the eighth house.[5]

Come, thou presbyter of the five members:[6] intelligence, thought, prudence, reflection, reasoning,[7]

Communicate with these young persons!

Come, spirit of holiness, and purify their veins and their hearts.[8]

And seal them in the name of the Father and of the Son and of the Holy Ghost."

And when they had been sealed, there appeared to them a young man holding a burning lamp, so that the (other) lamps were even darkened by the emanation of its light. And he went out, and disappeared from their sight. And the apostle said to the Lord, "Thy light is too great for us, Lord,

---

[2] "Which is above every name" is omitted in the Syriac.
[3] This line is omitted in the Syriac.
[4] Syriac: Communion of the blessing.
[5] Syriac: seven houses, which has found rest in the eighth house.
[6] Syr.: come, thou messenger of reconciliation.
[7] Syr. omits: intelligence . . . reasoning.
[8] Syr. omits this line and reads after "persons": and he sealed them, etc., etc.

and we cannot bear it. For it is too much for our sight." And when light came, and it was dawn, he brake bread, and made them partakers of the eucharist of the Messiah. And they rejoiced and exulted. And many others also believed, and were added (to the believers), and came to the refuge of the Saviour.

28. And the apostle ceased not preaching and saying to them, " Men and women, boys and girls, young men and maidens, vigorous and aged, both bond and free, withhold yourselves from fornication, covetousness, and gluttony. For under these three heads all wickedness comes. For fornication maims the mind and darkens the eyes of the soul, and becomes a hindrance of the due regulation of the body, changing the whole man into feebleness, and throwing the whole body into disease. Greediness puts the soul into fear and shame, being [inside of the body, and] robs what belongs to another, and suspects that in returning to the owners their property, it will be put to shame. Gluttony throws the soul into cares, troubles and griefs, fearing that it will be wanting, and reaches out for that which is far away. In refraining from these things, you are without care, without grief, and without fear, and there remains to you that which was said by the Saviour: Take no care for the morrow, for the morrow will take care of itself.[9] Remember also the word men-

---

[9] Matt. VI, 34.

tioned before: Look upon the ravens,[10] and behold the fowls of the heaven, that they neither sow nor reap, nor gather into barns, and God takes care of them; how much more, O ye of little faith! But look for his coming, have your hopes in him, and believe in his name. For he is the judge of the living and of the dead,[11] and he requites to each one according to his deeds.[12] And at his coming and appearance at last no one, who is about to be judged by him, has a word of excuse, as if he had not heard. For his heralds preach in the four quarters of the globe. Repent, therefore, and believe the preaching and take upon you an easy yoke and a light burden,[13] that you may live and not die. These things lay hold of; these things keep; come forth from the darkness, that the light may receive you! Come to him who is truly good, that from him you may receive grace, and place his sign upon your souls!"

29. When he had thus said, some of the bystanders said to him, "It is time for the creditor to receive his debt." And he said to them, "The creditor, indeed, always wishes to receive more, but let us give him what is proper." And [having blessed them] he took bread, oil, herbs, and salt, blessed it, and gave it to them. And he continued in his fastings, for the Lord's day was about to dawn. And on the night following,

---

[10] Comp. Luke XII, 24; Matt. VI, 26.
[11] Comp. Acts X, 42.
[12] Comp. Matt. XVI, 27.
[13] Comp. Matt. XI, 29, 30.

while he was asleep, the Lord came and stood by his head, and said, "Thomas, rise up early, and bless them all; and after the prayer and service go along the eastern road two miles, and there I will show my glory through thee. For because of the work, for which thou goest away, many will take refuge in me, and thou shalt reprove the nature and power of the enemy." And he rose from his sleep and said to the brethren who were with him, "Children and brethren, the Lord will this day perform something through me. Let us, however, pray and entreat him that nothing may be a hindrance to us toward him, but as at all times let it now also be done unto us according to his purpose and will. And having thus spoken, he laid his hands upon them and blessed them. And having broken the bread of the eucharist, he gave it to them, saying, "May this eucharist be to you for compassion and mercy, and not for judgment and retribution!" And they said, "Amen."

Third Deed.

ABOUT THE DRAGON.

(Aa. pp. 147–156).

30. And the apostle went forth to go where the Lord had bidden him. And when he came (near) the second milestone he turned a little out of the way, and saw the body of a beautiful youth lying, and he said, "Lord, was it this that thou brought-

est me out to come here, that I might see this trial? Thy will, therefore, be done, as thou purposest!" And he began to pray, and to say: "Lord, judge of the living and the dead, of the living who stand here, and of the dead, which are lying (here), and the Lord of all and Father— Father not of the souls that are still in bodies, but of those which have left them, because thou art Lord and Judge of the souls still in the bodies— come in this hour in which I call upon thee, and show thy glory upon him that is lying here." And he turned to his companions and said, "This work has not happened idly, but the enemy has wrought and effected this to make an assault, and you see that he has availed himself of no other form, and has wrought through no other living being, but through his subject."

31. And having said this, behold, a great dragon came forth from his den, knocking his head, and brandishing his tail down to the ground, and said with a loud voice to the apostle, "I will say before thee, why I have killed him, since thou hast come here to reprove my works." The apostle said, "Yes, say on." And the dragon: "There is a certain woman in this place exceedingly beautiful. And as she was once passing by, I saw her and fell in love with her, followed her and watched her. And I found this young man kissing her, and he also had intercourse with her, and did with her other shameful things. And to me it were an easy matter to tell thee this, <but I

dare not>. For I know that thou art the twin-brother of the Messiah, and always bringest our race to naught. Not wishing to harass her, I did not kill him in that hour, but I watched him passing by in the evening, struck him and killed him, and especially as he had dared to do this on Sunday." And the apostle inquired of him, saying, "Tell me, of what seed and of what race art thou?"

32. And he said to him, "I am the offspring of the serpent, and hurtful of the hurtful; I am a son of him who hurt and struck the four brothers that stood;[1] I am son of him who sits on the throne <and has power over the creature> which is under the heaven, that takes his own from those to whom he has lent; I am the son of him who encircles the globe; I am kinsman to him who is outside of the ocean, whose tail lies in his mouth; I am he who went into paradise through the hedge, and spoke with Eve what my father bade me speak to her;[2] I am he who inflamed and fired Cain to kill his brother,[3] and through me thorns and thistles sprang up in the ground;[4] I am he who cast down the angels from above, and bound them by the desire of women, that earthborn children might be produced by them, and that I might work

---

[1] The Syriac does not mention: the four brothers that stood; instead: I am the son of him who is like God in the eyes of those who obey him.
[2] Comp. Gen. III, 1.
[3] Gen. IV, 5–8.
[4] Comp. Gen. III, 18.

ACTS OF THOMAS 253

my will in them;[5] I am he who hardened Pharoah's heart, that he killed the children of Israel and subjugated them (the Israelites) through hard servitude;[6] I am he who deceived the multitude (the people in the desert, when they had made the golden calf;[7] I am he that fired Herod[8] and inflamed Caiaphas to the lying accusation before Pilate;[9] for this became me; I am he that inflamed Judas, and brought him to deliver the Messiah to death;[10] I am he that inhabits and holds the abyss of Tartarus,[11] and the Son of God has wronged me against my will and selected his own out of me; I am a kinsman of him who is to come from the east,[12] to whom also power is given to do whatever he will upon earth."

33. When the dragon had spoken these things before the ears of the multitude, the apostle lifted up his voice and said, "Stop now, O thou most impudent, and be ashamed that thou art wholly useless (weak). For thine end, the destruction has come. And do not dare to say what thou hast done through thy dependents. But I command thee in the name of that Jesus who even until now makes a fight against you for the sake of those who are his own, to suck out the poison

---

[5] Comp. Gen. VI, 1-4.
[6] Comp. Exod. I sqq.
[7] Comp. Exod. XXXII.
[8] Comp. Matt. II.
[9] Matt. XXVI, 3.
[10] Comp. Matt. XXVII, 11 seq.; XXVI, 14-16.
[11] Comp. Rev. IX, II.
[12] Antichrist is probably meant.

which thou hast put into this man, and to draw it forth and take it out of him!" And the dragon said, "The time of our destruction has not yet come, as thou didst say. Why dost thou force me to take out what I have put in him, and to die before the time? For my father shall also find his end when he draws forth and sucks out what he has put into the creation." And the apostle said to him, "Show now the nature of thy father! And the dragon came, put his mouth upon the wound of the young man and sucked the gall (the poison) out of it. And in a short time the color of the young man, which was like purple, grew white, and the dragon swelled. And when the dragon had drawn up all the gall into himself, the young man sprang up and stood, and ran and fell at the apostle's feet. And the dragon being swelled up shrieked out and died, and his poison and gall were poured forth. And in the place where his poison was poured forth there was made a great chasm, and the dragon was swallowed up. And the apostle said to the king and to his brother, "Take workmen, and fill up the place and lay foundations, and build houses above it, that there be a dwelling place for strangers."

34. And the young man said to the apostle with many tears, "What have I sinned against thee? For thou art a man having two forms, and wherever thou wishest, thou art found, and art not prevented by anyone, as I see. For I saw that man how he stood beside thee, and also

said to thee, 'I have many wonders to show by thee, and I have to accomplish great works through thee, by which thou shalt obtain a reward, and thou shalt make many to live, and they shall be in repose in eternal life, as the children of God. Do thou, therefore, said he, raise this young man — whereby he meant me — who has been cast cast down by the enemy and became his overseer at every time.' Thou hast done well to come hither, and again thou shalt well go away to him, being not at all forsaken by him. And I have been released from care and reproach, and a light rose upon me, (and I was released) from the care of the night and rested from the daily work; but I was also released from him who exasperated me to do these things. I sinned against him, who taught me the contrary, and I have destroyed that kinsman of the night, which forces me to sin by his own practices; but I found, however, that kinsman of mine who is like the light. I have destroyed him that darkens and obscures his subjects, that they know not what they do, and, ashamed of their works, they abandon them and their deeds have an end. But I found him, whose works are light and whose deeds are truth, of which no one repents, whoever does them. I was released from him, in whom falsehood abides, whom darkness as a covering goes before, and shame, impudent in idleness, follows after. But I found him, who revealed to me what is beautiful to lay hold of it, the Son of truth, the kinsman of concord, who, driving away the mist, enlightens his creation, heals its wounds, and overthrows its enemies. But I entreat thee, man of God, make me again to behold and see him who is now hidden from me, that I may hear also his voice, whose wonderfulness I cannot express. For it is not of the nature of this bodily organ."

35. And the apostle answered and said to him, "If thou hast released thyself from those things, whose nature, as thou hast said, thou hast known and knowest, who he is who has wrought these things in thee, and hast learned and become a follower of him,' after whom thou now longest through thy ardent love, thou shalt see him and be with him for ever in his repose and in his joy. But if thou art rather carelessly disposed toward him, and again returnest to thy former deeds, and lettest go that beauty and that beaming countenance which has now been displayed in thee, and if the splendor of his light, after which thou now longest, is entirely hidden from thee, thou shalt be deprived not only of this life, but also of the future, and thou shalt go to him of whom thou didst say that thou hast destroyed him, and thou shalt see him no more whom thou hast said thou hast found."

36. And when the apostle had said this, he went to the city, holding the young man by the hand, and saying "What thou hast seen, child, is only a little of the many things which God has. For not concerning these visible things preaches

he the gospel to us, but he promises to us greater things than these. So long as we are in the body, we cannot tell and say what he will give to our souls in the future. For if we say that he gives us light, this is something visible and we have it already. But if we say that he will give us riches, they exist and appear already in this world, and we name them and we long not for them, since it has been said: 'With difficulty will a rich man enter into the kingdom of heaven.'[13] And if we speak of fine cloaks, which the weaklings put on in this life, we name them, and it has been said, 'they that wear soft things are in Kings' houses.'[14] And when we speak of costly dinners, we mention things that exist, and concerning these we have received a commandment to take heed to ourselves, lest at any time our hearts be overcharged with surfeiting, and drunkenness and cares of this life;[15] and it has been said, 'Take no thought for your life, what ye shall eat or what ye shall drink; nor yet for your body, what ye shall put on. For the life is more than meat, and the body than raiment.[16] And if we speak of this temporary rest, its judgment has also been appointed. And we speak about the upper world, about God and angels, about watchmen and saints, about the ambrosial food and the drink of the true wine, about lasting and not obsolescent gar-

---

[13] Matt. XIX, 23.
[14] Matt. XI, 8
[15] Comp. Luke XXI, 34.
[16] Matt. VI, 25.

ments, about that which eye hath not seen, nor ear heard, nor hath come into the heart of sinful men what God has prepared for those that love him.[17] Of these things we speak, and concerning these things we preach the gospel. Do thou also, therefore, believe in him, that thou mayest live, and put thy trust in him, and thou shalt not die. For he is not to be persuaded by gifts, that thou shouldest offer them to him; nor does he need sacrifices, that thou sacrifice to him. But look to him, and he will not overlook thee; turn thou to him, and he will not forsake thee. For his comeliness and beauty will make thee love him, but it permits thee not to turn away from him."

37. And after the apostle had said this, much people were added to the young man. And looking about, the apostle noticed how they lifted themselves up to see him,[18] and they went up into elevated places. And the apostle said to them, "Ye men who have come to the assembly of the Messiah, and who wish to believe in Jesus, learn from this, and see that if you do not get high up you cannot see me, who am small, and cannot look at me, who am like yourselves. Now if you cannot see me, who am like yourselves, unless you raise yourselves a little from the earth, how can you see him who lives above and is [now] found below, unless you first raise yourselves out of your former behavior, and unprofitable deeds and desires, which

---

[17] Comp. 1 Cor. II, 9.
[18] Comp. Luke XIX, 4.

last not, and of your riches, which must be left behind, and of the possession which is of the earth and grows old, and of garments which spoil and of the beauty which ages and vanishes away, yea, even of the whole body, in which all this is kept, and it grows old and becomes dust, returning into its own nature? For all these things are only a support for the body. But rather believe in our Lord Jesus Christ, whom we proclaim, that your hope may be upon him and you have in him the eternal life, that he may be your companion in this land of wandering, a haven in this troublous sea and an overflowing fountain in this thirsty land and a house full of food in the place of the hungry, and rest for your souls, and also a physician of the bodies."

38. When the multitude of the assembled heard these things, they wept and said to the apostle, "Man of God, we dare not say that we belong to that God whom thou preachest, because our works which we have done are alien from him, not pleasing to him. But if he has compassion upon us and pities us, and delivers us, overlooking our former deeds and frees us from the evil which we have done, when we were in error, and takes not into account nor keeps the recollection of our former sins, we shall become his servants, and we shall do his will to the end." And the apostle answered and said to them, "He neither condemns you nor does he reckon against you the sins done by you, being in error, but he overlooks your transgressions which you have done ignorantly."

Fourth Deed.

Concerning the Colt.

(Aa. pp. 156-159.)

39. Whilst the apostle was still standing in the highway and spoke to the multitude, a colt of an ass came up to him and, opening its mouth, said, " Twin brother of the Messiah, apostle of the Most high and initiated into the hidden word of the Messiah, who receivest his secret utterances, coworker of the Son of God, who, though once free, hast been a servant, and being sold hast brought many to freedom, kinsman of the great race which condemns the enemy and redeemed its property (from him), who to many in the land of the Indians didst become a cause of life — because thou camest to erring men, and through thy appearance and thy divine words they now turn to the God of truth, who hast sent thee — mount, sit on me and rest, till thou comest to the city." And the apostle began and said, " O Jesus Christ, Son of the perfect mercy, O rest and calmness, and thou of whom even the unreasonable animals speak; O hidden rest, and thou who art manifest by the working as our Saviour and nourisher, who keepest us and makest us rest on strange bodies, Saviour of our souls, sweet and inexhaustible source, firm, pure fountain which is never troubled, helper and succor of thy servants in the struggle, who keepest and drivest away from us the enemy, who battlest for us in many battles, and makest

us victorious in all, our true and invincible athlete, our holy and victorious general, most glorious, who givest to thy people imperishable joy and rest, which knows of no affliction, good shepherd,[1] who didst offer thyself for thy sheep, didst overcome the wolf and hast redeemed thy sheep and led them to good pastures — we praise and glorify thee and thy invisible Father and thy Holy Spirit [and] the mother of all creatures."

40. When the apostle said this, the whole multitude looked at him waiting, to hear what he would answer the colt. And after the apostle remained silent for a time, like one being beside himself, and looking toward heaven, he said to the colt, "Who art thou, and whose art thou? For surprising and strange is that which was spoken by thee, which is also hidden to many." And the colt answered and said, "I am of that family which served Balaam,[2] and to which also belonged that colt on which sat thy Lord and thy Master.[3] And now I have been sent to give thee rest by thy sitting on me, that these may believe and I obtain that portion which I am about to receive by the service now offered to thee, and which shall be taken from me, if I do not serve thee." And the apostle answered, "He who gave thee this gift (of speech) can do, that it be given to thee and to those belonging to thy race unto the end. For as concerns this mystery I am powerless

---

[1] Comp. John X, 11.
[2] Comp. Numb. XXII, 21 sqq.
[3] Comp. Luke XIX, 30.

and weak." And he would not mount. But the colt entreated him that by riding on it he might bless it. And the apostle mounted and sat down, and all went with him, some going before, others following him, and they all ran, anxious to see how he would dismiss the colt.

41. And when he came near the gates of the city, he alighted and said, "Go and be kept where thou hast been." And immediately the colt fell to the ground and to the feet of the apostle and died. All of those that were present were sorrowing, and said to the apostle, "Make it alive." And he answered and said to them, "I could do it indeed through the name of Jesus. But this would not help it. For he who gave it the speech that it spoke, could also do it, that it did not die. I shall not raise it, not as if I could not do it, but because this is the best for it." And he ordered those present to dig a hole and bury the carcass. And they did as he bade them.

FIFTH DEED.

ABOUT THE DEMON THAT DWELT IN THE WOMAN.

(Aa. pp. 159-167.)

42. And the apostle went into the city, followed by all the multitude. And he thought of going to the parents of the young man whom he had revived, after having been killed by the dragon. For they entreated him very much to come and to abide in their house. Suddenly an exceedingly beautiful

woman cried out, "Apostle of the new God, who hast come to India, and servant of that holy and good God — for by thee he is proclaimed the Saviour of the souls of those which come to him, and by thee the bodies of those are healed which are punished by the enemy, and thou hast become the cause of life of all, which turn to him — command that I be brought to thee, that I may tell thee what happened to me, and that perhaps there may be hope to me and to those who stand by thee, to be more confirmed in the hope in that God whom thou preachest. For not a little have I already been tormented by the enemy for five years. As a woman I formerly had rest, surrounded everywhere by peace, [and I cared for nothing]. For I had none to care for.

43. "And one day when I left the bath, it happened that I met a man who looked troubled and disturbed. And his voice and answer seemed to be very weak and thin. And coming up to me he said, 'Let us unite in love and have intercourse with each other as a man with his wife.' And I answered and said, 'I had no intercourse with my betrothed, as I refused to be marrried — how should I give myself up to thee, that wishest to have intercourse with me as in adultery?' And having said this, I passed by. And to my maid I said, 'Didst thou see the young man and his impudence, how shamelessly and boldly he talked to me?' And she said, 'I saw an old man talking with thee.' When I had come to my house and had supped, my mind

suggested to me some suspicion, especially as he appeared to me in two forms. And with this in my thoughts, I fell asleep. In that night he came in to me and made me share in his filthy intercourse. I saw him also when it was day, and fled from him. According to his wont, he came at night and abused me. And now as thou seest me, I have been tormented by him five years, and he has not departed from me. But I know and am persuaded that even demons and spirits and monsters are subject to thee, and tremble at thy prayer. Pray, then, for me, and drive away from me the demon, that torments me continually, that I also may become free, and may be brought to my own kind, and receive the gift which has been granted to my kindred."

44. And the apostle said, "O irrepressible wickedness! O shamelessness of the enemy! O jealous one that is never at rest! O ugly one who subjects the beautiful ones! O many-formed one —he appears as he wishes, but his nature cannot be changed — ! O crafty and perfidious! O bitter tree, whose fruits are like it! O traducer, fighting over that which is not his! O deceit which uses impudence! O wickedness that creeps like a serpent and is related to it!" And when the apostle had thus spoken, the fiend stood before him, no one seeing him but the apostle and the woman, and said in the hearing of all with a very loud voice:

45. "What have we to do with thee, apostle of the Most High? What have we to do with thee, servant of Jesus Christ? What have we to do with

thee, counselor of the Holy Son of God? Why wilt thou destroy us before our time?[1] Why wilt thou take our power? For until the present hour we had hope and time left us. What have we to do with thee? Thou art powerful in thine own, and we in our own. Why wilt thou use tyranny against us, since thou teachest others not to use violence?[2] Why dost thou covet that which is not thine own like one who is not satisfied with what he has? Why dost thou liken thyself to the Son of God, who wronged us? For thou art like him altogether, as if thou hadst him for a father. For we thought to bring him also under the yoke, like the rest. But he turned, and left us under his power, because we knew him not. He deceived us by his very homely form and his poverty and want. For when we thus saw him, we thought him to be a man clothed with flesh, not knowing that it was he who makes men live. And he gave us power over our own, and for the time being not to give up our own, but to abide in it. But thou wishest to get more than is necessary and has been given thee and to do violence to us!"

46. And having thus spoken, the demon wept and said, "I leave thee, my most beautiful consort, which I found long ago and was at rest. I leave thee, my beloved, trusty sister, in which I was well pleased.[3] What I shall do or whom I shall call

---

[1] Comp. Mark I, 24; V, 7; Matt. VIII, 29.
[2] Comp. Luke III, 14.
[3] Comp. Matt. III, 17.

upon to hear me and protect me, I know not. I know what I shall do:[4] I shall go to the places where the fame of this man has not been heard; and in thy stead, my beloved, I may perhaps find one with another name." And lifting up his voice, he said, "Remain in peace who has taken refuge with him, that is greater than I. I will go away, and seek one like thee; and if I find her not, I shall return again to thee. For I know that when thou art near this man, thou hast a place of refuge in him; but when he has gone away, thou shalt be as thou wast before he appeared; and thou wilt forget him, but for me there will be again opportunity and boldness. But now I fear the name of him who has protected thee." And having thus spoken, the demon disappeared. And after he had gone fire and smoke were seen, and all present were struck with amazement.

47. And the apostle, seeing this, said to them, "Nothing strange or unusual has the demon shown, but the element by which he shall be burned. For the fire shall consume him, and its smoke shall be scattered abroad." And he began to say, "Jesus, hidden mystery which has been revealed unto us; thou art he who didst make known to us many secrets, who hast separated me from all my companions and told me three words with which I am set on fire, but which I cannot communicate to others; Jesus, man, slain, dead, buried; Jesus, God of God

---

[4] Comp. Luke XVI, 4.

ACTS OF THOMAS

and Saviour, who quickeneth the dead, and heals the sick;[5] Jesus, who appearest to be in want,[6] and savest as if in want of nothing, catching the fishes for the morning and evening meal,[7] and satisfying all with a little bread;[8] Jesus, who rests from the toil of the journey like a man, and walkest upon the waves as God;[9] Jesus Most High, voice arising from perfect compassion, Saviour of all, right hand of the light, prostrating the wicked through his own kind, and bringing all his kind into one place; polymorphous, who art the only begotten, the firstborn among many brethren;[10] God of God Most High and man, despised until now; Jesus Christ, who overlookest us not when we call upon thee; who hast become the cause of life to the whole human race; who wast judged for our sakes and kept in prison, whereas thou freest all that are in bonds; who wast called a deceiver,[11] whereas thou deliverest thine own from deception — I pray thee for these present and who believe on thee. They wish to obtain thy gifts, having a joyous hope in thy help and taking refuge in thy majesty. Their ears are opened to hear the words which are spoken to them. May thy peace come and dwell in them, and renew them by cleansing them from their former deeds, and let them put off the old man with his deeds,

---

[5] Comp. Luke IX, 52; VII, 14; John XI, 43; Rom. IV, 17.
[6] Comp. Matt. VIII, 20.
[7] Comp. Luke V, 1-11; John XXI, 6, 11, 12.
[8] Comp. Matt. XIV, 19; John IV, 6.
[9] Comp. Matt. XIV, 25.
[10] Comp. Rom. VIII, 29.
[11] Comp. Matt. XXVII, 63.

and put on the new man now declared to them by me!"[12]

49. And he laid his hands on them and blessed them, saying, "The grace of our Lord Jesus be upon you for ever!" And they said, "Amen."[13]

And the woman begged of him and said, "Apostle of the Most High, give me the seal, that that foe may not come back upon me again." And he made her come near to him, laid his hands on her, and sealed her in the name of the Father and of the Son and of the Holy Ghost. And many others were also sealed with her. And the apostle ordered his minister (deacon) to set out a table. And they set out a couch which they found there. And having spread a linen cloth upon it, he put on it the bread of the blessing (the blessed bread). And the apostle, standing by it, said, "Jesus, who hast deemed us worthy to partake of the eucharist of thy holy body and blood, see, we are emboldened to come to thy eucharist and to invoke thy holy name; come and commune with us."

50. And he commenced to say:

<" Come, gift of the Most High;>
Come, perfect compassion;
Come, communion with the male;[14]
<Come, Holy Spirit;>
Come, thou that knowest the mysteries of the chosen one;

---

[12] Comp. Eph. IV, 22, 24; Col. III, 9, 10.
[13] Comp. Rom. XVI, 20.   [14] Not in the Syriac.

Come, thou that communicatest in all the combats of
   the noble combatant;
<Come, treasury of glory;>
<Come, most Beloved of the mercy of the Most
   High;>
Come, rest,
That makest manifest the great deeds of the whole
   greatness;
Come, thou that disclosest secrets
And makest manifest the mysteries;
Come, holy dove,[14]
Which hast brought forth twin young;[14]
Come, thou secret mother;
Come, thou who art manifest in thy deeds;
Come thou giver of joy
And of-rest to those who are united to thee;
Come and commune with us in this eucharist,
Which we make in thy name,[15]
And in the love feast
For which we are united at thy calling."[16]

And having thus spoken, he made the sign of the
cross upon the bread, broke it and began to distribute it. And first he gave it to the woman, and
said, "This shall be to thee for remission of sins
and everlasting transgressions."[17] And after her,
he gave also to all the others who had received the
seal.

---

[14] Not in the Syriac.
[15] "In thy name" is wanting in the Syriac.
[16] Comp. Lipsius, *loc. cit.*, p. 317 f.
[17] In the Syriac: everlasting resurrection.

Sixth Deed.

CONCERNING THE YOUNG MAN WHO KILLED THE MAIDEN.

(Aa. pp. 167-178.)

51. And there was a certain young man, who had done a nefarious deed. And he also came and partook of the eucharist. And his two hands withered, so that he could no longer bring them to his mouth. When those present saw him, they told the apostle what had happened. And the apostle called him and said, " Tell me, my son, and be not afraid, what thou hast done, ere thou camest hither. For the eucharist of the Lord has convicted thee (of a bad deed). For this gift, by permeating them, brings healing to many, especially to those who come in faith and love; but thee it has withered away, and what has happened has happened not without some cause (on thy part.) " And the young man convicted by the eucharist of the Lord came up, fell to the apostle's feet, and prayed him, and said, " An evil deed has been done by me, whilst I thought to do something nice. I loved a woman who lived in an inn outside of the city, and she loved me also. And I having heard from thee, and believing that thou proclaimest the living God came and received the seal from thee along with the others. And thou didst say, " Whoever shall indulge in impure intercourse (with a woman), especially in adultery, shall not have life with the God

whom I preach. As I loved her very much, I entreated her and tried to persuade her to live with me in chaste and pure intercourse, as thou thyself teachest. And she would not. Since she would not, I took a sword and killed her. For I could not see her living in adultery with another."

52. When the apostle heard this, he said, "O maddening intercourse, how leadest thou to impudences! O unrestrained lust, how hast thou excited this one to do this! O work of the serpent, how art thou uplifted in thine own!" And the apostle ordered some water to be brought in a dish. And when the water had been brought, he said, " Come, waters from the living waters; everlasting, sent to us from the everlasting; rest, sent to us from the rest; power of salvation, proceeding from that power which overcomes all and subjects it to its will — come and dwell in these waters, that the gift of the Holy Spirit may be fully communicated to them!" And to the young man he said, "Go, wash thy hands in these waters." And having washed them they were restored. And the apostle said to him, " Believest thou on our Lord Jesus Christ, that he can do all things?" And he said, "Though I am very weak, yet I believe. But I did this in the hope of doing something good. For I entreated her, as I told thee already, but she would not be persuaded by me to keep herself chaste."

53. And the apostle said to him, " Come, let us go to the inn, where thou didst the work, and let us see what happened. And the young man went be-

fore the apostle on the road. When they had come to the inn, they found her lying. And when the apostle saw her, he was sad, for she was a beautiful maiden. And he ordered her to be brought into the middle of the inn. And having put her on a couch, they brought it, and set it in the midst of the courtyard of the inn. And the apostle laid his hand on her, and began to say, "Jesus, who always appearest to us — for this thou wishest that we should always seek thee and hast given us the permission to ask for us and to receive, and hast not only permitted us this, but hast also taught us how to pray [1] — who art not seen by us with the bodily eyes, but who art not altogether hidden from those of our soul, and who art hidden in thy form, but manifested to us by thy works; and by thy many deeds we have recognized thee as much as we comprehend, and thou hast given us thy gifts without measure, saying, 'Ask, and it shall be given you; seek, and ye shall find; knock and it shall be opened unto you.' [2] We pray, therefore, being afraid of our sins. And we ask of thee not riches, nor gold, nor silver, nor possessions, nor any of those things that come from earth and go into the earth again; but we beg of thee, and entreat that in thy holy name thou raise this woman lying here by thy power, to thy glory and to an awakening of faith in those which stand by."

54. And he said to the young man, having

---

[1] Matt. VII, 7.
[2] Comp. Acts of John, ch. 22.

marked him (with the sign of the cross), "Go and take her hand, and say to her, Through iron I killed thee with my hands, and with my hands I raise thee because of faith in Jesus." And the young man went and stood by her, saying, "I have believed in thee, O Christ Jesus." And looking upon Judas Thomas the apostle, he said to him, "Pray for me, that my Lord, upon whom I call, may come to my help." And having laid his hand on her hand, he said, "Come, Lord Jesus Christ, give her life and me the earnest of the faith in thee." And drawing her by the hand, she sprang up, and sat, looking at the great multitude standing around. And she also saw the apostle standing opposite to her, and having left her couch, she sprang up and fell at his feet, and took hold of his garments, saying, "I pray thee, lord, where is thy companion who has not left me to remain in that fearful and grievous place, but has given me up to thee, saying, Take this one, that she may be made perfect, and thereafter be brought into her own place?'

55. And the apostle said to her, "Tell us where thou hast been." And she answered, "Dost thou, who wast with me, to whom also I was intrusted, wish to hear?" And she commenced thus: "An ugly-looking man, all black, received me; and his dress was exceedingly filthy.[3] And he took me to a place where there were many chasms, and a great stench and most hateful odor were given forth

---

[3] For the following compare also the Apocalypse of Peter in Pick, *Paralipomena*, p. 120 f.

thence. And he made me look into each chasm, and I saw in the chasm blazing fire, and fiery wheels run there, and souls were hung upon these wheels, dashing against each other. And there was crying and great lamentation, and no Saviour was there. And that man said to me, These souls are akin to thee, and in the days of numbering they were given over to punishment and destruction. And then (when the torture of each is completed) others are brought in their places; in like manner all these are again succeeded by others. They are they who have exchanged the intercourse of man and wife. And again I looked down, and saw infants (newly born) heaped upon each other, and struggling and lying upon each other. And he said to me, These are their children and for this they are placed here for a testimony against them.

56. "And he brought me to another chasm, and as I looked into it, I saw mud and worms spouting forth, and souls wallowing there; and (I heard) a great gnashing of teeth thence from them. And that man said to me, These are the souls of women, which left their husbands (and of husbands which left their wives), and committed adultery with others, and which have been brought to this torment. And he showed me another chasm, and looking into it, I saw souls hung up, some by the tongue, some by the hair, some by the hands, others by the feet, head downward, and smoked with smoke and sulphur. Concerning these the man which accompanied me said the following:

ACTS OF THOMAS

the souls hung up by the tongue, are slanderers, and such as have spoken false and disgraceful words and are not ashamed of it. Those hung up by their hair are the shameless, who are not ashamed at all and go about with uncovered heads in the world. Those hung up by the hands are they which took that which did not belong to them and have stolen, and who never gave anything to the poor voluntarily, nor did they help the afflicted; but they so acted, because they wished to get everything, and cared neither for law nor right. And these hung up by the feet are those who lightly and eagerly walked in wicked ways and disorderly paths, not visiting the sick, neither burying those who departed this life. On this account each soul receives what it has done.

57. "And again he led me forth and showed me a very dark cavern, exhaling a very bad odor. Many souls were peeping out thence, wishing to get some share of the air. And their keepers would not let them peep out. And my companion said to me, This is the prison of these souls, which thou hast seen. For when they have fully received their punishment for that which each has done, others succeed them. Some are fully eaten up, others are given up to other punishments. And the keepers of the souls in the dark cavern said to the man that had charge of me, Give her to us, that we bring her to the others till the time comes when she is given up to punishment. But he said to them, I will not give her to you, because I am afraid of him who gave her

up to me. For I was not told to leave her here; I shall take her up with me, till I get an injunction about her. And he took me and brought me to another place, where there were men who were bitterly tortured. He that is like thee took me and gave me up to thee, saying to thee, Take her, for she is one of the sheep which have wandered away. And thou didst take me, and thus I now stand before thee. I beg, therefore, and supplicate thee that I may not come to those places of punishment which I have seen."

58. And the apostle said, "You have heard what this woman has recounted. And these are not the only punishments, but there are others worse than these. And you too, unless you turn to the God whom I preach, and abstain from your former works and the deeds which you did ignorantly, shall find your end in these punishments. Believe, therefore, in Christ Jesus, and he will forgive you the former sins and will cleanse you from all your bodily desires that abide in the earth, and will heal you from the faults that follow after you, and go along with you, and are found before you. Let every one of you put off the old man and put on the new,[4] and leave your former course of conduct and behavior. Those that steal, let them steal no more, but let them live, laboring and working.[5] The adulterers are no more to commit adultery, lest they give themselves up to everlasting punishment.

---

[4] Comp. Eph. II, 22; Col. III, 9.
[5] Comp. Eph. IV, 28.

For adultery is with God an evil altogether grievous above all other evils. Put away also from yourselves covetousness, and lying, and drunkenness, and slandering,[6] and rendering evil for evil![7] For all these are alien and strange to the God whom I preach. But walk ye rather in faith, and meekness, and holiness, and hope, in which God rejoices, that you may become of his household, expecting from him those gifts, which a few only receive."

59. The whole people therefore believed, and presented obedient souls to the living God and Jesus the Messiah, enjoying the blessed works of the Most High and his holy service. And they brought money for the service of the widows. For he had them collected in the cities, and he sent to all of them by his servants (deacons) the things necessary, both clothing as well as food. He himself ceased not to preach and to speak to them and to show that this Jesus is the Messiah, of whom the Scriptures have spoken,[8] that he should be crucified after his appearance and should be raised after three days from the dead. He also showed to them, explaining and beginning from the prophets, what was said concerning the Messiah,[9] that it was necessary for him to come, and that everything had to be accomplished, what was spoken of him beforehand. And the fame of him spread over all the cities and villages, and all who had sick persons or such as

---

[6] Comp. Eph. IV, 25.
[7] Comp. 1 Pet. III, 9.
[8] Comp. Acts XVIII, 28.
[9] Comp. Luke XXIV, 27.

were troubled by unclean spirits,[10] brought them to him; and some they laid on the road [11] by which he was to pass, and he healed all by the power of the Lord. And those that were healed by him said with one accord and one voice, " Glory to thee, Jesus, who in like manner hast given healing to all through thy servant and apostle Thomas! And being in good health, and rejoicing, we pray thee, that we may become members of thy flock and be counted among thy sheep. Receive us, therefore, O Lord, and consider not our trespasses and our former transgressions, which we have done, because we were in ignorance!" [12]

60. And the apostle said, " Glory be to the only-begotten of the Father; [13] glory to the first-born of many brethren; [14] glory to thee, the helper and succor of those who take their refuge to thee. Thou that sleepest not, and raising those that are asleep; that livest and bringest to life those that are lying in death: O God Jesus Christ, Son of the living God, redeemer and helper, refuge and rest of all those that labor in thy work, who affordest health to those who for thy name's sake bear the burden and heat of the day; [15] we give thanks for the gifts given to us by thee, and for the help from thee bestowed upon us, and thy providential care that has come upon us from thee.

---

[10] Comp. Luke VI, 18.
[11] Comp. Acts V, 15.
[12] Comp. Acts III, 17.
[13] Comp. John I, 14.
[14] Comp. Rom. VIII, 29.
[15] Comp. Matt. XX, 12.

61. "Perfect these things upon us, therefore, unto the end, that we may have confidence in thee. Look upon us (and see), because for thy sake we have left our houses and our patrimony, and for thy sake we have gladly and willingly become strangers.[16] Look upon us, O Lord (and see) that for thy sake we have given up our own possession, that we might obtain thee for a possession that shall not be taken away. Look upon us, O Lord, because we have left those related to us by ties of kindred, in order that we may be united in relationship to thee. Look upon us, O Lord, who have left our fathers and mothers and providers, that we behold thy father, and be satisfied with his divine nourishment. Look upon us, O Lord because for thy sake we left our bodily wives and our earthly fruit, in order that we may share in that true and lasting communion and bring forth true fruits, whose nature is from above, which no one can take from us, in which we abide and they abide with us."

Seventh Deed.

CONCERNING THE COMMANDER.

(Aa. pp. 178-185.)

62. When the apostle Judas Thomas was preaching in India the word of God, a commander of King Misdai (Masdai) came to him, and said to him, "I have heard of thee that thou dost receive no

---

[16] Comp. Matt. XIX, 27, 29.

reward, but givest to the poor what thou hast. For if thou wouldst receive a reward, I should have sent thee a sufficient sum of money and I had not come myself, since the king does nothing without me. For my possession is great and I am rich, one of the wealthy in India. But I never did anything wrong to anyone. But the reverse I have experienced. I have a wife and I had a daughter by her, and I love her (the wife)very much, as nature demands it, and I had no intercourse with another woman. And it happened that there was a wedding in our city, and those which made the wedding were good friends of mine. So they came and asked me (my consent) by inviting my wife and daughter. Being well befriended, I could not refuse it. So I sent her, though she did not care, and I sent also many slaves with them. So they went away, decked with much jewelry, she and her daughter.

63. And when it was evening, and the time had come to come home from the wedding, I sent lamps and torches for to meet them, and I stood by, looking out when they came, and I could see her and my daughter. And as I stood, I heard a lamentation. Woe to her! was heard from every mouth. And the slaves returned with torn garments and told me what had happened. We saw, said they, a man and a boy with him; the man had his hand upon thy wife, the boy upon thy daughter. But they ran away from them. And we wounded them with swords, but the swords fell to the ground and they (the women) also, gnashing with their teeth and

knocking their heads against the ground. And when we saw this, we came to tell thee. Upon hearing this, I tore my garment, and struck my face with the hands, and ran all the way like mad. And having gone away, I found them prostrated in the market. And I took them and brought them into my house, and having regained their senses after a while, they rose and sat down.

64. "I now began to ask my wife, What is it that had happened to thee? And she said, Dost thou not perceive what happened to me? For I asked of thee not to let me go to the wedding, since I did not feel very well. And as I walked by the way and came to the aqueduct, I saw a black man before me and his head shaking a little to me and a boy like him standing by his side. And I said to my daughter, Look at these two ugly-looking men, whose teeth are like milk and whose lips are like soot. And we left them at the aqueduct and went on. After sunset, having broken off from the wedding, and gone with the slaves through (the city), and when near the acqueduct, my daughter noticed them first and she came to me. And after her I saw them also, coming towards us, and we ran away from them. And the slaves also, which were with us ran away. (And they) beat us, and threw us down. And as she told me this, the demons came near again and threw her down. And since that hour they can go out no more, being locked up in one or in another house. And on their account I suffer much and am troubled. For

wherever they are they throw them down and uncover them. I ask thee, therefore, to pray to God: help me and have mercy upon me! For since three years no table (for the meal) has been set up in my house, and my wife and my daughter sat at no meal. Especially (I ask thee) for my unhappy daughter, which has not seen anything good yet in this world.

65. When the apostle heard this from the commander, he felt very sorry for him. And he said to him, "Believest thou that Jesus heals her?" And the commander said, "Yes." And the apostle said, "Commend thyself to Jesus, and he will heal and help her." Said the commander, "Show him to me, that I may ask him and believe on him." And the apostle said, "He appears not to these bodily eyes, but is only found with the eyes of the mind." And the commander lifted up his voice and said "I believe on thee, Jesus, and I beseech and ask of thee, help my little faith, which I have toward thee." The apostle commanded the deacon Xenophon [1] to assemble all in one place. And when the multitude was assembled, the apostle spoke, standing in the midst:

66. "My children and brethren, which believe on the Lord, remain in this faith, by preaching Jesus, who has been preached to you by me, and by putting your hope in him. Forsake him not, and he shall not forsake you. When you sleep in this

---

[1] Syriac: Xanthippus.

sleep weighing down the sleepers, he sleeps not and watches. And when you travel by sea and are in danger and there is none to help, he walks upon the waters and helps. I am now about to go from you, and it is uncertain whether I shall see you again in my body. Be not like the people of Israel, which fell when left alone for a short time by its shepherd.[2] I leave with you in my place deacon Xenophon, for he also preaches Jesus like myself. For neither am I something, nor he, but Jesus. For I also am a man, clothed with a body, a son of man, like one of you. I have also no riches, as some, which convince also the possessors of their entire uselessness, since they are left behind on earth, whence it came. But the trespasses which men take upon themselves on their account, and the filth of sin, they take with them. The rich are seldom found in the practice of mercy. But the merciful and the meek of heart — they shall inherit the Kingdom of God. Even beauty remains not with man. For they which rely upon it, when old age comes, shall suddenly be confounded. Everything has its time. There is a time to love, a time to hate.[3] Let the hope, therefore, be on Jesus Christ, the Son of God, who is always loved and desired, and remember us, as we remember you. For we also (Thomas and Xenophon), unless we carry the burden of the commandments, we are not

---

[2] Comp. Exod. XXXII.
[3] Eccles. III, 1, 8.

worthy to be preachers of that name, and shall be punished there afterward."

67. And having prayed with them and remained a long time in prayer and supplication, he commended them to the Lord and said: "Lord, the Lord of each soul, which dwelleth in a body; Lord, Father of the souls which hope in thee and wait for thy mercy, who redeemeth thy men from error, and freest from servitude and corruption those who are subject to thee and take refuge with thee, come to the fold of Xenophon, anoint them with holy oil, heal their wounds and keep them from the grievous wolves." And he laid his hands upon them and said, "The peace of the Lord come upon you and go also with us!"

Eighth Deed.

ABOUT THE WILD ASSES.

(Aa. pp. 185–197)

68. And the apostle went forth to go on his way. And all accompanied him with tears and adjured him to remember them in his prayers and not to forget them. And when he had mounted the wagon and all brethren were left behind, the commander came, ordered the driver to rise, and said, "I pray and supplicate to be deemed worthy to sit under his feet and to become his driver on this way, that he may become my companion on that way, in which only a few walk."

69. And having gone about two miles, the apostle bade the commander to rise and sit beside him, allowing the driver to take his own seat. And as they went on it happened that on account of the great heat the beasts of burden became tired and could move no more. And the commander became very sad and discouraged, and thought of running by foot to fetch other beasts of burden for the wagon. But the apostle said, "Let not your heart be troubled, neither let it be afraid;[1] but believe on Jesus Christ, whom I have preached to thee, and thou shalt see great wonders." And looking about he saw a herd of wild asses, grazing by the way. And he said to the commander, "If thou believest on Jesus Christ, go to the herd of wild asses and say, Judas Thomas, the apostle of the Messiah of the new God, saith, Let four of you come, because we need you!"

70. And the commander went, seized by fear, because they were so many. And as he went, they came to meet him. And having come near, he said to them, "Judas Thomas, the apostle of the new God, commands you that four of you should come, because I need them!" And the wild asses upon hearing this, came to him running with one accord; and having come, they fell upon their knees.[2] And the apostle said to them, "Peace be with you! Yoke four in place of these beasts of burden put aside!" And every one of them came and crowded

---

[1] Comp. John XIV, 27.
[2] The Syriac inserts here a hymn of the apostle.

to be yoked. But there were four stronger than the rest, and these were yoked. Of the others, some went before, some followed. And having gone a short distance, he dismissed them, saying, " To you, the inhabitants of the desert, I say, Go to your pastures! For if I needed all, you would all go with me. But now, go to your place, where you were." And they quietly went away, till they disappeared.

71. While the apostle, the commander, and the driver went on, the wild asses walked quietly and evenly, in order not to disquiet the apostle of God. And when they had come near the gate of the city, they turned aside and stopped before the house of the commander. And the commander said, " It is not possible to tell what happened, but I will await the end and then I will speak." And the whole city came, having seen the wild asses yoked. And the fame also spread that the apostle intended to remain here. The apostle asked the commander, " Where is thy dwelling, and whither art thou bringing us?" And he said to him, " Thou knowest thyself that we are at the door, and these which had come along at thy behest know it better than myself."

72. Having said this, they alighted from the wagon. And the apostle began to say, " Jesus Christ, whose knowledge is despised in this country; Jesus Christ, of whom nothing has been heard in this country; Jesus, who receivest all apostles in every country and every city, and by whom all

worthy of thee are glorified; Jesus, who has taken thee a form and becamest like a man and didst appear to all of us in order not to separate us from thy love; Lord, thou art he who hast given himself for us and has bought us with a price by his blood, as a precious possession. But what have we, Lord, to offer in exchange for thy life which thou hast given for us? For what we have is thy gift. <And thou demandest also nothing of us> than this, that we ask thee and (thereby) have life."

73. And having spoken thus, many came from all sides to see the apostle of the new God. And the apostle said again, "Why do we stand idle? Lord Jesus, the hour has come. What wishest thou that should be done? Command, therefore, that this be accomplished what must be done now." And the wife and daughter of the commander were very troubled by the demons, in such a wise that the inmates of the house thought that they would rise no more. For they would not allow them to eat anything at all, but threw them on their beds, and they recognized no one till the day on which the apostle came. The apostle said to one of the wild asses, which were yoked on the right side, "Go into the court, and there standing call the demons and say unto them, Judas Thomas, the apostle and disciple of Jesus Christ, says, Come out hither! For for your sakes and against your relatives have I been sent to destroy you and to persecute you to your place, till the time of consummation comes and you go down into your dark depth."

74. The wild ass, accompanied by many people, went in and said, "I say to you, the enemies of Jesus the Christ, I say to you which close the eyes not to see the light — since the worst nature cannot be changed for good — to you I say, the children of hell and destruction, (the children) of him who unceasingly does evil, who always renews his operations and that which becometh his nature, to you I say, most impudent, who shall be destroyed by yourselves — but what I should say concerning your destruction and end and what I should advise, I know not. For it is much and immense to hear it. But your trespasses are greater than the punishment which is reserved for you. But to thee, demon, and thy son, which follows thee — I say — for now I have been sent for your sakes — but why make many words about your nature and origin, which you know yourselves and are nevertheless impudent? Judas Thomas, the apostle of Jesus the Messiah, who has been sent hither out of much love and kindness, commands you, Go out in the presence of all the people here and tell me of what family you are!"

75. And immediately the woman and her daughter came forth, like dead and dishonored. And when the apostle saw them, he was sad, especially on account of the girl, and said to the demons, "Let no forgiveness and forbearance fall to your lot, for you also know no forbearance or compassion! But in the name of Jesus, leave them and go aside!" When the apostle had said this, the women fell

down and died. For they had neither breath, nor did they speak. And the demon began and said with a loud voice, " Hast thou come hither again, mocker of our nature and kindred? Hast thou come again to deface our tracks. And as I think, you will not suffer us at all to remain upcn earth. But this you cannot do at this time." The apostle, however, supposed that this demon was the same which was driven out from that woman.

76. And the demon said, " I beseech thee, suffer me to go and to dwell where thou wishest, and command me for that purpose, then I shall not fear him who has power over me. For as thou hast come to preach, so have I come to destroy. As he who sent thee punishes thee for not fulfilling his will, so, unless I do the will of him who has sent me, I am sent before the time and appointed season into my nature (exist no more as an individual). And as the Messiah helps thee in thy work, so helps me my father in that which I do. And as he prepares for thee the vessels, worthy that he dwell in them, so selects he (my father) vessels, by which I accomplish his deeds. And as he nourishes and provides his subjects, thus he (my father) prepares for me and those in which I dwell punishments and torments. And as he gives thee eternal life as reward for thy work, so he (my father) offers me as recompense for my works everlasting destruction. And as thou enjoyest thy prayer and good works and thy spiritual hymns, thus I enjoy murders and adulteries and the wine-offerings offered

upon the altars. And as thou turnest men over to everlasting life, I turn those which obey me to everlasting damnation and punishment. Thou receivest thy reward, I mine."

77. The demon having spoken this and the more, the apostle said, "Jesus commands thee and thy son through me, that you no more enter into a human dwelling but go out and go and dwell altogether outside of the dwelling of men!" And the demons said to him, "Thou hast given us a hard order. But what wilt thou do to those which are now hidden from thee? For the makers of idols (of wood and stone) enjoy them (the demons dwelling in them) more than thou, and the multitude worships them and does their will, bringing offerings to them and offering wine and water libations as food and presenting gifts." And the apostle said, "they shall now be destroyed with their deeds." And suddenly the demons became invisible. But the women did lie like dead upon the ground, having no voice.

78. And the wild asses stood together and separated not. But the wild ass which by the power of God was able to speak said to the apostle, whilst all were silent and looked on what they would do, "Why standest thou idle, apostle of the Most High, who waits that thou beseech him for the greatest knowledge? What dost thou delay? For thy teacher wishes to show his great deeds by thy hands. What standest thou, herald of the hidden One? For thy Master will make known through thee the

secret, reserving it for those, whom he deems worthy to hear it. What restest thou, who performs great deeds in the name of the Lord? For thy Lord encourages thee, by giving thee courage. Be not afraid therefore. For he will forsake no soul which according to kindred belongs to thee. Begin, therefore, to call upon him, and he shall willingly hear thee. What standest thou and admirest all his deeds and effects! For these things are small which he has shown by thee. And what wilt thou say of his great gifts? For thou shalt not be able to tell them fully. What dost thou wonder at his bodily healings, which pass, especially as thou knowest the true and lasting healing which he gives to those who belong to him? And why dost thou look at this temporal life, and thinkest not of the eternal?

79. "And to you, multitudes standing here and waiting that the prostrated women shall be raised, I say, Believe the apostle of Jesus Christ; believe the teacher of truth; believe him who shows you the truth; believe on Jesus; believe on the Messiah which was born, that the born have life through his life; who also became a child and was educated, that the perfect humanity appear through him. He taught his own teacher,[3] because he is the teacher of truth and the wisest of the wise; he offered sacrifice also in the temple, to show that every offering is hallowed (by him).[4] This here is his apostle, the

---

[3] Comp. Thomas' Gospel of the Infancy, ch. 6.
[4] Comp. Matt. XVII, 27.

revealer of truth. It is he who does the will of him who sent him. But lying apostles and prophets of lawlessness shall come,[5] whose end shall be according to their deeds, which indeed preach and give laws that one should flee lawlessness, but they are found at all times in sins. They are clothed indeed in sheep's clothing, but inwardly they are ravening wolves; they are not satisfied with one wife, but corrupt many women; they say that they despise children, yet ruin many children and suffer for them; they are not satisfied with what they have, but wish that everything useful should serve them alone, whereas they pretend to be his (Christ's) disciples; they say one thing with their mouth, but in their hearts they think otherwise; they command others to refrain from wickedness, but themselves they do nothing good; they are regarded as temperate and command others to abstain from fornication, theft, and avarice, but in secret they do all these things themselves, teaching others not to do these things."

80. While the wild ass was thus talking, all looked at it. And when it was silent, the apostle said, "What I am to think of thy beauty, O Jesus, and what to say about it, I know not; rather I cannot. For I am not able, O Christ, to utter it completely, O thou that restest and only One who art wise, who alone knowest what is in the heart and the contents of thought; — glory be to thee, merciful and tranquil; glory be to thee, wise word; glory

---

[5] Comp. Matt. VII, 15; 2 Pet. II, 1.

ACTS OF THOMAS

to thy mercy, which is shed over us; glory to thy compassion which is spread over us; glory to thy majesty, who didst come down for our sakes; glory to thy highest kingdom, which humbled itself for our sakes; glory to thy strength which became weak for our sakes; glory to thy deity which for our sakes appeared in the image of man; glory to thy humanity, which died for our sakes, to make us alive; glory to thy resurrection from the dead, for by it our souls shall share in the resurrection and rest; glory and praise to thy ascension into heaven, for by it thou didst show us the way to the highest after thou didst promise that we shall sit on thy right hand and judge with thee the twelve tribes of Israel. Thou art the heavenly word of the Father; thou art the hidden light of the mind; thou art he that shows the way of truth; O persecutor of darkness and destroyer of error."

81. When the apostle had spoken thus, he went to the women and said, "My Lord and my God, I doubt not in thee, nor do I call upon thee in unbelief, who art always our helper and assistance and restorer who givest us thy strength, encouragest us, and givest thy servants freedom in love. I beseech thee, let these women rise up healed, and become again as they were ere the demons struck them." Having spoken thus, the women turned and sat down. And the apostle ordered the commander that his servants take them and bring them in. And when they had come in, the apostle said to the wild asses, "Follow me." And they followed him till

outside of the gates. And having come out, he told them, "Go in peace to your pastures!" And the wild asses went away willingly, the apostle standing and seeing to it that no harm be done to them by anyone, till they had become invisible in the distance. And the apostle returned with the people into the house of the commander.

Ninth Deed.

About the Wife of Charis.

(Aa. pp. 197–229.)

82. It came to pass that a woman, (the wife) of Charis, the near relative of the king, named Mygdonia, came to see and to behold the new appearance of the new God, who was preached, and the new apostle, who abode in their country. And she was carried by her slaves, but could not be brought to him on account of the many people and the narrow space. So she sent to her husband for more servants. They came and went before her, pushing and striking the people. When the apostle perceived this, he said to them, "Why do you make these go away who come to hear the word and show willingness for it? You wish to be near me, whereas you are far—as it has been said of the people, which came to the Lord, Having eyes, and ye hear not.[1] And to the multitudes he said, He

---

[1] Mark VIII, 18.

that hath ears to hear, let him hear;[2] And, come unto me, all ye that labor and are heavy laden, and I will give you rest." [3]

83. And looking at her (Mygdonia's) carriers, he said to them, this beatitude, which was given to them, is now also given to you who are heavy laden. Ye are those which carry burdens, grievous to be borne,[4] and are driven onward by her (the woman's) behest. And whereas you are men they lay burdens upon you, as upon the unrational beasts, because your lords think that you are not men like themselves. <And they know not that all men are alike before God,> whether they be bond or free. <And God's judgment is just which comes upon all souls on earth, and none escapes it,> whether bond or free, poor or rich. For neither shall the riches help the rich, nor will poverty save the poor from judgment. For we received not a commandment which we cannot fulfill, nor did he put upon us heavy burdens grievous to be borne. He did neither put upon us such a building as men build it, nor stones to be hewn and houses to be established, as your artists make up by their intelligence, but we received the commandment from the Lord, that what is displeasing to us when done unto us by another, we should not do to another.

84. "First of all abstain from adultery, for it is the cause of every evil, <and of murder, on

---

[2] Matt. XI, 15.
[3] Matt. XI, 28.
[4] Comp. Matt. XXIII, 4.

which account the curse came upon Cain;> also of theft, which induced Judas Iscariot and caused that he hung himself; <and of gluttony, which caused the loss of primogenitureship, and of avarice,> for those that are given to avarice see not what they do; and of ostentation <and defamation> and all dirty deeds, especially of the carnal <and the dirty intercourse and couch of uncleanliness,> the end of which is eternal damnation. For this (uncleanliness) is the starting point of every evil. In like manner, it also leads those which are proud into servitude, drawing them down into the depth and subjecting them to their hands, that they see not what they do, on which account their deeds are unknown to them.

85. "Ye, however, <walk in holiness, for it is chosen more than any other good before God,> and become ye thereby well-pleasing to God, <and in moderation, which indicates the intercourse with God> and gives life eternal and despises death. And (walk) in kindness (meekness), for it overcomes the enemy and alone obtains the crown of victory. And in goodness and in helping, the poor and satisfying the want of the needy, by bringing (from your possession) and communicating to the needy. Especially walk in holiness, for before God it is the starting point of every good thing. <For he that is not sanctified can do nothing noble.> The holiness is of God, destroying fornication, overcoming the foe, well-pleasing to God. It is an invincible athlete, it is highly esteemed of God and

is glorified by many. It is the messenger of peace, by preaching peace. <Moderation, however> if one acquires it, he is without cares, because he pleases the Lord and waits for the time of redemption. For it does nothing which is wrong, and gives life and rest and joy to all which obtain it.

86. "And meekness has subdued death, bringing it under its power. Meekness has overcome the enemy. Meekness is a good yoke. Meekness fears none and resists not. Meekness is peace and joy and enjoying of rest. Remain, therefore, in holiness and take the freedom from care (proceeding from moderation) and approve meekness. For in these three main parts the Messiah is described, whom I preach to you. Holiness is the temple of the Messiah, and whoever lives in it obtains him as inhabitant. <And moderation is the rest (recreation) of God.> For he fasted forty days and forty nights, without tasting anything. And whoever keeps it shall live in it as upon a mountain. Meekness, however, is his glory, for he said to our fellow-apostle Peter, Turn back thy sword and put it up again into its place. For if I would do this could I not put more than twelve legions of angels from my Father on my side?"[5]

87. When the apostle spoke thus and the whole multitude heard it, they crowded and came near. But the wife of Charis, the relative of the king, started up from the palanquin, threw herself to the

---

[5] Comp. Matt. XXVI, 52, 53; John XVIII, 11.

ground before the apostle, took hold of his feet, beseeching and saying, "Disciple of the living God, thou hast come into a desert country. For we live in a desert, because by our life we are like the irrational animals; but now we shall be saved through thy hands. I beseech thee, therefore, care for me and pray for me, that the mercy of God, whom thou preachest, come upon me and I become his maid, and have part in the prayer and in the hope and in the faith on him, and receive also the seal and become a holy temple and he dwell in me."

88. And the apostle said, "I pray and ask for you all, brethren, which believe in the Lord, and for you, sisters, which hope in the Messiah, that the word of God may rest on you all and dwell in you; for we have no power over you." And he began to speak to the woman Mygdonia: "Rise up from the ground and consider. For this ornament which thou hast on will not help thee any, nor the beauty of thy body, nor thy garments. Neither the fame of the authority which surrounds thee, nor the power of this world, nor this filthy intercourse with thy husband will be of use to thee, if thou art deprived of the true intercourse. For the exhibition of jewelry is destroyed, and the body ages and changes, and the garments wax old, and the power and dominion pass by, accompanied by the responsibility for each's behavior in it (the rule). And the communion of begetting children also passes by, since it is an object of contempt. Jesus alone always remains and they which hope in him." When he had spoken this, he

said to the woman, " Go in peace, and the Lord will make thee worthy of his mysteries." And she said, " I am afraid to go away, fearing lest thou leavest me and goest to another people." And the apostle said to her, " Though I go away, I shall not leave thee alone, but Jesus will be with thee because of his compassion." And she fell down, worshipped him, and went to her house.

89. And Charis, the relative of King Misdai, after having bathed, went up to recline at dinner. And he inquired after his wife, where she was. For she had not come as usual from her chamber to meet him. And her servants said to him, " She is unwell." And he started up, went to the chamber and found her on the couch and covered. And he unveiled her, kissed her, and said to her, " Why art thou so sad?" And she said, " I am unwell." He said to her, " Why hast thou not observed the decency becoming a free woman and stay at home, but didst go and listen to the idle words and look at works of sorcery? But rise, dine with me, for I cannot eat without thee." But she said to him, " Excuse me for today, for I am very much afraid."

90. Upon hearing this from Mygdonia, Charis would not partake of the meal, but ordered his servants to bring her to eat with him. And having brought her, he demanded that she should eat with him. And she excused herself. As she would not, he ate alone, saying to her, " On thy account I refused to eat with King Misdai, and thou wouldst not eat with me?" And she said, " Because I am

unwell." Having risen up, Charis intended to associate with her after his custom. But she said, "Have I not told thee, that I refused for to-day?"

91. Upon hearing this he went away and went to sleep on another couch. When he awoke from his sleep he said, "My mistress Mygdonia, hear the dream which I have seen. I saw myself at meal near King Misdai and besides us stood a table containing everything. And I saw an eagle coming down from heaven taking away two partridges from the place before me and the king, which he carried into his nest. And he came near again fluttering about us. And the king ordered a bow to be brought to him. The eagle took again a dove and a turtle from the place before us. The king threw an arrow after him which pierced him from one side to the other without hurting him. And he flew to his nest. And raised from the sleep, I am frightened and very sad because I had tasted the partridge and he would not suffer me to bring it to my mouth." And Mygdonia said to him, "Thy dream is beautiful, for thou eatest partridges daily, whereas this eagle has till now not tasted a partridge."

92. When it was morning, Charis went and put the left shoe on the right foot. And stopping he said to Mygdonia, "What does this mean? For behold, the dream and this act!" Mygdonia said to him, "This also is not bad, but seems to me very beautiful: from a bad thing comes the better." Having washed his hands, he went to salute King Misdai.

ACTS OF THOMAS

93. In like manner also Mygdonia went early in the morning to salute the apostle Judas Thomas. She met him talking to the chief commander and the multitude. And he exhorted them by speaking of the woman which had received the Lord into her soul, and asked whose wife she was. The chief commander said, " She is the wife of Charis, the relative of King Misdai. And her husband is very severe and the king obeys him in everything which he says. And he allows her not to remain in the knowledge which she professes. He has also often praised her in the presence of the king by saying none were so good for love as she. [Everything of which thou speakest to her is strange to her."] And the apostle said, " If the Lord has truly and indeed risen in her soul (as sun) and she has received the sown seed, she will neither care for the earthly life nor fear death, nor will Charis be able to do any harm to her. For he whom she has received into her soul is greater, if indeed she has truly received him."

94. When Mygdonia heard this, she said to the apostle, " In truth, my lord, I have received the seed of thy words and shall bring forth fruits which are like the seed." Says the apostle, " Lord, these souls which are thine own, praise and thank thee; the bodies which thou didst deem worthy to be habitations of thy heavenly gift thank thee." And he also said to those about him, " Blessed are the saints, which have never been condemned by their souls (conscience); for because they have ob-

tained these (not condemning consciences), they doubt not in themselves. Blessed are the spirits of the saints which have safely received the heavenly crown for the fight commissioned to them. Blessed are the bodies of the saints, because they were deemed worthy to become temples of God, that Christ may dwell in them. Blessed are ye, because ye have power to remit sins. Blessed are ye, if ye lose not that which is committed to you, but take it with you with joy and gladness. Blessed are ye, saints, because it is given to you to ask and to receive. Blessed are ye, meek ones, because God has deemed you worthy to become heirs of the heavenly kingdom. Blessed are ye, meek ones, for ye have overcome the wicked one. Blessed are ye, meek ones, because ye shall see the face of the Lord. Blessed are ye who hunger for the Lord's sake, for rest is preserved for you, and your souls rejoice from now on. Blessed are ye quiet ones (because ye were found worthy) to be delivered from sin." When the apostle had said this in the hearing of the whole multitude, Mygdonia was more strengthened in the faith and in the glory and majesty of the Messiah.

95. And Charis, the king's relative and friend came to the breakfast and found not his wife at home. And he asked all in his house, "Whither has your mistress gone?" And one of them said, "She went to the stranger." Upon hearing this from the one servant, he was angry at the others, because they did not announce to him at once what

had happened. And he sat down and waited for her. And when it was evening and she entered into the house, he said to her, "Where hast thou been?" She answered and said, "To the physician?" He said, "Is the stranger a physician?" She said, "Yes, a physician of souls. Most physicians heal the bodies, which decay; but he heals the souls, which do not perish." When Charis heard this, he was inwardly very wroth at Mygdonia on account of the apostle. But he answered nothing, for he was afraid, as she was superior to him in riches and intelligence. He went to the meal, but she went to her chamber. And he said to one of his servants, "Call her to the meal." But she would not.

96. When he heard that she would not leave her chamber, he went in and said to her, "Why wilt thou not eat with me? And wilt thou not also have intercourse with me according to custom? And in this respect I am more suspicious. For I heard that that sorcerer and deceiver teaches that none should cohabit with his wife, and he reverses what nature demands and the deity has ordered." When Charis said this, Mygdonia held her peace. Again he says to her, "My lady and wife Mygdonia, be not deceived by deceitful and foolish words, nor by the works of sorcery which this man, as I heard, does in the name of the Father, of the Son, and of the Holy Ghost. In this world it has never been heard that one has raised the dead. But as I hear, he is reported to raise the dead. And as he neither eats

nor drinks, think not, that he neither eats nor drinks for righteousness' sake. He rather does it because he has nothing. For what should he do who has not even the daily bread? And he has only one garment because he is poor. And as concerns this that he receives nothing from anyone he does it because he is aware that none has been made well by him."

97. When Charis said this, Mygdonia was dumb like a stone. She prayed, however, for daylight, that she might go to the apostle of the Messiah. He left her and sadly partook of his meal, for he was anxious to have intercourse with her. When he had left, she bent her knees and prayed thus: "Lord God, merciful Father, and Redeemer Christ, give me strength that I overcome the boldness of Charis, and grant unto me to keep the holiness which is well-pleasing to thee, that by it I may also find eternal life." Having thus prayed, she betook herself to her bed, being clothed.

98. Having eaten, Charis came near her. And she cried, "Henceforth thou hast no place beside me, for my Lord Jesus who is with me and rests in me is better than thou." And laughingly he said, "Well dost thou mock with these words at that sorcerer, and nicely dost thou laugh at him who says, You have no life with God unless you sanctify yourselves!" Having said this, he tried to go into her. But she would not suffer it, but cried out with a piercing voice, "I call upon thee, Lord Jesus, forsake me not! I have taken refuge in thee! As I

have perceived that it is thou who seekest those which are in ignorance and savest those which are kept in error, so I pray thee now of whose report I heard and in whom I believed, Come to my assistance and save me from Charis's insolence, that his impurity have no power over me." And she put her hands (to her face), and ran away uncovered. And upon leaving she tore down the curtain of her chamber, put it around her, went to the nurse, and slept with her.

99. And Charis spent the whole night in sadness, striking his face with the hands. And he thought of going immediately to the king and to report to him of the power which surrounds him. But considering he said within himself, "If the great sadness which now fills my heart obliges me to go to the king, who will introduce me to him? For I know that, had not evil report thrown me down from my pride and vaunt and greatness and brought me into this smallness and separated my sister Mygdonia from me, I should not have come out at this time (of the night) even if the king stood at the door and give him an answer. But I shall wait till it is day. I know that the king will grant what I ask of him. And I will speak of the madness of the stranger, whose tyranny throws the great and illustrious into the abyss. For it pains me not that I am deprived of her intercourse, but I sorrow for her, because her noble soul has been humbled. She, a woman of comeliness, in which none of the servants has ever detected an unseemliness, ran uncov-

ered from her chamber, and I know not whither she went. But it is possible that having been made mad by that sorcerer, in her madness she went to the market to seek him. For nothing seems to her lovely but that man and his words."

100. Having spoken thus, he began to moan and say, "Woe to me, wife, and woe to thee also! For too soon have I been deprived of thee! Woe to me, most beloved, for thou art better than my whole kindred. For I had neither a son nor a daughter from thee that I could enjoy them. Thou hast not even lived with me a year, and an envious eye has torn thee from me. Had the power of death taken thee away, I should have counted myself a king and leader! But that I should suffer this at the hand of a stranger! And, possibly, he is a slave, who ran away to my harm and to that of my most unhappy soul. But let nothing come in my way till I have destroyed him and avenged this night. And let King Misdai not (again) find pleasure in me unless he gives me revenge in the head of the stranger and in the commander Sifôr, who became her cause of destruction. For through him he came here and stays with him. And many go in and out there whom he teaches a new doctrine by saying that none can live unless he frees himself from all his possessions and like himself becomes an abstainer. And he endeavors to get many friends.

101. As Charis was considering this, it became day. And having passed the night waking, he put

on a cheap dress, and shoes on his feet, and, looking sad and dejected, he went to salute the king. Upon seeing him, the king said, "Why art thou so sad, and why didst thou come in such an attire? And thy face is also changed." Charis answered and said to the king, "I have to tell thee of something new, and of a new devastation which the commander Sifôr has brought upon India: a Hebrew magician whom he has in his house and who leaves him not. Many go to him, whom he teaches a new God and gives them new laws, of which no one has ever heard, by saying, 'It is impossible that you enter into the eternal life which I preach to you, unless you give up your wives, and the wives also give up their husbands. It happened that my unhappy wife also went to him and heard his words. And she believed them, left me during the night, and ran to the stranger. But let Sifôr and the sorcerer hidden in his house be brought to thee, and punish them, that not all of our people perish."

102. When his friend Misdai heard this, he said to him, "Be not sad and discouraged! I will have them brought here, and I will avenge thee, and thou shalt have thy wife again. For if I avenge others who cannot avenge themselves, I will avenge thee above all." And the king went out and sat upon the seat of judgment. Being seated, he ordered to call Sifôr, the commander. And having come into his house, they found him at the right hand of the apostle, and Mygdonia at his feet, listening with the whole people. And the king's messengers came

near to Sifôr and said, "Thou are sitting here listening to foolish words, and King Misdai is enraged thinking how to destroy thee because of this sorcerer and deceiver, whom thou hast brought into thy house!" Upon hearing this, Sifôr was discouraged, not because of the king's threat against him, but on account of the apostle, because the king was opposed to him. And he said to the apostle, "I am distressed for thee. For I told thee from the beginning that that woman is the wife of Charis, the relative and friend of the King, and that he does not suffer her to do what is promised, and that the king grants him everything which he asks." And the apostle said to Sifôr, "Fear nothing, but believe in Jesus, who comes to our defense. For we have been gathered to his place of refuge." Upon hearing this, and having put on his cloak, Sifôr went to King Misdai.

103. And the apostle inquired of Mygdonia, "What is the cause that thy husband is so enraged and has prepared these devices against us?" She said, "Because I did not yield to his desire. In the evening he wanted to force me and to subject me to that passion in which he indulges. But he to whom I commended my soul delivered me from his hands. And naked I ran away and slept with my nurse. But what happened to him that he made these cunning devices, I know not." The apostle saith, "This shall not hurt us. Believe in Jesus, and he will destroy the wrath in Charis and his

madness and his passion, and he will be thy companion on the dangerous road and bring thee into his kingdom; and he shall bring thee into eternal life, by giving thee a sure hope, which passes not away and changes not."

104. And Sifôr stood before the king, who asked him, "Who and whence is and what teaches that magician whom thou hast in thy house?" And Sifôr answered the king, "O King, thou art hardly ignorant of the trouble and sadness which I and my friends suffered because of my wife, which thou knowest and which others remember, and because of my daughter, which I regard more than all my possessions, what time of trial I had to undergo. For I became an object of derision and curse for our whole country. But I heard of that man, went to him, besought him and took him and brought him hither. And on the way I perceived wonderful and surprising things, and here many heard of the wild ass and of the demon which he drove out; and he healed my wife and daughter, and now they are well. He asks no reward, but demands faith and holiness that they become coworkers in his work. He teaches to honor and fear one God, the Lord of all, and Jesus Christ, his Son, that they may have life eternal. He only eats bread and salt, and drinks water from even to even; and he prays much, and whatever he asks of God is given to him. And he teaches that this God is holy and mighty, and that the Messiah is life and makes alive.

Therefore he exhorts also those which are with him to come to him (God) in holiness, purity, love and faith."

105. When Sifôr had spoken thus, King Misdai sent many soldiers into the house of Sifôr, the commander, to bring Thomas, and all those which should be found there. And when the messengers came into the house, they found him teaching a great multitude, and Mygdonia sitting at his feet. And when the messengers saw the multitude they were afraid, went to the king, and said, "We ventured not to say anything to him on account of the many people around him; Mygdonia also was listening to his words, sitting at his feet." When the King Misdai and Charis heard these things, Charis started up, took many people with him, and said, "I shall bring him, O King, and Mygdonia, whose mind he has disturbed." And with great unrest he came into the house of Sifôr. And he found him teaching; but Mygdonia he found not, because she had returned to her house, having perceived that her husband knew of her presence there.

106. And Charis said to the apostle, "Rise, wicked one and destroyer and enemy of my house, for thy sorcery harms me not; and I shall put thy sorcery upon thy head." Having said this, the apostle looked at him and said, "Thy threats shall turn against thee, for thou shalt not harm me. For greater than thee and thy king and thy whole army is the Lord Jesus Christ, in whom I put my hope." And Charis took a wrapper of one of his servants,

put it on the neck of the apostle, and said, "Drag and take him away; I shall see whether God can save him from my hands." And they dragged and took him to King Misdai. When the apostle came into the presence of the king, the king said to him, "Tell me who thou art and by what power thou doest these things?" But the apostle held his peace. And the king ordered his subjects to scourge him one hundred and twenty-eight times and cast him bound into the prison. And they bound him and led him away. And the king and Charis considered how to kill him. But the multitude worshipped him upon the knees like a God. And they had in their mind to say this: "The stranger acted wickedly against the king, and is a deceiver."

107. And when the apostle went to the prison, he said with gladness and rejoicing, "I thank thee, Jesus, that thou hast not only deemed me worthy to believe on thee, but also to suffer much for thee. I thank thee, Lord, that thou hast cared for me and hast given me patience. I thank thee, Lord, that on thy account I have been called a sorcerer and magician. May I also receive of the beatitudes of the lowly, and of the rest of the weary, and of the beatitudes of those whom men hate and persecute and revile by speaking evil against them. For, behold, on thy account I am hated; behold, on thy account I am avoided by the multitude, and on thy account they call me what I am not."

108. And all prisoners saw him pray and asked him to pray for them. After having prayed, and

having been seated, he began to repeat the following psalm:[6]

"When I was a minor
And in the palace [7] of my Father,
Enjoying the riches and abundance
Of those who brought me up,
From the East, our home,
The parents having equipped me, sent me away.
From the richness of their [8] treasuries
They supplied a burden,
Great and yet light,
That I alone could carry it.
Gold is the burden from above,[9]
And silver from the great treasuries [10]
And Chalcedon stones from India,
And pearls from the land of Kosan.[11]
And they supplied me with a diamond
<Which can break the iron.>

---

[6] The hymn or psalm, which is here inserted and which is only found in the Syriac and in one Greek manuscript, has erroneously been called "the hymn of the soul." It rather describes the descent of the Saviour to the earth (= Egypt), his deliverance of those souls which were there in the prison of the evil (= matter) and his return to the heavenly kingdom of light. The whole may be designated as a Gnostic development and expansion of Phil. II, 5-11. The hymn can be divided into the following sections: 1, the preparations for the journey; 2, the journey; 3, the abode in Egypt; 4, the return. Some have ascribed the authorship of this hymn to the Syrian Bardesanes; see Lipsius, *loc. cit.*, p. 292 f.; Preuschen, *loc. cit.*, p. 45 f., where an exposition is attempted.

[7] Syriac: in the kingdom.
[8] Syriac: our.
[9] Syriac: from the country of Gilan.
[10] Syriac: from Gazak.
[11] Syriac: Kushan.

And took off my garment wrought in gold and jeweled
Which they had made in their love,
And the cloak as yellow as gold,
Which answered my size.
And they agreed with me
And wrote it into my heart, that I should not forget it;
' When thou goest down into Egypt
To fetch thence the one pearl
Which is there <in the midst of the sea,>
Which the devouring serpent surrounds —
Thou shalt put on the jeweled garment
And the cloak, which thou hast enjoyed,
And with thy brother <our nearest kin,>
Thou shalt be heir in our kingdom.'

109. I came from the East <and went down>
On a difficult, dangerous road,
Accompanied by two guides,
For I was unexperienced, to travel on it.
I passed by the border of Mesêne,
The stopping place of the merchants of the East,
Came into the land of the Babylonians
<And entered within the walls of Sarbug.>
And when I had come to Egypt,
The guides, my fellow-travelers, left me,
I betook myself by the shortest road to the serpent,
Settled about its cave,
And waited till it slept
That I might secretly take my pearl.
And when I was alone

And in my appearance appeared strange to my roommates,
I noticed there was a countryman from the East,
The free, a young man, lovely and beautiful
A Son of the nobles.[12] He came, lived with me and became my companion,
And I made him a friend and comrade of my undertaking.
But I cautioned him against the Egyptians
And against the communion with these unclean ones.
But I dressed like them
Not to appear to them as a stranger,
As one who came from abroad
To obtain the pearl
That the Egyptians excited not the serpent against me.
But from some cause, whatever it be,
They learned that I was not from their country,
And with deceit and cunning they rose up against me,
And I partook of their meals.
I knew no more than I was a king's son,
And served their king,
And forgot also the pearl,
For which my parents had sent me,
And owing to the heaviness of their food
I sunk into a deep sleep.
  110.   When I suffered thus

---

[12] Syriac: one anointed.

My parents perceived it and were afflicted for me.
And a message was announced in our kingdom,
That all should come to the gates.
And the kings and worthies of Parthia
And all the great ones of the East
Passed a resolution on my account,
That I should not remain in Egypt.
And those in power wrote also to me,
By signing their names, as follows:
' From thy father, the king of kings,
And from thy mother, which rules the East,
And from thy brother, the second after us,
To our son in Egypt, Greeting!
Arise and wake up from the sleep
And hear the words of the letter
And consider that thou art a king's son.
<Behold,> thou hast taken upon thee a slave's yoke!
Think of the pearl,
On whose account thou wert sent to Egypt,
Think of thy gold-wrought garment,
<Think of the glorious toga
Which thou art to put on and with which thou art to adorn thyself.>
Thy name was mentioned in the book of life [18]
And with thy brother <our substitute, thou shalt be>
In our kingdom.
   111. <My letter is a letter,>

---

[18] Syriac: book of the valiants.

Which the king has sealed
Because of the wicked Babylonians
And the tyrannical demons of Labyrinth.[14]
<It (i. e. the letter) flew like the eagle,
The king of all fowls.
It flew and came down to me
And was all speech.>
Through its voice and its audible sound
I started up from the sleep,
Took it and kissel it,
<Broke its seal> and read.
Its contents agreed with that
Which was written in my heart.
At once I remembered that I am a king's son,
And my free origin longed after its kind,
I also remembered the pearl,
For which I was sent to Egypt;
And with sayings I began <to enchant>
The fearful <and devouring> serpent.
I lulled it asleep <and sunk it into slumber,>
For I mentioned the name of my father over it,
<And the name of our second one
And of my mother, the queen of the East.>
And I seized the pearl
And returned to bring it to my parents.
And I took off the dirty garment
And left it behind in its country.
And immediately I directed my way
To the light of my country in the East.

---

[14] Syriac: Sarbug.

And on the way I found my letter <before me,>
Which had started me.
And as it started me who was asleep, by its voice
It also led me through the light proceeding from it.
For the royal letter made of Serean [15] tissue
Shone sometimes before my eyes
<And by its voice and guidance
It encouraged again my haste.>
And love leading and drawing me
I passed by Labyrinth,[16]
Left Babylon to my left
And came to the great Mesêne,
<The port of the merchants,>
Situated at the seashore.
<And my precious garment, which I had taken off,
And the cloak, with which I was clothed —
From the heights of Warkan my parents had sent
By their treasurers,
Whom they had intrusted with them because of their faithfulness.>

112. But I remembered no more its splendor
For as a young boy I left it in the palace of the father.
Suddenly I saw the <glorious> garment
Looking like a mirror of mine.
I beheld it entirely in me,
I knew and saw myself wholly by it.

---

[15] According to Pliny *hist. nat.* VI, 17 (20), 54 f.; XXXVI, 14 (41), the ancients received their silken materials from Sēr, in northwestern China.
[16] Syriac: Sarbug.

<We were two, different from each other,>
And yet again one, in one form.
Yea, the treasures also I saw as two,
Which had brought the garment,
And yet they had one form:
Both wore a royal symbol.
The treasure and riches they had in hands
And returned, what belonged to me,
The glorious garment,
Adorned in shining colors
With gold and precious stones
And pearls in apparent color —
They were fastened above,
<And with diamonds all its seams were put together.>
And the picture of the King of kings
Was fully on the entire garment,
And sapphire stones were fittingly fastened above.[17]

113. And again I saw
That the impulses of knowledge proceeded from the whole
And it was ready to speak.
I heard, however, how it spoke
<With those which had brought it>:
'I descend from the bravest of all men,
On which account I was educated by the father himself,
And I perceived myself how my greatness
Grew in correspondence to his energy.'

---

[17] Syriac: like sapphire stones glitter its colors.

And with its royal motions
It wholly moved toward me.
From their (the bearers') hand it hastened away,
Striving after him, who should receive it.
An ardent desire seized me also
To go to meet it and to receive it,
And I stretched myself and took it,
And adorned myself with the beauty of its colors,
And my cloak, which surpassed that of a king,
I wholly put around me.
And having put it on, I was lifted up
To the gate of salutation and adoration
And I bowed my head and worshiped
The splendor of the Father, who had sent it to me
Whose behests I had executed.
In like manner he also did as he had promised.
And in the gates of his palace
I mingled among his great ones.
And he rejoiced over me and received me,
<And I was with him> in his palace.
All his subjects, however,
Praise him with joyous voices.
And he promised me that to the gate
Of the King <of kings> I should go with him,
That with my offerings and the pearl
Together with him I appear before the king " [18]

---

[18] In the Syriac follows now a lengthy song of praise by the apostle Thomas.— Concerning our song Lipsius remarks (p. 296): "The preservation of this precious remainder of Gnostic poetry we owe to the happy ignorance of the Catholic reviser, who had no idea what heretical serpent is hidden beneath the lovely flowers of this poetry."

114. Charis went home rejoicing, believing that his wife would live with him again and be as she was before, ere she heard the divine word and believed in Jesus. Coming back, he found her hair cut off and her garment rent. Seeing her, he said to her, " My lady Mygdonia, why does this nauseous disease take possession of thee? And why hast thou done this? I am thy husband since the time of thy virginity, and the gods as well as the laws give me the right to rule over thee. What is this great madness of thine that makes thee ridiculous in the eyes of all the people? Put away the anxiety which comes from that sorcerer. I shall remove his sight, that thou shalt see him no more."

115. When Mygdonia heard these words, she gave vent to her feelings and sighed and lamented. And Charis said again, " I must have greatly sinned against the gods, that they have entangled me into such a disease. I pray thee, Mygdonia, torment not my soul by this thy lamentable sight and humble appearance, and make my heart not heavy through the anxiety for thee. I am thy husband Charis, whom all the people honor and fear. What shall I do? I know not how to act. What shall I think? Shall I keep silence and bear? And who can bear it when his treasure is taken from him? And who could tolerate to be deprived of thy good manners? Thy sweet savor is in my nostrils and thy cheerful face is in my eyes. They take away my soul, and the very beautiful body which I enjoyed when I saw it, they destroy and blind the sharp looking eye and

cut off my right hand. My joy is turned into sadness, and my life into death, the light is dipped into darkness. None of my relatives shall see me any more, none of whom have helped me, and the gods of the East I shall worship no more, which have surrounded me with such great misfortune. And indeed I shall no more pray to them nor sacrifice to them, having been deprived of my wife. What else shall I ask of them? All my glory has been taken away. And I am a prince, the second in the government of the king. All this Mygdonia has taken from me by rejecting me. No matter if they knock my eyes out, if only thou turnest thy eyes upon me in the accustomed manner!"

116. While Charis was sepaking thus with tears, Mygdonia sat silent and looked on the ground. He came near and said, "My most beloved lady Mygdonia, remember that of all the women in India I selected thee as the most beautiful and took thee, although I could have married others, more beautiful than thee. But no, I lie, Mygdonia. For by the gods it is impcsible to find one like thee in the land of the Indians. Woe to me ever, that thou dost not even answer me! Abuse me, if it pleases thee, but speak. Look at me (and see), that I am by far better and more beautiful than that sorcerer. I have riches and honor, and all know that none has such a family as mine. But thou art my riches and honor, thou art family and kindred. And behold, he separates thee from me."

117. When Charis had said this, Mygdonia said

to him, "He whom I love is better than thee and thy possession. For thy possession, being earthly, returns to earth. But he whom I love is heavenly and shall bring me also into heaven. Thy riches shall pass away, and thy beauty shall be destroyed, so likewise thy garments and thy many works. And thou remainest alone with thy trespasses. But remind me not of thy actions to me. For I pray to the Lord that thou wouldest forget and think no more of the former pleasures and the bodily connection, which shall pass like a shadow. Jesus alone remains forever, and the souls which trust in him. Jesus himself shall free me from the filthy deeds which I did before with thee."

Upon hearing this, Charis, broken in his soul, turned to sleep, saying to her, "Think the matter over during the night! If thou wilt be with me as before, ere thou didst see the sorcerer, I will fulfill all thy wishes, and if it pleases thee on account of thy kind disposition toward him, I shall release him from the prison and set him free and let him go to another country. And I shall not grieve thee, for I know how much thou thinkest of the stranger. He made not a beginning with thee, but like thee he also deceived many other women. These have come to their senses and think differently. Now consider my words and make me not a reproach in the land of the Indians."

118. Thus speaking, he fell asleep. And she took ten denarii, and went secretly away to give them to the keepers of the prison in order to be per-

mitted to go to the apostle. By the way Judas Thomas met her, who went to her. Upon seeing him, she was afraid, because she took him for one of the princes, as much light went before him. And running away, she said within herself, "I have ruined thee, poor soul, for thou shalt not again see Judas, the apostle of the living God, and hast not received the holy seal." And running away she went to a narrow place and hid herself there, saying, "It is better to be caught by poorer ones, which one can persuade, than to meet with this powerful prince, who despises presents."

Tenth Deed.

How Mygdonia receives baptism.

(Aa. pp. 229-240.)

119. As Mygdonia was considering this within herself, Judas came in and went to her. And seeing him, she was afraid, and fell down like dead. He came to her, took her by the hand, and said to her, "Fear not, Mygdonia; Jesus will not forsake thee, and thy Lord will not neglect thee, to whom thou hast given thyself; his merciful rest will not fail thee; the kind will not forsake thee on account of his great kindness, and the good because of his goodness. Arise from the ground, since thou art raised above it. Behold the light, for the Lord suffers not those which love him, to walk in darkness. Look at the companion of his servants, be-

cause he is their fellow-combatant in dangers." And Mygdonia rose up, looked at him, and said, "Whither didst thou go, my lord? And who is it which took thee out from prison to see the sun?" Says Judas Thomas to her, "My Lord Jesus is more powerful than all powers and kings and princes."

120. And Mygdonia said, "Give me the seal of Jesus Christ, and let me receive a gift from thy hands before thou departest the life!" And she took him, went into the court, awoke the nurse, and said to her, "My mother and nurse Marcia,[1] all helps and joys, which thou hast given me from childhood, were vain, and I owe thee (only) temporary thanks. And now show me a favor, that thou mayest ever receive recompense from him who gives the great gifts." Upon this Marcia said, "What is thy wish, my daughter Mygdonia, and what can be done for thy pleasure? The honors which thou didst promise to me before, the stranger did not suffer thee to show, and thou hast made me a reproach among the whole people. And now — what new thing dost thou ask of me?" Mygdonia said, "Be thou my partner for eternal life, that I receive from thee perfect nourishment. Take a loaf and bring it to me, also a very small measure of water, having forbearing regard for my free birth." And the nurse said, "I will bring thee many loaves, and instead of (the very small measure of) water I will bring measures of wine and fulfill thy wish." And

---

[1] The Syriac: Narcia; the Latin (*Miracula beati Thomæ* ed. Gregory of Tours, in Fabricius II, 687 ff). Narchia.

she said to the nurse, "I need no measures, nor also the many loaves, but this only bring: a small measure of water, a loaf and oil."

121. When Marcia had brought these things, Mygdonia stood before the apostle with uncovered head. And he took the oil, poured it upon her head, and said, " Holy oil, given to us for sanctification; hidden mystery, in which the cross is shown to us; thou art the extender of the bent members; thou art the humbler of the hard works; thou dost point out the hidden treasures; thou art the sproud of goodness. Let thy power come and rest on thy servant Mygdonia, and heal her by this liberty."[2] Having poured out the oil, he bade the nurse to undress her and to put around her a linen dress. And there was in that place a spring to which the apostle went and baptized Mygdonia in the name of the Father and of the Son and of the Holy Ghost. And when she was baptized and had dressed herself, he broke bread, took a cup of water, made her partake of the body of the Messiah and of the cup of the Son of God, saying, " Thou hast received thy seal and obtained eternal life!" And instantly a voice was heard from above, saying, "Yea, Amen!" When Marcia heard this voice, she became afraid, and asked the apostle to give her the seal also, and the apostle did, and said, " May the zeal of the Lord encompass thee like the others!"

---

[2] This is the reading of the text, which is no doubt corrupt. The reading ought to be something which denotes anointing with oil.

122. When the apostle had done this, he returned to the prison, found the doors open and the keepers sleeping. And Thomas said, "Who is like thee, God, who keepest thy tender love and thy zeal from none; who is like thee, merciful, who hast saved thy creatures from the evil? Life, which has overcome death; rest, which ends the toil! Glory be to the only-begotten of the Father; glory to the Merciful, who was sent out of mercy!" Having said this, the keepers woke up and saw all the doors opened, but the prisoners within. And they said within themselves, "Have we not secured the doors? How are they now opened and the prisoners within?"

123. When it was day, Charis went to Mygdonia. And he found them (both) praying and saying, "New God which has come to us through the stranger; God, hidden from the inhabitants of India; God, who hast shown thy glory through thy apostle Thomas; God, of whom we heard and in whom we believe; God, to whom we have come to be saved; God, who out of kindness and compassion didst come down to our weakness; God, who didst seek us when we did not know thee; God, who dwellest in the heights and art not hidden from the depths, take from us the madness of Charis." Upon hearing this, Charis said to Mygdonia, "Justly thou callest me bad and ugly and mad! For had I not tolerated thy disobedience and given thee freedom, thou shouldest not have called against me and remembered my name before God. But be-

lieve, Mygdonia, that nothing is to be gained from the sorcerer, and that he cannot do what he promises. But I do everything that I promise before thine eyes, that thou shouldest believe and endure my words and be toward me as before."

124. And coming near, he asked her again, and said, "If thou obeyest me, I shall have no more pains. Remember that day on which we first met. Tell the truth: did I not appear to thee then more beautiful than Jesus now?" And Mygdonia said, "That time required its own, and this requires its own. That time was that of the beginning, but this is that of the end. That time was that of the earthly life, this that of the everlasting. That was one of a temporary pleasure, this that of an everlasting. That was that of the day and of the night, this that of the day without night. Thou hast seen the wedding which passed over and remains here (on earth.) This wedding remains in eternity. That communion was that of destruction, this is that of eternal life. Those groomsmen and bridesmaids are temporary men and women; the present, however, remain unto the end. That wedding <is founded upon earth, in which oppression spread, this stands in the transition through fire, to which grace was sprinkled.> That bride-chamber passes away, but this remains for ever. That bed was covered with mantles, but this with charity and faith. Thou art a bridegroom, which passes away, and is destroyed, but Jesus is the true bridegroom, remaining immortal in eternity. That bridal present was

treasures and garments which wax old; this, however, is living words which never pass away."

125. Having heard this, Charis went to the king, and told him all. And the king ordered to bring Judas for a trial and to kill him. But Charis said, "Have a little patience, O king; frighten the man first by words, and persuade him to induce Mygdonia that she become toward me as before." And Misdai sent for the apostle of the Messiah and had him brought from the prison. And all prisoners were sad because the apostle went away from them — for they all loved him very much — and said, "Even this consolation which we had is taken from us!"

126. And Misdai said to the apostle, "Why teachest thou this new doctrine, which gods and men hate and in which there is no profit?" And Judas said, "What bad thing do I teach?" Misdai said, "Thou teachest that it is impossible for men to have life with God unless they keep pure to the God whom thou preachest." Judas said, "Thou speakest true, O king; this I teach indeed. For tell me: art thou not indignant when thy soldiers accompany thee in filthy garments? Now, if thou, who art an earthly king and returnest to earth, demandest that thy subjects are decent in their exterior, how couldst thou be angry and say that I teach evil by saying: those who serve my king must be holy and pure and free from every sadness and care for children and unnecessary riches and transitory

unrest? Thou requirest thy subjects to follow thee in conversation and manners, and when they despise thy commandments, thou punishest them; how much more ought they which believe on my God serve him with much holiness, purity and chastity, free from all fleshly pleasures, from adultery and dissipation, theft, drunkenness, gluttony, and (other) dishonorable acts!"

127. When Misdai heard these things, he said, "Behold, I set thee free. Go and persuade Mygdonia, Charis's wife, that she separate not from him." Said Judas to him, "Delay not, if thou meanest to do something (against me). For if she has received that in a right way, which she has learned, neither iron, nor fire, nor anything else which is stronger than these things will be able to harm her nor to separate him (from her) whom she retains in her soul." Said Misdai to Judas, "Some remedies make others without effect, and theriac makes bites of an adder ineffective. And if thou only wishest thou canst make ineffective the charms (formerly applied by thee), and bring about peace and concord among husband and wife. For by doing this thou savest thyself. For thou hast not yet lived thy life to the full. And know, if thou persuadest her not, I shall tear thee away from this life welcomed by all." And Judas said, "This life is given to us as a loan, and this time changes. The life, however, which I teach is imperishable, whereas beauty and visible youth shall be no more

after a short time." And the king said, "I advised thee what is profitable, but thou makest thy position worse."

128. When the apostle had left the king, Charis came and said to him beseechingly, "I pray thee, O man — for I never did anything wrong to thee or someone else nor against the gods — why hast thou brought such great misery upon me? Why hast thou excited such a sedition against my house? And what profit hast thou thereof? But if thou thinkest to profit by it, tell me what kind of profit it is, and I will obtain it for thee without trouble. Why make me mad, and destroy thyself? For if thou persuadest her not I shall lay my hand on thee and finally kill myself. But if, as thou sayest, there is life and death after this life, besides also a condemnation and victory and a judgment, I shall appear there also and be judged with thee, and if God, whom thou preachest, is just and judges justly, I know that I shall be vindicated. For thou didst harm me, without ever having been harmed by anyone. Here I can avenge myself for everything that thou didst against me. Obey me, therefore, and go into my house and persuade Mygdonia to behave toward me as before, ere she saw thee. Judas said to him, "Believe me, my son, if men loved God as much as one another, they would receive from him everything that they ask, without being forced by anyone."

129. While Thomas was saying this, they came into the house of Charis and found Mygdonia sit-

ting, and Marcia standing by her and with her hand on Mygdonia's cheek. And she said, "Mother, O that the remaining days of my life be shortened and all hours be like one hour, and I could leave this life to depart sooner and see that beautiful One of whom I heard from hearsay, the Living who gives life to all, that believe on him, go (thither) where there is neither day and night nor light and darkness, neither good and bad nor poor and rich, male and female, free or bond, not a proud and one neglecting the meek." And while she was thus speaking, the apostle came to her. And immediately she rose up and fell down before him. And Charis said to him, "Seest thou how she fears and honors thee, and willingly does what thou commandest?"

130. Having said this, Judas said to Mygdonia, "Obey, my daughter Mygdonia, what Brother Charis saith." And Mygdonia saith, "If thou couldst not express the thing by a word, how wilt thou force me to suffer the deed? For I heard thee say that this life is only a loan, and that this rest is only temporary and these possessions transient. And again thou didst say, that he who turns away from this life shall receive the everlasting, and whoever hates the light of the day and of the night shall see light which is not broken, and that he who despises these treasures shall find others, everlasting treasures. And now thou sayest this, because thou art afraid. Who changes a work which he has executed and in which he glories? <Who builds a tower and> destroys it again? Who covers again

a water fountain, which he dug in a dry place? Who finds a treasure and uses it not?" Upon hearing this, Charis said, "I shall not imitate you nor hasten to destroy you. As for thee, since I have the power, I will put thee in fetters and not permit thee to speak with the sorcerer. And if thou obeyest me <it is well; if not,> I know what I have to do."

131. Judas left the house of Charis and went to the house of Sifôr, and abode with him. And Sifôr said, "I will prepare for him a dining room in which he shall teach." And he did so. And Sifôr said, "I and my wife and my daughter shall from now on live in holiness, in purity, and in one mind. I pray thee, give us the seal that we become servants of the true God and such as belong to his lambs." And Judas said, "I fear to say what I think. I know something, and what I know I cannot express."

132. And he began to speak of baptism: "This baptism is forgiveness of sins. It is a light shed abroad everywhere. It generates the new man, <renews the thoughts, mixes soul and body,> establishes in a threefold [3] manner the new man, and is partaking of forgiveness of sin. Praise be to thee, hidden power, which is united with us by baptism! Praise be to thee, invisible power, which is in the baptism! Praise be to thee, renovation, by which those to be baptized are renewed,[4] taking

---

[3] Syriac: in the Trinity.
[4] Comp. Titus III, 5.

hold of thee with love." And having said this, he poured oil upon their heads, and said, "Praise be to thee, love of mercy! Praise be to thee, name of the Messiah! Praise be to thee, power, which dwellest in Christ!" And he had a basin brought and baptized them in the name of the Father and of the Son and of the Holy Ghost.

133. And when they were baptized and had dressed, he put bread on the table, and blessing it, said, "Bread of life, whose eaters shall be imperishable; bread which satisfies hungry souls with its blessedness — thou hast been deemed worthy to receive a gift, that thou becomest to us a forgiveness of sins, and those that eat thee, immortal; we name over thee the name of the mother, the hidden mystery of the hidden dominions and powers, we name over thee the name of Jesus." And he said, "Let the power of the blessing rest upon the bread, that all souls which partake of it be delivered from their sins." And he brake the bread and gave it to Sifôr and to his wife and daughter.

Eleventh Deed.

Concerning the Wife of Misdai.

(Aa. pp. 240–245.)

134. After King Misdai had dismissed Judas, he went to his house to partake of the meal and told his wife what had happened to their relative Charis, saying, "See what happened to the unfortunate one!

Thou knowest thyself, my sister Tertia, that the man has nothing more beautiful than his wife, which he enjoys. Now it happened that his wife went to the sorcerer, of whom thou hast heard that he came as a stranger into the land of the Indians, and she became enticed by his sorceries and separated from her husband. And he knows not what to do. And as I was about to destroy the wicked fellow, he would not allow it. But go thou and advise her to turn again to her husband, and to keep away from the foolish words of the sorcerer."

135. And Tertia rose up immediately and went to the house of Charis, the relative of her husband. And she found Mygdonia prostrated upon the ground resting on a sack and ashes. And she prayed that the Lord would pardon her her former sins and quickly take her from this life. And Tertia says to her, "Mygdonia, most beloved sister and companion, what disease has taken hold of thee? Know thyself and return again. Draw near to thy numerous family, and save thy husband Charis, and do not what is unbecoming thy free birth!" Says Mygdonia to her, "O Tertia, thou hast not yet heard the preacher of life! His voice has not yet come to thy ears, neither hast thou tasted the medicine of life, nor hast thou been delivered from destructive sighs. Since thou standest in the temporary life, thou knowest not the life eternal and the redemption, and without perceiving the imperishable communion <thou art tormented by corruptible communion>. Thou standest here clad in

garments which wax old, and longest not for the eternal. Thou art proud of thy beauty which shall be destroyed, and considerest not the ugliness of the soul. Thou art rich in slaves. <but freest not thyself from slavery.> Thou art proud of the glory of the multitude, but freest not thyself from the condemnation of death."

136. When Mygdonia had spoken thus, Tertia said, "I pray thee, sister, bring me to the stranger, who teaches these great things, that I may also go and hear him and be taught to worship the God whom he preaches and take part in his prayers and in that of which thou hast spoken to me." Mygdonia says to her, "He is in the house of Sifôr the commander, who became the cause of life for all who are saved in India." Upon hearing this, Tertia went hastily to the house of Sifôr to see the new apostle which had come into the land. When she entered, Judas said to her, "What hast thou come to see? A stranger and poor and despised and beggar, who has neither riches nor possession? But one possession I have which neither a king nor a prince can take away, which is neither destroyed nor does it cease, which is Jesus, the redeemer of mankind, the Son of the living God, who gave life to all which believe on him and take their refuge to him, and who is known by the number of his servants." Says Tertia to him, "Let me have part in this life, which, as thou promisest, all shall receive which come to the shelter of God." And the apostle said, "The treasury of the holy King is opened,

and they which worthily take part of the treasures deposited there rest, and by resting they reign. But no unclean and bad comes to him. For he knows our heart and the depth of thoughts, and none can be hidden from him. Thou also, if else thou truly believest on him shall be deemed worthy of his mysteries, and he will make thee great and rich and an heir of his Kingdom."

137. Having heard this, Tertia returned to her house rejoicing. And she found her husband, who, without having breakfasted, had waited for her. When Misdai saw her, he said, "Why is thy coming in so much more beautiful to-day? And why didst thou come on foot, which is unbecoming a person like thee?" Tertia says to him, "I am under great obligation to thee for having sent me to Mygdonia. For by going there I heard of the new life and saw the apostle of the new God, who gives life to them who believe on him and fulfill his commandments. I owe it to thee on my part also to recompense this grace by a good exhortation. For thou shalt be a great king in heaven, if thou obeyest me and fearest the God preached by the stranger and keepest thyself holy to the living God. For this kingdom passes away, and thy rest (recreation) will be turned into sadness. But go to that man and believe him, and thou shalt live unto the end." When Misdai heard this from his wife, he struck his face with the hands, tore his garment, and said, " Let the soul of Charis have no rest, because he has struck me at the soul, and let him have no hope, be-

ACTS OF THOMAS 337

cause he has taken away my hope." And he went away hence perplexed.

138. In the market he found his friend Charis, and said, "Why didst thou throw me as thy companion into Hell? Why hast thou robbed me and caused loss to me without having profited anything thyself? Why hast thou hurt me without having any benefit? Why hast thou killed me without having life thyself? Why hast thou wronged me without having obtained the right thyself? Why didst thou not suffer me to kill the sorcerer, ere he destroyed my house by his sorcery?" And he quarreled with Charis, and Charis said, "What has happened to thee?" And Misdai said, "He has bewitched Tertia!" And both went to the house of the commander Sifôr. And they found Judas sitting and teaching. And those present rose up before the king, but he (Judas) did not get up. And Misdai knew that it was he, took the seat and upturned it, and in lifting up the chair with the two hands, he struck him so hard on the head that he wounded him. And he delivered him to his soldiers with the words, "Drag him along by force without regard to him, that his impudence may become known to all." And they dragged him to a place where Misdai was in the habit of judging. There he stood, held by the soldiers of Misdai.

Twelfth Deed.

CONCERNING VAZAN, MISDAI'S SON.

(Aa. pp. 245–258)

139. And Vazan, Misdai's son, went to the soldiers and said, "Give him to me that I may speak to him till the king comes." And they handed him over. And he led him to the place where the king used to judge. And Vazan says, "Knowest thou that I am the son of Misdai the king, and that I am at liberty to say to the king what I will, and that <when I tell him,> he will spare thy life? Tell me, therefore, who thy God is, and on whose power thou reliest and in which thou gloriest? For if it is a power and are of sorcery, tell it and teach it, and I set thee free." Says Judas to him, "Thou art the son of King Misdai, who is a temporal king. I am, however, the servant of Jesus Christ, the eternal King. Thou art at liberty to tell thy father that he spare those whom thou wishest in this temporal life, in which men remain not, though thou and thy father give it to them. I, however, beseech my Lord and implore him for men, and he gives them new life, which abides forever. Thou gloriest in possession, slaves, garments, revelry, and unclean couch; but I glory in poverty, love of wisdom, humility, fasting, and prayer, and communion with the Holy Spirit and with my brethren, which are worthy of God, and I glory in an eternal life. Thou hast taken thy refuge in a man like thee, who

is unable to save his soul from judgment and from death; but I have taken refuge in the living God, in the Redeemer of kings and princes, the Judge of all. To-day you may live, but not to-morrow; but I have taken refuge in him who remains in eternity, who knows all our times and circumstances. But if thou wilt become a servant of this God, thou canst become it soon. And that thou art a servant of him, thou wilt show in the following things: first in sanctification, which is the principal part of all good things; then in the communion with this God whom I preach, in the love of wisdom, in simplicity, in love, in faith, by the hope in him and by the purity of a pure conversation."

140. And the young man, who became convinced by the Lord, sought an opportunity how he could help Thomas escape. Whilst meditating upon it, the king came. And the soldiers took Thomas and brought him forth. And Vazan also went with him and stood beside him. And the king took his seat and had Judas brought in with his hands tied behind him. Being led into the midst, he stood still. And the king said, " Tell me who thou art and by whose power thou doest these things?" Judas said to him, "I am a man like thyself, and do these things by the power of Jesus Christ." And Misdai says, " Tell the truth, ere I destroy thee." Judas says, " Thou hast no power over me, as thou thinkest, and wilt hurt me in nothing." Indignant over the words, the king ordered to heat (iron) plates and to put him bare-

footed on them. And when the soldiers untied his shoes, he said, "The wisdom of God is better than the wisdom of men. Thou, Lord and King, and thy goodness oppose his (the king's) wrath!" And they brought the plates which were like fire, and put the apostle on them. And straightway water rushed forth from the ground, that the plates were swallowed. And they which held him let him go and went back.

141. When the king saw the great amount of water, he said to Judas, "Pray thy God that he deliver me from this death, that I perish not by the flood." And the apostle prayed and said, "Thou who hast bound this nature and hast united in one place and sendest to different countries; who hast brought it out of disorder to order, who doest great deeds and great miracles by the hands of thy servant Judas; who hast pity on my soul, that I may always receive thy light; who givest reward to the weary; who savest my soul and bringest it again to its own nature not to unite with those that do harm; who art always author of life — calm this element that it rise not and destroy. For there are some here among those present who shall live, because they have believed on thee." Having prayed, the water was soon absorbed, and the place was dry. And when Misdai saw this he ordered him to be led to prison, "till I have decided what to do with him."

142. When Judas was taken to the prison,

Vazan, the King's son, went to the right and Sifôr to the left. Having entered into the prison, he sat down, also Vazan and Sifôr, and the latter persuaded his wife and his daughter to sit down. For they had also come to hear the word of life. For they knew that Misdai would kill him because of his very great wrath. And Judas began to say: " Deliverer of my soul from the servitude of the multitude, because I suffered myself to be sold, behold, I rejoice and am glad, since I know that the times are fulfilled, that I go in and receive <thee>. See, I am freed from earthly cares. Behold, I complete the hope and receive truth. Behold, I am delivered from sadness and have joy only. Behold, I am free from care and pain and live in rest. Behold, I am free from servitude and I am called to liberty. Behold, I have served times and seasons of time and have been lifted up above times and seasons. Behold, I receive <my reward> from the rewarder, who gives without counting, because his riches are sufficient for his gifts. <Behold, I undress myself and I dress myself,> and shall not again be undressed. Behold, I sleep and wake up, and shall not sleep again. Behold, I die and return to life, and shall not taste death again. Behold, with gladness they wait that I come, and rejoicing with them I shall be put as a flower into their wreath. Behold, I reign in the Kingdom, for which I hoped hence. <Behold, the wicked are confounded who have imagined to sub-

ject me to their power.> Behold, the disobedient fall before me, because I have escaped them. Behold, it is peace to which all come."

143. When the apostle spoke thus, all those present listened, believing that he was to depart his life in this hour. And he continued, saying, "Believe in the physician of everything visible and invisible and in the redeemer of souls which need his help. He is free, descending from kings. He is the Physician of his creatures. It is he who is reviled by his own servants. He is the Father of the height and the Lord and Judge of nature. He became the highest from the greatest, the only-begotten Son of the depth.[1] And he was called son of the virgin Mary and son of the carpenter Joseph; he whose lowliness we beheld with our bodily eyes, whose majesty, however, we have known by faith and saw it in his works; whose human body we also touched with hands,[2] whose changed appearance we saw with our eyes, whose heavenly form, however, we could not see on the mountain;[3] he who perplexed the princes and overcame death; he who is infallible truth and paid tribute <and> head-piece for himself and his disciples;[4] he at whose sight the prince became afraid and the powers combined with him were confounded. And the prince testified who and whence he was, and he did not tell him the truth, since he is a stranger to

---

[1] Syriac omits: the only . . . depth.
[2] Comp. 1 John I, 1; Luke XXIV, 39.
[3] Comp. Matt. XVII, 1–13.
[4] Comp. Matt. XVII, 24–27.

truth;[5] though having power over the world and its pleasures, treasures and enjoyments, he <abstains from> all these things and urges on his subjects to make no use thereof."

144. Having finished his address, he rose and prayed thus: " Our Father in the heavens, hallowed be thy name; thy Kingdom come; thy will be done as in heaven, so also on earth; <give us continually the daily bread;> forgive us our trespasses as we have forgiven our debtors; and lead us not into temptation, but deliver us from the evil.[6] My Lord and my God,[7] hope and trust and teacher <and my encourager,> thou hast taught me thus to pray. Behold, I pray this prayer and fulfill thy behest. Be thou with me unto the end. Thou hast planted life in me from my infancy and hast kept me from destruction. Thou hast led me into the poverty of the world and hast invited me to the true riches. Thou hast manifested thyself to me and shown me that I am thine; and I kept aloof from a woman, in order that the things which thou demandest be not found in pollution.

145. " My mouth is unable to thank thee, and my mind unable to consider thy zeal for me; who hast shown me, whilst I wished to become rich and to acquire, that riches become a punishment for many on earth. But I believed thy revelation and remained in the poverty of the world till thou, the

---

[5] Comp. John VIII, 44.
[6] Comp. Matt. VI, 9–13.
[7] John XX, 28.

true riches, didst come and didst fill me and those worthy of thee with riches and didst deliver us from indigence, care and avarice. Behold, therefore, I have accomplished thy work and executed thy behest and became poor, needy, strange, a slave, despised, imprisoned, hungry, thirsty, naked, and weary. Let the fulfillment of my trust not be lost, and may my hope in thee not be confounded! Let my toils not be in vain! Let my continual prayers and fastings not be lost, and let my deeds for thee not be lessened! Let not the devil take the seed of the wheat from the land,[8] <and [9] his tares be found in it; for thy land receives not his tares, and they cannot be gathered into the barns.[10]

146. <" I planted thy vine in the ground, let its sprouts spread in the ground and its shoots go up to heaven. May it be seen on earth, and may those enjoy them which are worthy of thee and which thou hast acquired. Thy silver which thou gavest to me I put on the table (of the exchangers);[11] call it in and return it to me with interest, as thou hast promised. With thy pound I gained by trading ten others, may they be added to me, as thou hast commanded. I released the debtors the pound — let it not be sought in my hand, which I

---

[8] Comp. Matt. XIII, 25.
[9] From here on to the beginning of 149 the text in the main manuscript is not altogether complete. Bonnet gives also a text from another MS., from which as well as from the Syriac the matter within brackets is given.
[10] Comp. Matt. XXV, 27.
[11] It will be noticed that here and in the following, references are made to the gospels, but in a manner which suits the whole tendency.

have released. Invited to the supper, I came at once, and excused me not with the piece of ground and the yoke of oxen and wife. May I not be rebuked by him, and may I not eat of it only after compulsion. I was invited to the marriage and put on white garments. May I be worthy of them and not be obliged to go into the outer darkness, hand and foot bound. My lamp radiates in its light; may its lord keep it (burning) till he leaves the wedding house and I receive him. May I not see that it smokes for want of oil. May my eyes receive thee, and my heart rejoice, because I have fulfilled thy will and carried out thy commandments. May I be likened unto that faithful and wise servant which is very careful in his watchfulness. Watching the whole night, I endeavored to guard the house from robbers, that one dig not through it.

147. <"My loins are girt about with truth, and my shoes are firmly tied to my feet. May I not see their bands untied. My hand I put to my plow and looked not back, that my furrows be not crooked. My fields are white and long ago ready for the harvest. May I receive my reward! The garment waxing old I used, and the work which brings rest I have finished. I kept my first, second and third watch, and may I receive thy face and worship before thy holy splendor. I have destroyed my storehouses and devastated them upon earth; may I receive from thy treasure, which diminishes not! The fountain running in me I dried up; may I rest at thy living fountain and find rest

there! The bound (prisoner) [12] which thou didst give to me I have killed; deliver the unbound in me, and may my soul not be deprived of its trust! The inner I made the outer, and the outer the inner.[13] May thy will be accomplished in all my limbs! I turned not backward, but reached forth unto the things which are before, let me not become a wonder or sign! The dead I made not [14] alive, and the living I killed not, and the needy I filled not. May we receive the crown of victory, O thou powerful over both worlds! Disgrace I received upon earth — get me the reward in heaven.

148. <Let the powers not perceive me, and those having power not resolve upon me; let the publicans not see me and the tax-gatherers not trouble me! Let the lowly not despise me, nor the wicked, the considerate and humble; and the slave and the despised and the great, riding the high horse, let them not dare to stand before me because of thy victorious power, Jesus, which encompasses me. For they flee and hide from it, because they cannot look at it. For unawares they fall upon those which obey them. One part of the children

---

[12] i.e. the body opposed to the unbound, i.e. the soul.
[13] Comp. Gospel of the Egyptians in Pick, *Paralipomena*, p. 21.
[14] The Greek has not the negation; in the Syriac the first two have the negation, not the third. In the Latin recension of *de miraculis B. Thomæ* (ed. Bonnet, 1883, p. 129) the third has also the negative form. If as Lipsius (I. 330) remarks, that by the dead (and needy) is meant the material body, by the living the pneumatic soul, then all three parts of the sentence must have the negation; we have translated accordingly.

of the evil one cries and reproves them, and none remains hidden, because their nature makes itself known.[15] The wicked are separated; the tree of their fruits is bitterness. Let me quietly pass by their place and come to thee. May joy and peace support me, and may I stand before thy glory! Let not the calumniator look at me, but let his eyes be dazzled by thy light in which I dwell, and may his lying mouth be shut, because he has nothing against me!"

149. <And turning to those who were in the prison by him, he said, "Believe, my children, on this God whom I preach; believe in Jesus Christ, whom I proclaim; believe in him who makes alive and helps his servants;> believe in the redeemer of those who toiled in his service. For my soul already rejoices, because my time is at hand to receive him. Being beautiful, he makes me always speak of his beauty, of what manner it is, although I cannot speak of it as I wish and ought. Thou who art the light of my poverty, and the supplier of my want and the provider of my need — be thou with me till I come and receive thee in eternity."

---

[15] One MS. reads: the part of these bad children cries and betrays; wherefore none can remain hidden from them; another MS.: but the part of the children of the evil one cries and convinces them, but none of them remains hidden from them, for their nature makes itself known.

Thirteenth Deed.

HOW VAZAN AND THE OTHERS WERE BAPTIZED.

(Aa. pp. 259–261.)

150. And the young man Vazan asked the apostle and said, I pray thee, man,[1] apostle of God, allow me to go out and I shall persuade the jailer to let thee go to my house, that from thee I may receive the seal and become thy servant and one that keeps the commandment of God whom thou preachest. For previously I walked already in accordance with thy preaching till my father forced me and bound me to a woman named Mnêsar. Being twenty-one years of age, I have been married to her seven years. Before she became my wife, I knew no other woman. On this account my father considered me also as unprofitable. And neither son nor daughter was ever born to me by this wife. But my wife also lived all this time in chastity with me, and to-day I know that if she were well and heard thy words, that I should have rest and she would receive eternal life. But danger and many sufferings try her. I will therefore persuade the keeper, provided thou wilt come with me. For I live all alone. At the same time thou healest the unfortunate." Upon hearing this, Judas, the apostle of the Most High, said to Vazan, "If thou be-

---

[1] Syriac: holy man.

lievest, thou shalt see the wonders of God, and how he saves his servants."

151. And as they were thus conversing, Tertia and Mygdonia and Marcia stood in the door of the prison, and having given three hundred and sixty-three silver pieces to the jailer, they went in to Judas. And they found Vazan and Sifôr and his wife and his daughter and all prisoners, sitting and listening to the word. And as they came to him, he said to them, "Who allowed you to come to us, and who opened the sealed door to go out?" Says Tertia to him, "Hast thou not opened the door and bidden us to go to the prison, where we should find our brethren and see the Lord's glory? And as we came near the door, thou wast separated from us — I know not how — and being hidden from us, thou camest here first, where we heard the noise of the door, as thou didst shut us out. We gave money to the keepers and thus we got in, and now we are here and beseech thee to let us help thee to go away from here, till the anger of the king against thee ceases." And Thomas said to her, "Tell us first how you were locked up."

152. And she says to him, "Thou wert with us, and didst not leave us even for an hour, and thou canst ask how we were locked up? But if thou wilt hear, listen: King Misdai sent for me and said, the magician has not yet become master over thee, because as I hear, he enchants the people by oil, water and bread, but he has not yet enchanted thee. Now obey me, otherwise I shall lock thee up and strike

thee, and destroy him. For I know that so long as he has not yet given thee oil, water and bread, he has not been able to have power over thee. And I said to him, Thou hast power over my body; do unto it as thou pleasest; but my soul I will not destroy with thee. Upon hearing this, he locked me up in a room. And Charis also brought Mygdonia and locked her up with me. And thou hast brought us forth and brought us hither to this assembly. Now give us the seal that the hopes of Misdai, who intends this, be destroyed."

153. Upon hearing this, the apostle said, " Glory to thee, polymorphous Jesus; praise to thee, who appearest like our poor humanity! Praise to thee, who givest to us courage and strength and joy, and comfort and help in all dangers and strength in our weakness." When he had said this, the jailer came in and said, " Put your lamps away, lest we be reported to the king." Having extinguished the lamps, they turned to sleep. And the apostle spoke with the Lord, " Now it is for thee, Jesus, to hasten, or, behold, the children of darkness put us into their darkness. Illuminate us by the light of thy nature!" And suddenly the whole prison was as light as the day. And while all those that were in the prison were asleep, they who believed on the Lord were awake.

154. And Judas said to Vazan, " Go before and prepare everything necessary." Says Vazan, " And who shall open the prison gates? for the keepers have closed them and are asleep." And

Judas said, "Believe on Jesus, and thou shalt find the gates opened." When he left them to go forth, the others followed him. And as Vazan went ahead, he met his wife Mnêsar, who went to the prison. And as she recognized him, she said to him, "My brother Vazan, is it thou?" He says, "Yea. And thou art Mnêsar?" She says, "Yea." And Vazan said to her, "Whither art thou going and at this time? And how didst thou get up?" And she said, "This young man put his hand upon me, raised me up, and in my sleep I saw that I should go where the stranger was to recover fully." Says Vazan to her, "What young man is with thee?" She says, "Seest thou not him which leadeth me by the right hand?"

155. And as they were thus conversing, Judas came with Sifôr and his wife and his daughter and Tertia and Mygdonia and Marcia into the house of Vazan. And when Mnêsar, Vazan's wife, saw it, she fell upon her knees and said, "Hast thou come to save us from the heavy disease? Thou art he whom I saw in the night as he gave me this young man to bring me to the prison. But thy goodness would not suffer it to trouble myself, but thou hast come to me thyself." And when she said this and turned around, she no more saw the young man. And not finding him, she said to the apostle, "I cannot go alone. The young man is not here, which thou hast given to me." And Judas said, "Jesus shall lead thee." And she went before them. And when they had come into the house of Vazan, the

son of King Misdai, much light shone to them, which was spread around them, although it was yet night.

156. And Judas began to pray and to say, "Companion and associate, hope of the weak and trust of the poor, refuge and shelter of the weary, voice which went forth from on high, comforter which dwells <among us,> shelter and haven of those which travel through dark countries, physician that heals without money, who hast been crucified by men for many, who didst descend into Hades with great might, whose look the princes of death could not bear, and didst ascend with much glory, and didst gather all who take refuge with thee and didst prepare the way, and in thy steps all went whom thou hast redeemed and didst lead them to thy fold and unite with them thy sheep; Son of mercy, Son sent to us out of philanthropy from the upper, the perfect fatherland; Lord of undefiled possessions; who ministerest unto thy servants that they live; who hast filled the creation with thy riches; poor one, which was in need and hungered forty days; who satisfies thirsty souls with thy goods — be thou with Vazan, Misdai's son, and Tertia and Mnêsar, and gather them into thy fold and unite them with thy number; be their guide in the land of error, their physician in the land of sickness, their rest in the land of the weary; sanctify them in the impure country, be the physician of their bodies and souls, make them for thy holy temples, and let thy Holy Spirit dwell in them!"

157. Having thus prayed for them, the apostle said to Mygdonia, "Undress thy sisters!" She undressed them and put aprons about them and brought them. And Vazan had gone first and they followed. And Judas took oil in a silver cup, and spoke thus: "Fruit, more beautiful than the other fruits, with which no other can be united; thou most compassionate; thou which burnest by the power of the word; power of the wood (cross), with which men by putting it on (by anointing themselves with it), overcome their enemies; which crowns the victors; token and joy of the weary; which has brought to men the good news of their salvation; which showest light to those that are in darkness; which art bitter as to the leaves, but sweet as to the fruit; which art rough as to the appearance, but tender as to the use; which seems weak, but carries the all-seeing power by the extraordinariness of thy power; Jesus, let thy victorious power come and rest upon this oil as it once rested upon the wood (cross) related to it — and thy crucifiers could not bear the word; let also come the gift by which thou didst blow at thy enemies and thereby didst bring about that they went back and fell downward, and may it dwell in this oil over which we call thy holy name!" And after the apostle had said this, he poured it first upon the head of Vazan, then upon the women, saying, "In thy name, Jesus Christ, let it be to these souls for forgiveness of sins and for keeping away of the enemy and for the salvation of their souls!"

And he bade Mygdonia to anoint them (the women), himself anointing Vazan. And having anointed them, he made them go down into the water in the name of the Father and of the Son and of the Holy Ghost.

158. And when they came out of the water, he took bread and cup, blessed, and said, "We eat thy holy body, crucified for us; and we drink thy blood, shed for us for redemption. May thy body be redemption for us, and thy blood for the forgiveness of sins! For the gall[2] which thou didst drink for our sakes, may the gall of the devil around us, be taken away; and for the vinegar, which thou didst drink for us, may our weakness be strengthened; for the spittle[3] which thou didst receive for our sakes, may we receive the dew of thy goodness, and for the reed[4] with which they struck thee for our sakes, may we receive the perfect house! And that thou didst receive a crown of thorns[5] for our sakes, may we that loved thee crown ourselves with an imperishable crown! And for the linen,[6] in which thou wast wrapped, let us be clothed with thy invincible power; for the new tomb[7] and burial let our souls receive renewal of the soul and of the body. That thou didst rise again and revive, let us rise again and live and stand before thee in righte-

---

[2] Comp. Matt. XXVII, 34.
[3] Comp. Matt. XXVII, 30.
[4] Comp. Matt. XXVII, 29.
[5] Comp. Matt. XXVII, 29.
[6] Comp. Matt. XXVII, 59.
[7] Comp. Matt. XXVII, 60.

ous judgment!" And he brake the bread of the eucharist, gave thanks,[8] and gave it to Vazan, Tertia, Mnêsar, and to the wife and daughter of Sifôr, and said, "May this eucharist be to your salvation and joy and to the healing of your souls!" And they said, "Amen." And a voice was heard, saying "Amen. Be not afraid, only believe!"[9]

Martyrdom of the Holy and Famous Apostle Thomas.

(AS. pp. 269–288.)

159. And after this Judas went away to be locked up. And Tertia, Mygdonia and Marcia also went to be locked up. And Judas said to them, "My daughters, servants of Jesus Christ, listen to me on this my last day on which I shall finish my word among you, because I shall no more speak in the body (to you). For, lo, I am taken up to my Lord Jesus, who has had pity upon me, who humbled himself even to my weakness and has brought me to the service of his majesty and deemed me worthy to become his minister. And I rejoice that the time is at hand for my deliverance, that I may depart and receive my reward in the end. For my rewarder is just; he knows how to recompense.

---

[8] Comp. Matt. XXVI, 26.
[9] In the Syriac the chapter closes thus: "And they said, 'Amen.' And a voice was heard, saying, "Yea and Amen." And upon hearing this voice, they fell upon their face. And again a voice was heard saying, "Be not afraid . . ."

For he is not envious, but liberal with his goods, relying on his great riches.

160. "I am not Jesus, but a servant of Jesus. I am not Christ, but a servant of Christ. I am not the Son of God, but I pray to be deemed worthy of him. Abide in the faith in Jesus Christ! Wait for the hope of the Son of God! Hesitate not in times of need, and doubt not when you see that I am reviled, imprisoned and die. For in this body I only do what is bidden me by the Lord. For if I wished not to die, you know that I can do it. But this death is no death, but deliverance and loosening from the body. And I will joyfully expect it that I may go and receive the Beautiful and Merciful. For I have become weary of the service which I did to him, and by that which I executed by his grace, and now he will not leave me. You, however, see to it that he comes not into you which enters in and brings doubts to the thoughts. For he is mightier whom you have received. Wait for his coming, that he may come and receive you. For after your departure you shall see him."

161. Having finished this discourse, he entered into the dark house, and said, "My Saviour, who hast endured much for our sake, let these doors be as they were and their seals unbroken!" And he left the women and went to be locked up. And they grieved and wept, knowing that King Misdai would destroy him.

162. And Judas went and found the jailers fighting, and saying, "What wrong have we done

ACTS OF THOMAS 357

to that sorcerer, that, availing himself of his magical art, he has opened the doors of the prison, and wishes to set all the prisoners free? But let us go and report to the king, and let him also know about his wife and his son." Whilst the keepers meditated upon this, Judas listened silently. And at dawn they went to King Misdai and said, "Lord, release that sorcerer, or cause him to be shut elsewhere. <For we cannot keep him.> For twice has thy fortune (only) kept the prisoners. When we lock the doors at the night time, we find them opened when we rise. Nay, more; thy wife and son will not keep away from the man any more than the rest of them." And when the king heard this, he went to look at the seals which he put to the doors. And he found the seals as they were, and said to the jailers, "Why are you telling lies? for certainly these seals are quite safe. And how do you say that Tertia and Mygdonia go within the prison?" And the wardens said, "We have told thee the truth."

163. And after this the king went to the house of judgment and sent for Judas. And when he came, they stripped him, and girded him with an apron, and set him before the king. And Misdai said to him, "Art thou a slave or a freeman?" Judas said, "I am a slave, but thou hast no power over me whatever." And Misdai said, "How hast thou run away and come to this country?" Judas said, "I came here that I might save many, and that I might by thy hands depart from this body,"

Misdai says to him, "Who is thy master? and what is his name? and over what country does he rule?" "My Lord," says Thomas, "is my Master and thine, being the Lord of heaven and earth." And Misdai said, "What is he called?" And Judas said, "Thou canst not know his true name at this time, but the name which has been given for a time is Jesus the Messiah." Misdai said, "I have been in no hurry to destroy thee, but have restrained myself; but thou hast added to thy deeds, so that thy sorceries have been heard of in all the country. But now I will so act that thy sorceries may also perish with thee, that our nation may be purified from them. And Judas said, "These sorceries, as thou callest them, shall never be removed from the people here."

164. And after this was said, Misdai reflected how to put him to death. For he was afraid of the people standing around, many, even some of the chief men, having believed in him. And he arose, and took Judas outside of the city; and a few soldiers accommpanied him with their arms. And the multitude thought that the king was wishing to learn something from him; and they stood and observed him closely. And when they had gone forth three stadia, he delivered him to four soldiers, and to one of the chief officeres, and ordered them to take him up into the mountain and spear him. And he returned to the city.

165. And those who were present ran to Judas, eager to rescue him; but he was led away, accom-

panied by four soldiers, two on each side, their spears in the hands, whilst the chief officer held him by the hand and led him. And Judas walking along, said, "O the hidden mysteries of thee, for even to the close of life are they fulfilled in us! O the riches of thy grace, which does not allow us to feel the bodily pains! For, lo, how four have laid hold of me, since of the four elements I have been made! And one leads me, since I belong to One to whom I am going. But now I learn that my Lord, who was of one, was pierced by one,[1] but I, consisting of four, am pierced by four."

166. And as they came to the place where they were to spear him, Judas said to those that held him. "Hear me now, at least, when I am departing from the body; and let not your eyes be darkened in understanding, nor your ears shut up, so as not to hear! Believe in the God whom I preach, after being delivered in your souls from rashness; and behave in a manner becoming those who are free, having glory with men and life with God."

167. And he said to Vazan, "Son of the earthly king and servant of Jesus Christ, give to those who execute the behest of King Misdai what is due to them, in order that I may go apart from them and pray." And when Vazan had persuaded the soldiers, Judas betook himself to prayer. And it was as follows: "My Lord and my God, my Hope and my Redeemer, and my Leader and

---

[1] Comp. John XIX, 34.

Guide in all countries, be thou with all who serve thee, and do thou guide me this day, that I may come to thee! Let no one take my soul, which I have given to thee! Let no publicans look at me and the tribute-gatherers falsely accuse me! Let not the serpent see me, and the children of the dragon hiss at me! Behold, O Lord, I have fulfilled thy work and accomplished thy behest. I have become a slave, wherefore I receive freedom this day. Do then give it to me perfect! And this I say not as one who doubts, but that they may hear it who need to hear."

168. And having prayed, he said to the soldiers, "Come, execute the command of him who sent you!" And the four pierced him at once and killed him. But all the brethren wept and wrapped him in beautiful shawls, and many linen cloths, and laid him in the tomb in which the former kings were buried.

169. And Sifôr and Vazan would not go down to the city, but, having spent there the whole day, spent the night there also. And Judas appeared unto them and said, "I am not here.[2] Why do you sit here and watch me? For I have gone up, and received what I hoped for. But rise up and walk, and after a short time you shall be gathered to me." And Misdai and Charis greatly afflicted Tertia and Mygdonia, but did not persuade them to abandon their opinion. And Judas appeared

---

[2] Comp. Matt. XXVIII, 6.

ACTS OF THOMAS

unto them and said, "Forget not the former things! For Jesus, the Holy and Living, will himself help you." And as Misdai and Charis and those around them did not persuade them, they allowed them to live according to their own will. And all the brethren there assembled together. For, when Judas was led to death, he had made Sifôr a presbyter in the mountain, and Vazan a deacon. And the Lord helped them and increased the faith by means of them.

170. And after a long time it happened that one of the sons of King Misdai was a demoniac; and the demon being stubborn, no one was able to treat him. And Misdai considered and said, "I will go and open the grave and take one of the bones of the apostle of God and touch my son with it, and I know that he shall be cured." And he went away to do what he intended. And Judas appeared unto him and said, "Since thou hast not believed in the living, how wilt thou believe in the dead? But be not afraid. Jesus the Messiah is kindly disposed to thee through his great goodness." And Misdai found not the bones. For one of the brethren had taken them away secretly and carried them into the regions of the West.[8] And he took dust from the place where the bones of the apostle had lain, touched his son with it, and said, "I now believe on thee, Jesus, after he has forsaken me, who always confuses men, that they see

---

[8] According to tradition: to Edessa.

not thy light." And when the son was healed in this manner, he (Misdai) took part in the assemblies of the brethren, submitting to Sifôr. And he asked all brethren to pray for him that he might obtain mercy from our Lord Jesus Christ.

171. [End of the deeds of the apostle Judas Thomas, which he did in the land of the Indians, fulfilling the command of Him who sent him, to whom be glory for ever and ever! Amen.]

THE END

I. INDEX TO TEXTS

Genesis	PAGE
iii, 1	252
18	252
iv, 5–8	252
vi, 1–4	253

Exodus	
i ff.	253
xxxii	253, 283

Numbers	
xxii, 21 ff.	261

Psalms	
cxviii, 22	97

Proverbs	
xxi, 1	130

Ecclesiastes	
iii, 1, 8	283

Isaiah	
vii, 13	96
xxviii, 16	97
liii, 2	96
4	90
8	96

Daniel	
ii, 34	97
vii, 13	97

Matthew	
ii	253
iii, 17	265
iv, 18	200
v, 4	16
7	16
8	15
vi, 9–13	343
25	257
26	249
34	248
vii, 7	272
15	292
viii, 20	267
29	265

	PAGE
x, 3	223
42	16
xi, 8	257
15	295
28	295
29	16
29, 30	249
xiii, 25	344
xiv, 19	267
25	267
31	76
xvi, 12–19	95
27	249
xvii, 1–13	342
11	89
20	76
24–27	342
27	291
xix, 23	257
27, 29	279
xx, 12	278
xxi, 21	76
42	97
xxiii, 4	295
xxiv, 30	97
xxv, 27	344
34	16
xxvi, 3	253
14–16	253
26	355
52, 53	297
64	97
xxvii, 11 ff.	253
29	354
30	354
34	354
59	354
60	354
63	267
xxviii, 6	360

Mark

	PAGE
i, 16	200
24	265
v, 7	265
vi, 3	96
viii, 18	294
xi, 23	76
xiii, 3	200

Luke

iii, 14	265
v, 1–11	267
23	100
vi, 18	278
vii, 11	98
14	100, 267
ix, 52	267
xii, 24	249
xvi, 4	266
xix, 4	258
30	261
xxi, 34	257
xxiii, 18	22
xxiv, 27	277
39	342

John

i, 14	278
40, 44	200
iv, 6	267
vi, 9	200
viii, 44	343
x, 11	261
38	90
xi, 16	223
43	267
xii, 22	200
xiv, 22	223
27	285
xvii, 21	90
xviii, 11	297
xix, 26	183
34	359
xx, 24	223
28	343
xxi, 2	223
6, 11, 12	267

Acts

i, 13	223
iii, 17	278
v, 15	278
viii, 18–20	95
x, 42	249
xviii, 28	277
xxviii, 16	57
30	57

Romans

iv, 17	267
viii, 17	16
29	267, 278
xii	60
xvi, 20	268

I Corinthians

ii, 9	120, 258
vi, 3	16
18, 19	15
vii, 29	16
31	16
xi, 27, 29	59

Galatians

v, 19–21	60
22, 23	60

Ephesians

ii, 22	276
iv, 22, 24	268
25	277
28	268
31	60
v, 3	60

Philippians

ii, 5–11	312

Colossians

i, 19	90
ii, 9	90
iii, 8	60
9	276
9, 10	268
12–16	60
iv, 14	13

II Timothy

i, 15	13
16	14
ii, 18	19
iv, 10	13

Titus

iii, 5	332

Philemon

24	13

I Peter	PAGE	I John	PAGE
ii, 4, 6	93	i, 1	342
iii, 9	277	Hebrews	
II Peter		xi, 5	16
i, 16	89	Revelation	
ii, 1	292	ix, 11	253

II. INDEX TO SUBJECTS

Abban, a merchant, buys the Apostle Thomas from the Lord, to be a carpenter for Gundafor, an Indian King, 226; thrown into prison by Gundafor, 241; released, 244.
Abdias, 125.
Achaia, 218.
Acts, apocryphal, introduction to, vii; origin, ix; purpose, xi; character, xii.
  of Andrew, 200 ff.
  of John, 123 ff.
  of Paul, 1 ff.
  of Peter, 50 ff.
  of Thomas, 222 ff.
Adam, 206.
Aegeates, refused by Maximilla, plots to kill Andrew, 211; has Andrew fastened to the cross, 216; the people cry out against, 218; visits Andrew on the cross and desires to release him, 219; the miserable death of, 221.
Aeons, 172, 188.
Africanus, 125.
Agrippa, 112.
Agrippina, 112.
Agrippinus, 85.
Albinus intends to kill Peter, 113; advises Agrippa to do the same, 114.
Alexander Severus, 223.
Alexander, the Syriarch, falls in love with Thecla, and brings her before the governor of Antioch, 25; his atrocious conduct towards her, 27 f.
Aline (Alype), 5.
Alphaeus, 225.
Amphion, 6.
Anchares, 4.
Andrapolis, 227.
Andrew, 225.
Andrew, Acts of, 200 ff., in prison is visited by the brethren, by Maximilla and Iphidamia, 204; is threatened by Aegeates, 205; encourages Maximilla not to yield to Aegeates, 205; strengthens Stratocles, 209; predicts his crucifixion, 211; speaks of his mission, 212; of his fate, 213; apostrophizes the cross, 215; is fastened to the cross, 216; smiles and discourses to the people from the cross, 217; refuses to be released from the cross, 219; his death, 220; his body taken down by Maximilla and Stratocles, 221.
Andronicus, 146, 159.
Animals, speaking, 74, 260, 288, 290.
Antioch, 4, 13, 24.
Antulus, 83.
Apollophanes, 7.
Apostles, the, apportion the regions of the world between them, 225.
Apostolics, 201, 223.
Apotactici, 201.

INDEX

Aricia, 62; Simon Magus dies there, 112.
Aristeus, 61.
Aristippus, 160.
Aristobula, 160.
Aristodemus, 136, 142.
Ariston, 66.
Armenian Bible, 36.
Artemilla, 3.
Artemis — temple, destroyed, 148.
Authors or authorities referred to:
Abdias, 161, 175.
Acta Concil. Nic., 144.
Acta Nerei et Achillei, 56.
Acta Philippi, 56.
Acts of Thomas, 75.
Actus Vercellenses, 51, 52.
Ambrose, 12.
Aphraates, 37.
Apocalypse of Peter, 273.
Ascensio Jesaiæ, 96.
Augustine, 56, 183, 195, 201, 223.
Bardesanes, 312.
Barhebræus, 223.
Basil, 10.
Bedjan, 224.
Berger, 37.
Binder, 195.
Bonnet, 9, 124, 125, 126, 144, 175, 192, 201, 221, 223, 225, 344.
Book of Jubilees, 59.
Bratke, 37.
Budge, 224.
Carriere, 37.
Cassian, 158.
Chrysostom, 12.
Clem. Alexandrinus, 96, 120, 124, 125, 179, 196.
Clementine Homilies, 108.
Clementine Recognitions, 108.
Codex Claromontanus, 3, 4.
Cyril of Jerusalem, 224.
Decretum Gelasianum, 4, 10.
De Rossi, 109.
Ephræm Syrus, 36.
Epiphanius, 12, 96, 201, 223.
Euodius of Uzala, 201.
Eusebius, 3, 51, 56, 200, 201, 223.
Fabricius, 158, 151.
Ficker, 51.
Gieseler, 93.
Gospel of the Egyptians, 346.
Grabe, 9.
Gregory of Nazianzen, 11.
Gregory of Nyssa, 11.
Gregory of Tours, 324.
Harnack, 61.
Hennecke 8, 125, 201.
Herder, 196.
Hermas, 59.
Hilgenfeld, 56, 180.
Hippolytus, 2.
Innocentius I., 201.
Irenæus, 108.
Isidore of Pelusium, 12.
James, 3, 51, 175, 224.
Jerome, 10, 12, 56.
John of Damascus, 12.
John of Salisbury, 3.
Justin Martyr, 59, 75, 90.
Lazius, 125.
Leipoldt, 8, 51.
Lemm, 116.
Lightfoot, 109.
Lipsius, viii, xii, xiv, 9, 51, 97, 106, 125, 175, 180, 188, 195, 200, 201, 223, 226, 231, 241, 269, 312, 319, 346.
Lugano, 75, 109.
Luther, 15.
Malala, 14.
Malan, 224.
Methodius, 10.
Mösinger, 37.
Muratorian Fragment, 4, 200.
Neander, 126.
Nicephorus, 4, 124, 223.
Nicephorus Callisti, 2, 3, 14.
Nicetas of Paphlagonia, 10.
Orac. Sibyllina, 96.
Origen, 2, 93, 222.

Passio Petri et Pauli, 110.
Paul de Tamoueh, 93.
Pfleiderer, 180.
Philastrius of Brescia, 51, 201.
Photius x, 50, 223.
Pick, 11, 76, 107, 119, 120, 182, 273.
Pliny, 317, 346.
Preuschen, 231, 312.
Priscillian, 51.
Prochorus, 126.
Pseudo-Cyprian, 182.
Pseudo-Lucian, 14.
Ramsay, 14.
Resch, 96, 97.
Rinck, 36.
Roswitha, 161.
Schaefer, 56.
Schimmelpfeng, 221.
Schmidt, x, xi, 2, 4, 37, 51, 52, 201.
Schnudi, Life of, 93.
Simeon Metaphrastes, 10.
Sulpicius Severus, 12.
Sylvia of Aquitania, 12.
Tertullian, 7, 8, 10, 59, 96.
Thilo, 124, 158.
Thomas, Gospel of, 291.
Tillemont, 10.
Tischendorf, 9, 126, 188, 191, 195, 225.
Turribius of Astorga, 223.
Vetter, 36.
Walker, 223.
Wilson, 196.
Wright, 224.
Zahn, x, 51, 52, 124, 125, 126, 144, 159, 161, 171, 175, 179, 180, 183, 188, 192, 195, 223.
Zeno of Verona, 12.

Babylon, 317.
Balaam, 261.
Balbus, 61.
Baptism, 332.
Barnabas, 63.
Barrabas Justus, 45.
Barsabas, 48.
Bartholomew, 235.
Berenice, 61.
Berus, 145.
Bread, breaking of, 15, 191, 333, 355.

Cæsarea, 64.
Caiaphas, 72, 253.
Cain, 252, 296.
Callimachus tries to defile the body of Drusiana, is prevented by a snake, 166; is raised by John, 168; makes a full confession, 168.
Candida, 57.
Castellius, 19.
Cestus, 46, 48.
Chalcedon, 312.
Charis, 294; is refused by Mygdonia, 299; his dream, 300; enraged, goes to King Misdai, 307; drags Thomas before the King, 311; entreats Mygdonia again and again to live with him as before, 320; seeks the help of the apostle Thomas, 330.
Christ Jesus:
some events of his life, 69, 91, 291 f., 342.
his deity, 31, 172, 174, 189, 193, 245, 266, 278, 293, 342, 359.
incarnation and birth, 14, 39, 40, 69, 287.
transfiguration, 89, 178.
descent into Hades, 352.
resurrection, 14, 191, 293.
ascension, 187, 293.
names of, 90, 184, 191.
forms of, 90, 176 f, 247.
Chrysa, 6.
Chryse, what she is told in a dream, 106.
Chrysippus, 6.
Cleobius, 7, 38, 61, 136, 142, 159.

INDEX

Cleon, 5, 6.
Cleopatra, 137.
Coptic Acts of Paul, contents of, 4 ff.
Coptic Fragment of Acts of Peter, 52.
Corinth, 7.
Corinthians, correspondence with Paul, 35 ff.
Cross, Andrew's address to the, 215.

Daemonicus, 136, 142.
Dalmatia, 43.
Daniel, 2.
Daphne, 23.
Daphnus, 38.
David, 14, 40.
Demas and Hermogenes, 13; their evil counsel against Paul and Thecla, 19.
Demetrius, 61.
Demiurge, 216.
Demon, an unclear, which had tormented a woman for years, expelled by Thomas, 262 f.
Demoniac healed by John, 134.
Devil, an Ethiopian, xiii, 93.
Dion, 5.
Dionysius, 61.
Domitian follows Vespasian, 127; is excited by the Jews against the Christians, issues an edict against the Christians, 128 sends soldiers to Ephesus to arrest John, 128; his interview with John, 130; entreats John to heal a female slave seized by a demon, 134; sends John to Patmos, 135.
Doris, 112.
Dragon, story of the, which killed a young man, and is destroyed by Thomas, 250 ff.
Drusiana, 159; is coveted by a servant, 161; is ague-struck and dies, 162; her tomb is opened by the steward of Andronicus, 165; her grave clothes are taken from her, 166; a serpent prevents the foul deed of the servant, 166; she raises Fortunatus, 172.

Edessa, 222.
Egetes, 202.
Egypt, 313, 315.
Elijah, 42.
Elisha, 42.
Encratites, 201, 223.
Ephesus, 2, 3, 138.
Eubola, 83, 84.
Eubula, 3.
Eubulus, 38.
Eucharistic prayer, 268.
Euphemia, 112.
Eutropius, 125.
Eve, 206, 252.

Falconilla, 26.
Festus, 45.
Flaccus, 56.
Flute-girl, the Hebrew, and the Apostle Thomas, 229, 232.
Fortunatus, 167, 172 f, dies of blood-poisoning, 175.

Gad, the brother of King Gundafor, his sickness and death, 242; caught away by angels, he is shown the heavenly palace built for his brother by the Apostle Thomas, 242; is allowed to return to earth to obtain the heavenly palace from the King, 243; is permitted by the King to occupy the palace, 244; is sealed by Thomas, 246.
Gaul, 43.

Gemellus, 10.
Gennesaret, 179.
Gnostic dedication-prayer, 247.
Gomorrha, 6.
Gundafor, King of India, the Apostle Thomas bought for, as a carpenter, 226; engages Thomas to build a palace for him, 239; seeing no palace built, he throws Thomas and the merchant, who bought him, into prison, 242; on the death of his brother, he resolves to put Thomas to death, 242; the brother of, sees the palace in heaven built by Thomas and obtained liberty to return to secure it for himself, 243; grants his brother permission to dwell in the heavenly palace, 244; is baptized and sealed, 246.

Hades, 233.
Hermias, 31.
Hermippus, 5.
Hermocrates, 5.
Herod, 72, 253.
Hymns, 180 f, 230 f, 312 ff.

Iconium, 4, 14.
Iconoclasts appeal to the Acts of John, 124.
Image-worship, 143.
India, 222; falls to the lot of Thomas, 225.
Iphidamia, 202.
Iphitus, 61.
Italicus, 83.

James, son of Zebedee, 225.
Jerome, 3.
Jerusalem, 6; taken by Vespasian, 126.
Jesus, meets Peter departing from Rome to avoid persecution, and tells him He is coming to be crucified for him, 115; how described by John, 175 ff.
Jews cause the death of Christians, 128.
John, brother of James, 225.
John, Acts of, 123 ff; his fame reaches Domitian, 128; is sent for by the emperor, 128; accompanies the soldiers to Rome and inspires them with reverence for him, 129; his interview with Domitian, 130; takes deadly poison before Domitian without injury, 131; restores to life the condemned criminal whom the washing of poison cup had killed, 133; cures a slave of the emperor's who was tormented by a demon, 134; sent to Patmos, 135; in the reign of Trajan goes to Ephesus, 135; his ministry here, 135; appoints Polycarp bishop, 135; goes to Ephesus, 136; his work there, 137 f; restores to life Cleopatra and Lycomedes, 140 ff; sees his picture, 143; heals the old women, 145; tells why he came to Ephesus, 146; before leaving goes to the temple of Artemis, 149; addresses the people there, 149; at his prayer the temple falls down and kills one of the priests, 150; restores him to life, 153; meets a parricide, 154; restores to life the dead father, 156; is asked to come to Smyrna, 157; looks at a partridge, 158;

reproves a priest, 158; goes again to Ephesus, 159; is molested by bugs, 160; his words occasioned by the death of Drusiana, 163; in the tomb of Drusiana he sees a beautiful youth, Callimachus with a big snake on him, and the steward Fortunatus being dead, 167; he raises Callimachus, 168; also Drusiana, 170; prays in the tomb, 174; discourses on the person of Jesus, 175 ff; his last service and exhortation, 189 f; orders his grave to be dug, 192; his last prayer and death, 192 ff. —John and the robber, 196 ff (Appendix).
Jonah, 41, 42.
Judas, 72, 253, 296.
Judas, son of James, 225.

Kosan, 312.

Labyrinth, 316, 317.
Lectra, 14.
Leonidas, 201.
Leucius Charinus, x, xi, 10, 51, 124; called "discipulus diaboli," 201.
Longinus, 6.
Longus, 45, 48.
Luke, 43, 47, 48.
Lycomedes, 136; has a picture of John made, 142.
Lysimachus, 61.
Lystra, 14.

Macedonia, 3, 63.
Manichæans, xi, 201, 223.
Marcellus, influenced by Simon Magus blasphemes, 71; repents, 74; restores a broken statue, 78; attacks Simon, 80; invites Peter to his house, 87; what he sees in his sleep, 93; takes down the body of Peter from the cross and buries it, 121.
Marcia, the nurse of Mygdonia, 324; is baptized, 325.
Marcus the Gnostic, 108.
Martyrdom of Andrew, 216 f.
Martyrdom of Thomas, 355 f.
Mary, 39, 40.
Matthew, 225.
Maximilla, 202; takes the body of Andrew down from the cross, 221.
Mesene, 313, 317.
Miletus, 7.
Misdai (Masdai), king of India, his commander comes to Thomas, 279; sends his wife Tertia to Mygdonia, 334; tells Charis of what he learned from Tertia, 337; his demoniac son cured by the dust of the place where the bones of Thomas had lain, 361; is received into the church, 362.
Mnêsar, Vazan's wife, 348.
Mygdonia, wife of Charis, comes to Thomas, 294; refuses having intercourse with her husband, 299; is strengthened by Thomas, 301 ff; resists all efforts of Charis, 303; leaves the house at night and goes to her nurse, 305; goes to the house of Sifôr to hear Thomas, 307; resists all approaches of Charis, and while he is asleep goes to see Thomas, 322 f; is strengthened by the apostle and asks for baptism, 324; is baptized, 326; the apostle asks her

to obey Charis but in vain, 331.
Myra, 5.
Myrte, 7.

Narcissus, 61, 63; Peter in the house of, 69, 80.
Nature, lower, 185.
Nero, persecutes the Christians and orders the beheading of Paul, 45; blames Agrippa for having killed Peter, 121; seeks to destroy all whom Peter had had instructed, 122; but is warned in a vision, 122.
Nexocharis, 201.
Nicæa, Council of, 124.
Nicaria, 112.
Nicostratus, 101.
Numbers, Eight (Ogdoad) and Twelve, 181.
Nympha, 5.

Oil, anointing with, 246, 325, 353 f.
Onesiphorus, receives Paul, 14.
Origenians, 201.

Palace, the, built by Thomas the apostle for King Gundafor, 239.
Parthenius, 47.
Parthia, 222, 315.
Patmos, John sent to, by Domitian, 135.
Patroclus, 48.
Paul, Acts of, 1 ff; goes to Iconium where he is received by Onesiphorus — his personal appearance described, 13 f; converts Thecla, 17; cast into prison by the governor, 21; visited in prison by Thecla, 21; cast out of the city, 22; fasts with Onesiphorus, 23; goes with Thecla to Antioch, 24; corresponds with the Corinthians, 35 ff; revives Patroclus, Nero's cup bearer, 44; appears to Nero, 48; conversion of his persecutors, 49; at Rome converts Candida, wife of Quartus, 57; prepares to go to Spain, 58; preaches and prays before leaving, 59; is conducted to the harbor, 61; martyrdom of, 43 ff; is beheaded, 47.
Perge, 5.
Peter, Acts of, 50 ff; his paralytic daughter, 53; called Petronilla, 56; his affair with Simon, 57 ff; is directed to leave Jerusalem for Rome, 64; enters a ship at Cæsarea and baptizes Theon in the Adriatic Sea, 65; lands at Puteoli where he is welcomed by Ariston, 66 ff; hastens to Rome to meet Simon, 69; exhorts the Christians in the house of Narcissus, 69; is asked to overcome Simon, 71; goes to the house of Marcellus to see Simon but is refused, 73; sends a speaking dog to Simon, 74; drives out a demon, 77; causes a smoked tunny to swim; sends a suckling child to Simon that confounds him, 81; sees Jesus by night, 82; tells the brethren of Simon's doings in the house of Eubola, 83; how he was detected, 84; and why he left Judea, 86; goes to the house of

Marcellus, 87; heals a blind woman, 85; speaks of Jesus, 89; heals many blind women, 91; meets with Simon, whom he exposes before the Romans, 94; answers the blasphemy of Simon, 96; asks Simon to do a sign, 97; revives several dead people, 98 ff; preaches repentance, 105; goes into the house of Marcellus, 105; heals many, 108; refutes Simon, 108; sees him ascend, but asks Jesus to make him fall down, 111; preaches in Rome, 112; his life being endangered, is advised to leave the city, 114; meets the Lord outside of the gate, 115; returns to the city, is seized and brought before Agrippa, 115; his address to the cross, 116; asks to be crucified with the head downward, 118; explains the reason, 118 ff; his body taken down by Marcellus and buried, 121; appears to Marcellus by night, 121.
Petronilla, daughter of Peter, 56.
Pharaoh, 72, 253.
Pheretas, 47.
Phila, 4.
Philip, 225.
Philippi, 7, 39.
Philostrate, 61.
Phrontina, 67.
Pilate, 253.
Prayers, 60 f, 247, 268 f, 341, 343.
Prayers addressed to Jesus, 139, 190, 233, 352, 359.
Ptolemy, 54.

Punishments of the wicked, 273 f.
Puteoli, 66.

Quartus, 57.

Rome, 7.
Rufina, punished, 59.

Sarbug, 313.
Saul, 6.
Seleucia, 32.
Septimius Severus, xi.
Sidon, 5, 6.
Sifôr, 307; is summoned before King Misdai, 308; speaks of Thomas and his cures, 309; asks to be baptized with his wife and daughter, 332; made a presbyter by Thomas, 361.
Simmias, 14.
Simon, 7, 38.
Simon (Peter), 225.
Simon, the Canaanæan, 225.
Simon Magus, viii; his doings at Aricia, 62; at Rome, 63; in the house of Marcellus, 71; his contention with the dog, 78; is driven from the house of Marcellus, 81; goes to the house of Narcissus to contend with Peter, 81; is attacked by a suckling child and becomes speechless, 82; his trickery in the house of Eubola, 83; why he left Judea, 85; meets with Peter at Rome, 94; blasphemes Jesus, 95; is answered by Peter, 96; causes a lad to die, whom Peter revives, 99; tries to raise another dead, but in vain, 103; tries again many

tricks, but is refuted by Peter, 108; tries to fly but falls down and breaks his shank, 111; is taken to Aricia, where he dies, 112.
Sodom, 6.
Stephanus, 38.
Stratocles, 205, 221.
Stratonicus, 108.
Stratonike, 7, 39.
Suckling child confounds Simon Magus, 82.

Tertia, wife of Misdai, goes to Mgydonia, 334; is induced to hear Thomas, 335; tells Misdai of her meeting with Thomas, 336.
Thamyris provoked by the conduct of Thecla, his betrothed, 17 ff; brings Paul before the governor, 20.
Thecla, reference to her in patristic literature, 10 ff; hears Paul preaching, and is so entranced by him that she hearkens not to mother nor lover, 17 ff; evil counsels of Demas and Hermogenes against, 17; visits Paul in prison, 21; condemned to be burned, but is miraculously delivered, 22 f; goes with Paul to Antioch, 24; vile conduct of Alexander the Syrian towards, 25; condemned to be thrown to wild beasts, she receives the sympathy of Tryphæna, 26; thrown to the wild beasts, but they have no power to hurt her, 27; baptizes herself, 28; bound between two fierce bulls, but remains unhurt, 29; is set at liberty, 30; goes to Myra seeking Paul, 30; visits her mother at Iconium, 31; goes to Seleucia and takes up her abode in a cave, where she performs many cures, 32; plot laid for her by certain young men, from which she is miraculously delivered, 33; period of her life and age, 32, 34.
Theoclia, 17.
Thenœ, 38.
Theon baptized by Peter, 65.
Theophilus, 38.
Theudes, 6.
Thomas, Acts of, 222 ff; his kindness, 224; India falls to the lot of, 226; refuses to go and is sold by his Master as a carpenter for Gundafor, an Indian King, 226; submits to his Master's will, 227; reaches Andrapolis, and is obliged to attend a royal marriage feast, 228; struck by a cup-bearer, 229; the song of, 230; taken by the King to the bridal chamber to pray for the married couple, 233; the Lord converses with the bride and bridegroom in the form of, 234; the King is enraged with, 237; undertakes to build a palace for King Gundafor, 239; expends the money entrusted to him for the palace on the poor and afflicted, 240; the King, finding no palace built, throws him into prison, resolving to flay and burn him, 242; curi-

ous story of his release from prison, 244; baptizes King Gundafor, 246; continues preaching, 248; the Lord appears to, 250; story of, in relation to the young man and the dragon, 250 ff; is addressed by a colt, 260; a young woman tormented by an unclean demon delivered by, 262 ff; story of, in relation to the young man who killed the maiden, 270 ff; raises the maiden to life, who relates what she saw in the unseen world, 273 ff; his preaching, miracles and success, 277 ff; a commander comes to him beseeching him for his wife and daughter, 279 ff; becomes a believer, 282; accompanies Thomas on his journey, 284; wild asses come to the apostle's help, 285; stop at the house of the commander, 286; the apostle heals the commander's wife and daughter, 293; is visited by Mygdonia, 294; preaches to the multitude, 295; addresses Mygdonia, 298; is taken before King Misdai and imprisoned, 311; his psalm in prison, 312 ff; baptizes Mygdonia, 326; is summoned to appear before the King, 328; defends his teaching, 328; offered freedom provided he persuade Mygdonia to live with Charis, 329; returns to the house of Sifôr, 332; is taken to the tribunal of Misdai, 337; is visited by Vazan, the King's son, 338; is put barefooted on hot plates, 339; is asked by the King to pray for him and is taken back to the prison, 340; preaches and prays there, 341 f; is visited by Tertia, Mygdonia, and Marcia, 349; goes to the house of Vazan, 352; baptizes Vazan, Tertia, Mnêsar, 353; returns to the prison, 355; discourses on the person of Jesus, 356; is brought before the King, 357; is condemned to death, 358; his last words and prayer, 359; his death, 360; laid in a tomb, 360; the dust of the place where his bones had lain heals a demoniac son of Misdai, 361.

Thrasymachus, 5, 6.
Threptus, 38, 39.
Timothy, 63.
Titus, 14, 43, 47, 48.
Torments of the wicked, the 273 ff.
Tryphæna, how she befriends Thecla, 25, 26.
Tyre, 6.

Urion, 45.

Vazan, Misdai's son, asks Thomas concerning his God, 338; is convinced, seeks an opportunity to help Thomas escape, 339; asks Thomas for baptism, 348; made a deacon by the apostle, 361.
Vercelli, 51.
Vespasian is succeeded by Domitian, 127.

Warkan, 317.
Wicked, the place and the punishments of, 273 ff.
World, unseen, description of, 273 ff.

Xanthippe, 113.
Xenophon, 100, 282; appointed by Thomas to care for the commander and the other believers, 284.

Young man, the, who kills a maiden, the story of, 270 ff.

Zeno, 14, 38.